T0370431

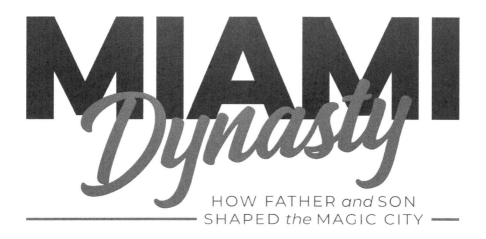

MIAMI *Dynasty*

HOW FATHER *and* SON SHAPED *the* MAGIC CITY

XAVIER L. SUAREZ

authorHOUSE®

AuthorHouse™
1663 Liberty Drive
Bloomington, IN 47403
www.authorhouse.com
Phone: 833-262-8899

Published by AuthorHouse 08/23/2024

ISBN: 979-8-8230-3051-9 (sc)
ISBN: 979-8-8230-3050-2 (e)

Contents

Prologue

It is the Ides of March 2020. My son, Francis Xavier Suarez, is the highest authority in the city I love—the city that has been my home since I moved here in 1975.

I am a lowly county commissioner in the same metropolis, called Miami-Dade County. The two jurisdictions, the city of Miami and the former Dade County, overlap to a great extent. In effect, we are joint venture partners in running what is now the world's most attractive, most diverse, and most interesting urban setting.

Miami seems to always be ground zero for something—whether refugees, drugs, or glamour. Today none of those things distinguish Miami. Today, what distinguishes Miami is a novel pandemic that goes by the name "coronavirus."

As I write this in 2020, Miami is not so much ground zero as the predicted next hot spot for the nightmarish rate of death and sickness that has been plaguing New York for a month now, resulting in about three thousand deaths. Miami is also ground zero for something more fortuitous.

Its mayor and my son, Francis X. Suarez, has become the face of government at the municipal level, just as New York governor Andrew Cuomo has become the face at the state level and President Donald Trump the face at the national level.

Mayor Francis (as I like to call him in public settings) is more than a face. He is very youngish-looking, very fit, bilingual father and husband whose wife and two kids are even better looking than he is.

But that's all about style. In terms of substance, he has done three things that distinguish him—and his city, by derivation. He was the first mayor to cancel two major festivals early on in the epidemiological cycle, the first and only mayor of a major city to contract the disease, and the first public figure to donate his own plasma, once he was cured, in order to cure others.

That's the ultimate trifecta.

Most of the strong measures that Francis took to control the spread of the virus were done on instinct. I was not consulted, and neither was the county's mayor, who did not take it well.

The county's mayor, Carlos Gimenez, is on paper a much more powerful figure than the city's mayor. He has what are called "strong mayor" powers, and he lords over twenty-nine thousand employees, not counting the eleven thousand employees of the public hospital.

In addition, Gimenez runs the world-class airport and the seaport, which is the largest cruise ship port in the world. Miami's mayor rules only the airwaves. And the airwaves are kind to him—to put it mildly.

A lot of this book will reflect the tension that exists between the city mayor and the county mayor.

My role is much less pronounced. I am one of thirteen county commissioners. I have no executive powers and no legislative committee chairmanships. I am a bit of an outcast on the thirteen-person commission, in part because I am the only nonpartisan member and in part because I can be outspoken in my criticism of both Gimenez and some of my commission colleagues.

Yet I, too, have powerful followers. My district has many millionaires and billionaires—perhaps more of the latter than any district of two hundred thousand residents in any part of the world that is not named Manhattan, London, Moscow, Hong Kong, or Tokyo.

And, I should add, before the coronavirus hit, a lot of those New York and foreign billionaires were eager to grab their bags and move to sunny, low-tax, glamorous Miami.

That was just a month ago; then the virus hit us in the face. And the first face was that of our young mayor, Francis, who apparently contracted it from a Brazilian diplomat who had come here with Brazil's right-of-center, populist president, Jair Bolsonaro.

Francis and I are both populists, in the sense that we make decisions with a view to what benefits the people we govern. In the current crisis, he has played things more conservatively than I would have, but—as the saying goes—the proof is in the pudding.

The measures he has taken have probably saved a lot of lives; ultimately, every other urban area and most states followed his precedent-setting orders requiring shutting down all but the most essential commercial activities and requiring everyone to stay at home.

I will leave for later in this book the telling of the final outcome of the viral outbreak that made the mayor of Miami, Francis Suarez, a viral figure. Suffice it to say that we worked together, argued very little, and ultimately did our best to solve both the health crisis and the ensuing economic crisis.

He paid more attention to the former; I paid more attention to the latter. In the end, I think we acted in unison and with amazing results, just as we have done for the past decade on other, more mundane issues, such as our ineffective mass transit system.

We are not a dynasty in the sense that either of us has inherited any kind of power. In fact, I had little power when Francis was elected to the city commission (2009), and he was only a city commissioner when I was elected to the county commission, in a special election in 2011.

There may be touches of dynastic succession in that I was mayor of Miami from 1985 to 1993. It's also possible that by the time this book is published, one of us will be mayor of the city and the other mayor of the county.

But believe me when I say there is nothing of an inherited right to reign or a dynastic succession in our situations. There are, I suspect, some inherited traits, though even with those, Francis and I have enormous stylistic differences.

Occasionally, we have substantive differences. Mostly, we dance around each other as if tied at the hip, but by a very elastic band that often stretches close to the breaking point, before it brings us back to a very cohesive and (hopefully) elegant dance.

My reader can judge.

Introduction

The summer of 2017 is about to begin in Miami. Our idle thoughts are concentrated on the beach and the lazy sport of baseball—once considered the national pastime.

In Miami, politics is always in season; *it is the national pastime.*

This is evident from the Venezuelan demonstrators I see downtown, as I get off the people mover for a lunch appointment. It is evident from the rush of legislative activity in Tallahassee, as the chief executive (Governor Rick Scott) and the heads of the Florida House of Representatives (Speaker Richard Corcoran) and Senate (President Joe Negron) huddle to craft a last-minute deal to avoid a lengthy and bitter special session.

Nationally, there is much ado about Trump's signaling a withdrawal from the Paris accord on carbon emissions and about the never-ending Russia-hacking investigation.

Locally, what is paramount is the end of the qualifying period for the city's mayoralty. That deadline comes at the end of the summer—soon after the August recess, when city and county both take a break from politics and presumably prepare for the budget hearings, which by law must happen in September.

With the election barely five months away, my son, Francis, still has not drawn an opponent. The city mayor's daughter, Raquel Regalado, has announced her candidacy for the U.S. Congress, in the seat that has been held for three decades by the illustrious Ileana Ros-Lehtinen. Ros-Lehtinen's recent press release on her planned retirement in 2018 has created a vacuum that has sucked potential opponents away from considering a challenge to Francis in the quickly approaching November mayoral election.

Hard as it is to believe, we are well into the summer and the young would-be mayor of Miami is still unopposed. The *Miami Herald* interviews Francis, and he casually remarks that it's a miracle.

But he doesn't mean it in the sense of divine intervention. I have always emphasized to my kids that praying to God is mainly to seek the counsel of the Almighty as to how *we can do miraculous things with the gifts we have received.*

Still, it's a miracle that on this Friday in 2017, Francis and I find ourselves in Miami's oldest church, called Gesù. Like its namesake in Rome, it was built by the Jesuit order, the same institution that gave birth to so many Middle Ages scientists and to the current pope, who chose the name Francis from St. Francis of Assisi, though it could just as easily have been chosen from St. Francis Xavier, one of the founders of the order.

My son, Francis Xavier, was named after both great saints. He was baptized by a Franciscan (Capuchin) priest who is now a cardinal (Boston's Seán O'Malley). Could it be that my son was destined to possess a combination of Jesuit erudition and Franciscan inclination to service?

My reader can judge. Francis certainly has traces of advanced analytical skills, mixed in with people skills that have not been seen (in these parts) since Maurice Ferré, who was mayor of Miami in the seventies and early eighties, and whom I somehow defeated in 1985.

On this Friday, Francis and I find ourselves, by pure coincidence, in a temple of worship that depicts, on a ceiling that emulates the Sistine Chapel's, the Jesuit martyrs who brought Christianity to Florida.

Gesù is the oldest parish in Miami and the only one left downtown. The Jesuits still serve as the parish priests. The church is beautiful—particularly on the inside, where freshly restored frescoes adorn almost every segment of the upper walls and every nook and cranny of the ceiling.

The Mass is ready to start, but I am here for confession, and that ends when the Mass begins, which means I may have to wait another half hour to have my confession heard. But I am lucky on this day, as the previous confessant walks out and the priest ushers me in, announcing that I am the last person he will hear. The bell rings the beginning of noon Mass, and as I hasten into the confessional box, I note the entrance of my son, who has decided to hear Mass on this very same day, at this very same time, and in this very same church.

Francis and I don't coordinate our spiritual calendars in this way. Hell, we don't even coordinate our political calendars. He marches to a totally different beat and a totally different drummer: His music is frenzied and his calendar is crowded. He is rock-and-roll, and I am classical.

My schedule is much more relaxed. My days as a 24/7 politician-cum-father-of-four have long since ended. My law practice requires about half of the hours that it did when I was mayor.

Compared to Francis, I have a lot of free time. On this day, we just happen to be at the same church at the same time, though in search of totally distinct sacraments. We embrace quickly, and I whisper, "What are you doing for lunch after mass?" He whispers back, "I am doing lunch with Vince [Lago] at the little restaurant next to my law office; you are welcome to join us."

It's a good thing that we've seen each other. Vince Lago is one of our stable of young Turks in Miami politics, and he is intense on this day—seething with impatience at the county's inability to solve our transportation woes. As a commissioner in the neighboring city of Coral Gables, Lago is at his wit's end when discussing the debacle that is our metropolitan transportation system.

That topic permeates this book; in various chapters I will describe the county's transportation incompetence, which has managed to squander yearly revenues of a quarter-billion dollars for about a decade now. Today Francis and I are both presumably at Gesù to pray for a little help from the almighty God, who is not supposed to meddle in politics.

That is what the First Amendment says.

And yet, here we are, less than ninety days from the end of the qualifying period for mayoral candidates, and there are no challengers to this young man—the boy wonder of Miami politics. What is it that makes Francis so special that he might be the first-ever mayor of a major city to be elected by acclamation?

It is impossible for me to be objective when answering this question, of course, as he is my son.

But my reader should remember that my analysis is made a little more objective by my own travails. It took me four tries to be elected mayor; my first three campaigns for public office all ended in defeat. The Miami dynasty is not at all like that of the Kennedys in that sense; my dad was neither an ambassador nor wealthy.

He was a refugee from Cuba and Fidel Castro's Communism who arrived in Washington, D.C., in 1961 with fourteen kids. His first job paid him exactly $500 a month. Later on, I will tell the story of his engineering wizardry, which took him from being the protégé of Clyde Cowan at Catholic University to designing nuclear power plants with Bechtel Corporation.

My old man was a brilliant, tough, didactic technocrat who instilled in me a love of both science and politics, including the very theoretical tenets of political philosophy. But I was a refugee myself and had to start from scratch.

Let me tell you how low that starting point was. The first apartment my parents had, in Hyattsville, Maryland, was a two-bedroom, and only three children were allowed per couple. The management was sure that my parents had six kids living there, but they actually had nine!

To get into the pool area, you needed to show picture IDs. So three of us would get in and then pass the IDs under the fence to the next three.

Despite our lack of money, my dad decided that I should study at the best school in the nation's capital. His boss, Clyde Cowan, told him that was St. Anselm's Abbey School, a bastion of liberal arts scholarship that was hidden on a wooded promontory in the northeast area of D.C. So my dad took me there and explained to the headmaster that he had been dean of engineering at an Augustinian university in Havana, Cuba, called Villanueva. He also told the headmaster that he himself had studied civil engineering at Villanova University in Philadelphia.

The headmaster said that was all well and good, but that at St. Anselm's, students were accepted on their own merits, not their father's. And I had to take an admissions test, with the usual math and verbal components.

The headmaster brought my dad the test results and remarked, "It's a good thing your son is advanced in math, because his English is abysmal." He showed my dad an example of a wrong answer to a rather basic question, which I shall never forget: The question was, "Of the following four words, which one is not in the same category with the others?" The words were "stream," "river," "creek," and "mustard."

I got the answer wrong, and the headmaster highlighted my deficiency by putting a big red circle around it. But he admitted me to the school, and soon I was learning English, French, Latin, and Greek, as well as earning a presidential scholarship to Villanova. There, at my father's alma mater, began my university experience, which would end up lasting no less than eight years.

Fourteen years after my arrival in this country, I arrived in Miami with a seventy-five-dollar Buick and an unusual combination of degrees: in mechanical engineering, law, and public policy. Even though the last two were from Harvard, I was proudest of my engineering degree, because I was the only one who had graduated *summa cum laude* in the entire college of engineering.

I was at the very top of the academic world but at the very bottom of the political world when I arrived in Miami in 1975.

And the road to the top rung in municipal politics was very rocky, to say the least. It took me four tries to be elected mayor of Miami. Overall, I have lost more elections (seven) than I have won (six). Other vicissitudes followed in 1997.

I served as mayor of Miami for three terms, from 1985 to 1993. The media referred to those in a positive way, saying that I had been a "popular" mayor. That much could be corroborated in polls, though it glosses over the expected pitfalls that I navigated as mayor of a city that was experiencing every kind of ethnic and sociological upheaval during my tenure.

It also glosses over the unexpected—and unnecessary, as well as mostly undeserved—battles with the *Miami Herald* during those eight years. But that is a topic I will treat lightly.

Suffice it to say that the *Herald* is part of the mainstream media that consider their task to be "adversarial" to the politicians instead of collaborative. It is a remarkable turnaround from the role played by the media in the 1950s and 1960s, as described in David Halberstam's book *The Powers That Be*.

(It is a book worth reading, as it illustrates the effect that collaborative media can have on the rise of politicians like John F. Kennedy and Richard

Nixon. All of that ended with Watergate, of course, and one wonders what positive things might have come out of the presidencies of Bill Clinton and George H. W. Bush, had the media not totally changed their approach...)

But that is a story for another day. My narrative is about Francis and myself, as we have sought and occupied public office for the past three decades. And that narrative continues from where I left off above with a brief respite (1993 to 1997) when I took time off to mind my business and my growing family.

In 1997, I was elected the first executive mayor of Miami and then unelected by a court, which gave the seat to my opponent. For thirteen years after that low point in 1997–98, I languished in a time similar to what Winston Churchill called his "years in the wilderness." I could not win a race to be a dogcatcher, let alone mayor of Miami or Miami-Dade.

My son did much better. In his first try at the city commission, he won. That was in 2009. Then, two years later, he helped me get on the county commission, where I have served for nine years, while he served on the city commission.

I guess you could say that I passed the torch to him, as the second man in the relay, and then waited for him to pass it back to me so I could do the "anchor" (fourth and last) leg in the relay.

Few politicians get to do that—occupy posts in local government in tandem with their offspring. I am not aware of this happening in any other major American city.

Another first in American history is what I managed to do when I became the mayor of a major city a scant twenty-five years after arriving as a refugee to these shores. My story is thus unique from beginning to end. And the uniqueness speaks more to the greatness of this nation than to my own personal qualities.

And, of course, there was a lot of serendipity, which is the name we nowadays give to what used to be called fate, or destiny, or what believers call Providence.

Whatever you call it, the fact is that I was greeted in this country by an exile mecca that the Native Americans called Miami, which means "fresh water," as in the river that divides Miami in half.

To a great extent, the north side of the river is populated by folks who are of what is called the working class, whereas the south side of the river is inhabited mostly by well-to-do folks, the wealthiest of whom live close to the southern shores of the peninsula called Florida.

But that is all way too simplistic. Like all cities, Miami is a matrix, with multiple variables describing location and other variables defining occupation, living style, and culture. The one variable that is common is that 80 percent of us were not born here. We came from points north, looking for sunshine, and from points south, looking for freedom and the American dream.

I guess I am the embodiment of the American dream. My son, and his peers, are the lucky second act of that mostly felicitous drama.

This is the story of how we tried to share that dream with the rest of our fellow citizens.

1

The Passing of the Torch

The beginning of this century, as experienced in Miami, not only coincides with the passing of the torch by Cuban exiles to their U.S.-born children, but also marks the point in which Cuban-Americans consolidated corporate power with political power.

By the time I was elected mayor in 1985, the Cuban exile community had grown to a critical mass that wielded political power effectively; it was a function not only of sheer numerical strength but also of the peculiar affinity for politics that Cuban-Americans have.

Whereas other ethnic groups might have a 25 percent turnout in local elections, Cuban-Americans can reach 60 percent and even 70 percent.

Such electoral fever is probably shared by other immigrant groups—particularly those that flee totalitarian regimes and find in the U.S. the blessings of one-person-one-vote democracy.

Cubans also thrive when it comes to entrepreneurial endeavors. This phenomenon has been most evident in the construction industry. You could see a skilled worker (plumber, electrician, plasterer, cabinetmaker) start off working for an established builder and soon get certified as a contractor in the field.

If someone's English wasn't good enough to pass the state's contractor exam, that person would partner with someone who had the license. Within the first two decades after Castro, Cuban-American builders were a powerful force in Miami's private sector. After four decades, a handful of Cuban developers had become billionaires.

By the year 2000 there were Cuban-owned banks, furniture companies, drugstore and food-store chains, clinics and managed-care companies, hospitals, real estate firms, law firms, and every kind of freight and shipping business.

Miami soon had by far the highest regional concentration of Hispanic-owned businesses in the nation. Cuban-Americans had taken over the corporate world in what was—as far as I could tell—a unique phenomenon for any migrant group, on any continent, during the modern era.

Neither the Irish in Boston nor the Mexicans in the Southwest, nor Italians or Jews anywhere, have laid claim to a city's corporate machinery in a mere forty years. By the beginning of the twenty-first century, Cuban Americans had done it in Miami.

And it had been predicted by one very smart American politician more than two decades before. His name is Bill Bradley.

A couple of decades ago, just as I was getting ready to bow out as mayor of what is perhaps the world's most interesting city, we were visited by former U.S. senator Bill Bradley. The occasion was a small gathering of socially minded Cuban-American leaders; Bradley was our speaker for the day—though it was really more like an intimate roundtable discussion.

Bradley posed a poignant question to us: "What will happen when you Cubans consolidate your civic and corporate power? Will you forget other minorities, or will you help lift them up into the economic and political mainstream?"

Bradley is one of my heroes: a great basketball player, an Ivy Leaguer, and a consummate, literate politician of unquestioned integrity. That is an irresistible combination for me.

When he asked the question, I could only stammer, "Senator, only you could ask a question like that." Then I added, "All I can say is that I hope we will not forget the other minorities, the other refugees, like the Haitian Americans, Nicaraguans, and our forebears, who came here involuntarily, the African Americans, who—because of our numbers—look to us for leadership in areas such as affirmative action."

I have often thought about that question, and about that answer. There was no hypocrisy in my answer, but there was an element of ambiguity, of subjectivity.

My reader can judge whether I succeeded in being impartial; of necessity, that comment and my commentary in general relate to my personal experiences.

In recent weeks, one personal decision involved the endings of both my first full term as a commissioner and the county mayor's first full term as mayor. For five years, we had served together in those capacities, and it was not the best of times but also not the worst of times.

The municipal ship of state had sailed on a fairly even keel, though not with any great vigor. On the issue affecting our county the most—transportation—we had taken only baby steps. Yet the establishment (the developers, bankers, lobbyists, lawyers, and well-heeled entrepreneurs) was happy with the incumbent, Gimenez, and had lavished a campaign fortune on him, almost assuring his reelection.

In the meantime, I had drawn only token opposition as a commissioner. The *Miami Herald*, satisfied that Gimenez and I had both avoided scandal and balanced the budgets for five years, endorsed us both. (It didn't seem to bother the editorial writers that in many ways I am the antithesis of Gimenez, as will be seen in the rest of this book.)

Thankfully, my son gets along with Mayor Gimenez. Ironically, I get along with Gimenez's bitter enemy, Mayor Tomás Regalado, who heads the older, better-known municipality of Miami.

The city of Miami and Miami-Dade County should by all rights be peas in a pod. They should be well-meshed parts of the same municipal machinery. In fact, they should be consolidated, as has been done in places like Jacksonville, Florida, and Toronto, Canada.

Some day they probably will be. For now, they are often at odds, often at war, often at cross-purposes. Only the *patience of one man and the pasta of his son* have allowed the city and county to make any progress at all during the past nine years.

How Francis and I have crafted major reforms in mass transit, housing, and education during the nine years we have served together is the stuff of which great stories are made.

Buzz Bissinger told a story like it about Ed Rendell in Philadelphia. Mike Royko told it about Richard Daley in Chicago. Robert Caro and Alyn Brodsky told it about the great La Guardia in New York. Ed Koch and Rudy Giuliani had to tell it about themselves.

At least my son has someone else telling his story, which is interwoven with my own story. I suppose that I should be happy to have lived to tell this wonderful story of a father and a son who love not only their city but the people who live in it.

In the final analysis, what counts for a democratic leader—maybe for any kind of leader, including a benevolent monarch—is that he loves his people. Adlai Stevenson said that about John F. Kennedy. He said, "Like the ancient Prophets, [JFK] loved the People enough to warn them of their errors; and the man who loves his country best will hold it to its highest standards."

Francis and I love Miami, and we feel obligated to hold its people to the highest standards of democracy.

Only the future will tell whether we will succeed. But this book will shed some light on how we have tried.

2

Francis on the Eve of Becoming Mayor

We are still in 2017 in our narrative; it has been eight years since Francis was elected to the city commission. He became chairman four years later, at the age of thirty-five—the youngest commissioner ever to be in charge of the legislative assembly of this great global city.

Now, eight years after he was first elected, he is poised to be the next mayor of Miami, at thirty-nine years of age. He has never lost a race, though he did withdraw from one, announcing an early retreat after encountering minor media storms, in 2013. The storms passed quickly, and it seemed like the gods favored his withdrawal; it was the most graceful, most successful exit from a campaign that anyone in these parts had ever seen.

Perhaps that is a reason for his success four years later.

Perhaps he compressed, in one abandoned race, what I learned in seven defeats.

The main lesson, I think, is that politics is not by any means an exact science. It is more art than science, more dependent on circumstance than on substance, more a matter of timing than of planning.

But this book is not particularly about political strategy or campaigning. This book is about a father and a son who are consumed by public service, who have similar genes and ideology but are still so different.

Francis and I are similar in our faith, in our ideals, in our analytical skills. But we are so different in style. Where Francis is a born politician, I am a made politician. He is gregarious; I am studious. He loves to mingle with people; I love to read and write books. He is disorganized and naturally charismatic; I am a logistical contraption, and whatever charisma I display was learned from him and other great leaders, whom I imitate by sheer force of will.

On the road to some appointment is where our stylistic differences are most on display. I plan my drive to each appointment about a week in advance; I drive myself and know exactly what route I am taking, plus the possible alternatives in case of unexpected congestion on the chosen route. I even know what lanes I am taking for each anticipated turn.

By contrast, Francis plans everything at the last minute—assuming he plans it at all. A recent incident illustrates why I say he is logistically challenged. Francis and I had a joint appearance on a morning television program. I arrived early, as usual. He arrived right as the program started, with wife and baby in tow.

He excused himself by saying he had forgotten that his car was not at home, which meant his wife had to drive him to the program, with pajama-clad baby in the back. Then he confided, "I left my car at the car wash...two days ago!"

Such personal traits aside, my son and I are substantively very similar. We both base our philosophy of government on the same political scientists. He's a little bit right of center and I am a little left of center, but neither of us is a classic liberal or a classic conservative. We are both inspired by a strong faith, though he's more observant than I am.

And we're both athletes—competitively so. We both love basketball, played point guard in high school, and excelled in passing and sheer athleticism. Besides basketball, where we always were a winning combo in two-on-two, we have competed (and still do, to some extent) in tennis, swimming, and track.

One type of workout we don't compete in is CrossFit. While I continue to practice my swimming, he incessantly practices the rigorous CrossFit exercises, akin to weight-lifting. Here, I don't even dream of competing, given the frailty of my seventy-year-old joints. He, on the other hand, can dead-lift 455 pounds, which is more than the combined weight of his wife, himself, and his two children.

The fact that he has excelled in physical training, that he's much stronger than his father, is, I suspect, a source of pride for him. So is the fact that he has become a better speaker—at least in English.

Politically we're competitive but not rivals. We argue and occasionally get defensive as to our modes of leadership. But in the end, we want to make each other look good.

Besides the natural love that exists between father and son, there is a hidden factor at play that makes us want to collaborate more and compete less. It is the simple fact that in this county of almost three million people, with thirty-four cities, an $8 billion budget, the world's largest passenger port, and an airport with more international connections that any other in the country—a metropolis that is currently headed by two politicians (Regalado and Gimenez) who detest each other—if we don't perform like synchronized swimmers, the entire machinery of government simply comes to a halt.

Being in office simultaneously in the same metropolis is an unusual opportunity—a privilege very few families have ever had. Ours is not a typical father-son relationship, because I get to emulate him as much as he does me. So far, we do that as commissioners of city and county, respectively.

Perhaps in 2020 I will get to be mayor of the county while he is still mayor of the city.

For the moment, as I've said, I'm a county commissioner watching him perform as a city commissioner on his way to the mayoralty.

In the process, I've been doing my best to copy my son's people skills, which are Kennedyesque. I suppose he strives to keep up with my analytical skills. In at least two areas, affordable housing and mass transportation, he has exceeded them.

The fact of the matter is, he learns from me—particularly in policy— and I learn from him—particularly in politics. You might ask, how can that be? How can a thirtysomething city commissioner teach a wizened, three-term mayor about politics?

Well, he does. A lot.

And what makes this interesting is that we are both having enormous success in both policy and politics. The proof, as to politics, is that Francis has been reelected twice without opposition, in 2011 and 2015, to the city commission. I also have been reelected twice: once with no opposition, in 2012, and once with only token opposition, in 2016.

Now, in 2017, Francis seems to have no opponent as he climbs the municipal ladder to reach for the mayoralty of the world's newest and most exciting global city. It is hard to believe, but he looks to waltz right in. If so, it will be unprecedented in these parts—unless the incumbent terms out.

Two months out from the end of the qualifying period, there is only one potential opponent; he sits with Francis on the city commission and his last name is Carollo.

This is not "Crazy Joe" Carollo, who briefly served as Miami's mayor, but his younger brother, Frank. The *Miami Herald* characterizes them as another one of Miami's dynasties. But that one, hopefully, is about to end.

The Suarez dynasty, if my reckoning is right, will continue until the City of Miami and the County of Miami-Dade have governments that work, that are both compassionate and efficient.

This book is about the father-and-son team that worked to make that happen, during a period that spanned more than three decades. Two genetically similar but stylistically different politicians have learned from each other, competed amicably with each other, and ultimately fused their skills to take Miami from what *Time* magazine called "Paradise Lost" in 1981 to what is now a marvelous fusion of the best of America with the best of Europe and a touch of Africa and Asia.

The story is about policy as much as, if not more than, politics. Most pundits (including media and political consultants) don't pay much attention to policy. Historians do.

And so do the people.

In a democracy, the civil society—including and perhaps primarily the media—should frame the "Great Debate" between electors and elected such that the electors choose from policy options. In reality, for reasons that bear on the various flaws in our current system, the Great Debate is often a battle of money, media, and the masses, with the latter being pushed and pulled by negative ads on the one hand, and glossy pictures of the candidate with his or her family and pet on the other.

Luckily, in a city where only forty to fifty thousand citizens turn out to vote in odd years, when the mayoral race takes place, the connection of the politician to the voter is so close, so intimate, so near, that the system becomes almost like a direct democracy, as in ancient Greece.

I call it "in-your-face democracy."

Everyone knows the saying by former speaker Tip O'Neill to the effect that "all politics is local." I would say all politics *should be local.* In Miami, for the reasons stated, as well as others that have to do with a very lively Spanish media, all politics tend to be that way.

And that means that candidates cannot simply be created by money or media. They have to be time-tested and come from the very earthy streets of the city. It helps, of course, to have a well-known last name.

For Francis in 2017, that means being on the lookout for the current mayor's daughter (named Regalado, like her father) and the current city commissioner, whose older brother is the previously mentioned Joe Carollo.

As I mentioned, Regalado has recently eliminated herself from contention by filing for a congressional election that will take place in 2018. So city commissioner Frank Carollo is the only viable threat. He is the younger brother of someone who has haunted Miami politics for more than three decades, causing mischief and sowing discord along the way. The two of them make an odd pair.

3

The Carollo Brothers

Joe Carollo is undoubtedly a macabre folk figure in Miami's history. He was a city commissioner who made my life miserable for two years until I defeated him in what I called the ABC ("Anybody but Carollo") campaign in 1987. I won that battle rather readily. He was defeated and you might think he'd be out of politics forever.

Think again.

A decade later, he managed to get back on the city commission, finagled a special election to replace the venerable Mayor Stephen P. Clark, who had passed away, and defeated an opponent who—he said—had beaten his wife with a coat hanger.

Somehow, by hook or crook, Joe Carollo became mayor of Miami in 1996. Then, in 1997 and 1998, he declared Miami to be in a fiscal emergency that didn't really exist and managed to get the courts to reverse an election in which I had beaten him in the polls. (This all deserves a separate book, but maybe one written by others.)

Better to roll forward to the present.

Carollo, once again, is the bad boy of Miami politics, whose true colors are now pretty clear for all to see.

Unfortunately, they were not always so clear. In fact, by a combination of media manipulation and political legerdemain, Joe Carollo ultimately had me ousted from the mayoralty and installed himself. His reign of terror lasted only four years (1997 to 2001), but the negative effect on my reputation took more than a decade to wear off.

In the meantime, his younger brother had achieved political success as a city commissioner.

Frank Carollo, Joe's younger brother by a decade, is something his older, feistier brother never was: a true-blue, state-certified cop.

He also differs from his brother in that he is a family man; his marriage seems solid and his devotion to his little daughter quite apparent, as he dotes on her at eleven o'clock mass at my parish, called Saints Peter and Paul Church. (Joe Carollo, by contrast, has had a number of stormy marriages and breakups, including a notorious one in which, as mayor, he ended up spending a night in jail after throwing a tea canister at his wife.)

Frank is also not as much of a demagogue as Joe. He professes to care about government spending and inefficiency. His professional background, beyond law enforcement, is in forensic accounting. His employer, Tony Argiz, runs a very successful certified public accounting firm in town and tells everyone that Frank is a real accountant, not just your typical "politician for hire."

"Politicians for hire" is my term for well-heeled politicians who are hired typically by law firms to bring in business, while doing as little as possible to resemble real professionals in the legal field. This is a frequent arrangement in Miami—perhaps more than anywhere else in the nation. The tradition was started four decades ago by a fellow named Armando Lacasa, who somehow convinced the Florida Bar that he should be admitted to practice law based on a questionable certification that had him being admitted to practice law in Cuba.

Lacasa was a piece of work. He was appointed to the Miami city commission in the late seventies and immediately began to grow his personal wealth. This is not unusual for public officials in these parts nowadays, but back then the salary was minuscule, only $5,000 a year.

Needless to say, Lacasa didn't get rich through earnings from city hall or his law practice. He got rich by investing in real estate that was in the midst of being rezoned by the very city commission on which he sat.

The most celebrated of those rezoning capers involved a project planned for the mouth of the Miami River, as it meets with the street that is arguably Miami's equivalent of Park Avenue. It's called Brickell, and I am lucky to have bought a condo unit there in the year 2000 for a mere $199,000.

But back to Commissioner Lacasa. The guy put deposits on a couple of units being planned on Brickell and the Miami River. This is choice property: two blocks from downtown and next to glorious Biscayne Bay.

The only problem with the project is that it was not zoned for a high-rise condominium. The city commission had to approve that, and Lacasa was sitting on the five-member board of commissioners.

That, of course, was a direct conflict now that he had contracted to buy a couple of units there. At the time, if you had a good reputation or good credit or both, you could do that for as little as $10,000; you could also resell your option to buy and keep the difference in price, even though you never actually bought the unit. (It's called "flipping" the real estate.)

That is exactly what Lacasa did. Then he abstained from voting on the rezoning, which left the decision to four others. Then, when the rezoning was approved, he promptly assigned his right to buy the units for a much higher price. Presto, he became perhaps a half-million dollars richer.

This transaction was later reported by a *Herald* reporter named Luis Feldstein-Soto. He embellished the investigative story with a moniker he invented for Commissioner Armando Lacasa: "Armando LaCondo."

Lacasa ultimately became my opponent in three city elections. In the second one, he was defeated by a fellow named Demetrio Perez, in an election in which both Perez and I had outpolled him; Perez had edged me in the runoff. In a city with no electoral (single-member) districts, he occupied the "Cuban" seat. Later, as the city's Cuban voters increased, there were two or more Cuban-American commissioners.

Nowadays, the city has five district commissioners. One of them, who represents the heart of Little Havana, is Frank Carollo, Joe's brother. I could tell myriad stories about Joe Carollo but will limit myself to salient ones that impinge on current events.

Ostensibly, Frank Carollo is a real professional. On the city commission dais, he acts professionally enough; his mumbled tirades are not nearly as vitriolic as his older brother's used to be. Unlike Joe, he does not seem to see himself as a prosecutor.

But there ends the dissimilarity. Though perhaps not as mercurial and unstable as his brother, Frank is nevertheless one weird dude.

To begin with, he refuses to list his home address in public records—based on a state statute that exempts certified law enforcement officers from having to reveal their addresses. Apparently, it has not occurred to him that his service on a five-member board of commissioners that governs a major city of half a million people entitles the public to know whether he even lives in the district he represents.

Unlike his brother, who was investigated for all kinds of ethical conflicts in his business dealings (plus some wild divorce proceedings and the previously mentioned domestic violence arrest), Frank has had only one minor brush with the law. It happened when he was stopped by police for a moving violation and promptly alerted the chief of police, who immediately had the traffic ticket voided. It was an abuse of power and led to some sort of disciplinary fine by the local ethics commission.

But it did not affect his reputation as a fairly diligent, sober, and populist commissioner. (I think, on the issue of the traffic ticket, that the public in general assumes that city commissioners are immune from being charged for minor traffic infractions.)

But let's be honest and state the truth about this man. The best that can be said of Frank Carollo as a commissioner is what they used to say about mediocre Hollywood actors: that he's good to his wife and daughter. This guy's main (and only) accomplishment as a commissioner for eight years (2009 to 2017) was being the John Hancock of the commission. What I mean is that when a public works job was done in his district, using bonds approved before he even sat on the commission, his name took up the space of three or four other names on the neighborhood signs that gave credit to the city government.

Well, that is a bit of an exaggeration; I forgot his other legislative accomplishment. Having a newborn daughter whom he took everywhere, this guy decided that changing diapers in public restrooms should not be the task of mothers only. At his urging, the city passed an ordinance requiring men's bathrooms to be equally equipped with the diaper-changing tables that many ladies' rooms have!

And the world became much safer after that.

As the mayoral election of 2017 approached, a development project in the island next to downtown, called Watson Island, became a cause célèbre. It was a bit of déjà vu, since the development of Watson Island had been my first brush with the other Carollo brother, back in 1985.

Now it was being revisited in what could have been an eerie replay of the Carollo confrontation, three decades later. Francis, as always, not only avoided a confrontation with his commission colleague but showed his debating skills in a way that deflated Frank.

One sensed that the Carollo legacy of feigned concern for Watson Island would be Frank's big opportunity to challenge Francis and tarnish his reputation as a good-government politician. I say "Carollo legacy" because way back, in 1986–87, Joe Carollo had done his best to embarrass me about a very copacetic plan to improve Watson Island, a jewel resulting from the dredging of sea-lanes needed for the neighboring cruise seaport known as Dodge Island.

That story would take up too much space here. Suffice it to say that prior to my election as mayor in 1985, the city fathers and mothers (with Joe Carollo as part of the government) had approved a very rustic and low-intensity marine exhibition center on Watson Island. When I saw the plans (which were blessed by all the environmental groups as being a logical use of the island), I had inquired about the financing capability of the winning bidder.

Told that there was none, I enlisted some heavyweights to form a consortium of investors to do the project. I also ensured that the public component of the improvements, which was a seaside drive (like Havana's Malecón), would be built first; thus, if the marine expo center was never financed and built, the public would at least inherit a beautiful promenade providing spectacular views of the bay.

It was beautiful, it was appropriate, and it was now financially feasible, with the inclusion of a very reputable contractor: Bechtel Corporation.

It was so good that it had to be blown up by Joe Carollo. And blow it up he did, with gusto! By the time the accusations were over, Carollo had dug up some leftist leanings on the part of one of the investors and had challenged another one of the investors (the formidable Cuban exile leader Jorge Mas Canosa) to a duel.

As the *Miami Herald*'s Dave Barry would say, I am not making this up.

That all happened thirty years ago, and for the succeeding three decades, Watson Island saw some reasonably compatible development, including the relocation of the former Parrot Jungle and a children's museum. More recently, it was the locus of a rather imposing tunnel entrance and the previously mentioned project.

Thirty years after Joe had sunk an appropriate, enviro-friendly redevelopment of Watson Island, Frank was presumably poised to sink a totally inappropriate and concrete-laden development on the same island.

It was the right decision by the wrong person, as we shall see.

4

Watson Island Revisited

The redevelopment project approved for Watson Island this time around was totally absurd—except perhaps for one component, which was a mega-yacht marina. The city of Miami has really distinguished itself, as a builder and an operator, only where it concerns marinas. The reason for this is evident: Even governments, which as a rule are not particularly efficient, can take advantage of cornering the market for some good or service. In the case of marinas, the city owns most of the waterfront rights where marinas can be built; because of the high demand and low supply, it doesn't take a genius to make a buck from offering marina slips at a price that covers the cost of construction and the operation of the marina.

This is particularly true when the cost of acquisition is pretty much zero, as the waterfront property, in the case of "dredge islands" like Watson, was zero to begin with.

So far so good. Beginning early in the century and lasting until the present (a span of almost sixteen years), Miami managed to concoct a phased-in project in which the first phase was the only one that made sense and had proven financing (probably for the reasons mentioned above about the high demand and low supply of marinas).

The next phase of the Watson Island project involved a six-hundred-room hotel, plus extensive retail stores and 1,500 parking spaces.

Say what? Why would the city use what was left of this small but spectacularly located waterfront paradise for more hotels and stores, when it would necessarily compete with mega-projects being built in downtown Miami, Brickell, and the Omni area?

And why would you pour concrete for 1,500 parking spaces just when we were about to start providing mass transit service to Watson Island, as part of the Baylink project linking the mainland to Miami Beach? Not to mention the folly of creating an incentive for people to drive and park on what should be as much public space as possible, in this precious resource inherited from the state...

The commission had to decide whether or not to waive the breach incurred by the developer because of deadlines missed in starting the second phase of the project. Delays in construction, of course, have multiple, often justifiable causes. But the suspicion was that the delays were not just logistical but financial. Francis prepared for the commission discussion by immersing himself in the lease and the master agreement that the city and developer had signed.

The most glaring deficiency was precisely in the failure of the developer to have a signed and sealed construction loan with a reputable bank, which would call for regular cash disbursements as the project proceeded. It helped Francis enormously that real estate financing was precisely his niche in the practice of law.

The man knew his stuff.

You have to see the video of this virtuoso performance. I say that because he's my son, and there is inevitable bias. I expect that by the time this book is published, the available technology will permit my readers to click a link that allows them to see for themselves.

In the meantime, let me describe it with only a modicum of (justifiable) fawning.

As I said before, Francis was as well prepared as a lawyer doing a cross-examination in court. He had all the relevant sections of the various agreements at his fingertips and quoted each with precision.

In rather clear terms, the signed documents required that the developer have a construction loan in place, providing financing in the amount of $31.2 million.

Period. No ifs, ands, or buts.

For whatever reason, the developer was not able to prove the existence of a construction loan. Instead, he chose to substitute an affidavit of liquidity, claiming that he had that much money in the bank.

Francis laid into that claim. "Let's assume," he said, "that I gave you my affidavit saying that I had thirty-one point two million dollars and could do this project. Would you accept my affidavit?"

That one question, that one hypothetical, won the day. It reminded me of the famous question by defense counsel Joseph Welch in the Joe McCarthy congressional hearings of the House Un-American Activities Committee: "Have you no decency, sir, at long last?"

If I had been doing the questioning, I probably would have raised the question by using a fictional hypothetical. I would probably have said, "Sir, would you accept an affidavit of financial wherewithal from Joe Blow?" Which would have some effect but not the sting that Francis's hypothetical had.

As a true, instinctive politician, Francis knows how to personalize a technical issue. By saying "Would you accept *my* affidavit," he was telling these bigwigs that we, the people, knew their game. A city commissioner who's on his way to being mayor of Miami, and has raised close to $3 million, is a trustworthy individual.

But *an affidavit* is no substitute for a construction loan—even if it comes from a well-respected government official.

The blow had been struck. It was followed by additional question-and-answer dialogue between Francis on one side and the big-time lawyers and lobbyists on the other. When the lobbyist suggested that the money was in the bank, Francis pointed out that a bank account, unless it's in escrow, can be withdrawn on a moment's notice. When Francis pointed out that the developer had also breached the terms by failing to pay close to a million dollars in real estate taxes on time, the lobbyist said it was not a default because it had been accepted late by the city two years in a row.

Rather than argue the point, Francis simply asked, "But why was the payment late?" The lobbyist had no answer.

There were other fine moments by Francis during his questioning. Perhaps the best was when he explained that the requirement of a construction loan, even though modified somewhat by a subsequent document, was inalterable because the master agreement made clear that its provisions could not be modified by any subsequent verbal or written amendment, and thus represented the will of the commission.

It wasn't just that he won the technical argument with the big-time lawyers and lobbyists, as well as with his own city manager. *It was the way he did it, with stern but respectful language.* It was the precision he used to explain what documents govern or control when there is an apparent contradiction.

And it was his elegant but forceful chiding of the city administration for even trying to modify the clear terms of the master agreement approved by the commission.

It was so masterful that both the city manager and the developer's lobbyists and lawyers were left to stammer in near incoherence.

Poor Frank Carollo had to follow that performance, and he began by acknowledging that "Commissioner Suarez has made a compelling argument."

He followed that with a rather obtuse and tangential discussion of a totally different project in which the city manager had almost allowed a developer to skirt the requirement of building a fire station.

That tangential diatribe was accompanied by all kinds of obsequious compliments directed at the very administrators that he was criticizing. That, in turn, brings to mind a key problem that plagues local governments.

In Miami, for reasons I cannot fathom, the bureaucrats are extremely well paid, extremely respected by the media, and borderline incompetent.

Of all the defects in the structure of local government, this is the most salient one and will be discussed in various subsequent chapters.

For now, though, I prefer to delve into some success stories. As I constantly tell my staff, what counts is not the bad projects we shoot down; what counts is the good projects we make happen.

In his first seven years as a commissioner (five of which coincided with my tenure on the county commission), Francis accomplished some great things—particularly in the area of transportation.

He did that while having no executive power, no bully pulpit, and no geographical jurisdiction over the projects in question.

A lot of it was based on pure charisma.

People who see us together, or who hear us separately on radio or television, would never guess the drastically different styles that we have. As I said earlier, where Francis is a born politician, I am a made politician.

It took us half a decade to kick-start a mass transit plan for Miami-Dade. The impediments were enormous.

The lack of leadership by most of the putative leaders was abysmal.

But I am getting ahead of myself. Right now, I want to focus on the phenomenon that is Francis Xavier Suarez.

It is not all based on charisma, or on a great-looking wife and child. There are myriad other factors, which I will analyze throughout the book.

But it must be admitted that charisma is important in politics. Extremely important. Some people just don't have it. Others ooze it. In the next few chapters, I'll analyze some well-known personalities in terms of charisma. Later in the book, I will touch upon charisma as possessed by the political character du jour in the particular narrative.

One of my most interesting encounters with a national figure happened in 1997, when I met Donald Trump.

5

A Close Encounter
with Donald Trump

had only one opportunity to rub elbows with Donald Trump prior to his entering politics. It happened in New York City, during a stormy period in my political career, when I traveled to the Big Apple in an effort to force Wall Street to "let my people go."

Let me explain.

The city of Miami in 1997 was in a declared state of fiscal emergency. The mayor, none other than the previously mentioned Joe Carollo, had used all his demagogic wiles to convince the establishment (all the way to the governor in Tallahassee) that the city's finances were in shambles. Miami, argued Carollo, could not pay its bills.

Carollo used a couple of emissaries to convince the governor of this. One happens to be a good friend of mine; he is a prominent lawyer named Sonny Holtzman, and he was a confidant of Governor Lawton Chiles. Sonny never took the time to judge for himself whether what Carollo (and his erstwhile city manager, Merrett Stierheim) thought about the city's finances was even remotely right. He just conveyed the alarming facts to the kind old man, whose mental faculties were already on the wane.

Chiles consulted the state's auditor general, who actually reports to the legislature—and went with the auditor's advice. The city, they all argued, was $65 million in the hole.

It would be fun to take apart the entire quantitative argument. For example, I could mention that the city's finance department was double-listing one of the city's outstanding bonds, in the approximate amount of $64 million. *The darn thing was listed twice in the city's net worth statement.* (This by itself nullified the $65 million deficit.)

I could also mention that the negative balances included $110 million in contingent liabilities—a number that was previously reported as $15 million per year in annualized, pay-as-you-go reserve funds. (This had been done to comply with an accounting rule called GASB 12. It is kind of silly, when you think about it. Municipal governments are shielded from civil suits by sovereign immunity, which caps a claim at $100,000. Unless some city employee negligently runs over a crowd of people and kills scores of them, judgments against the city will usually not exceed a couple of million dollars a year.)

But those were not as fictional as the $75 million deficit listed for the city's "enterprise fund," which was really just the accumulated accounting losses of the solid waste department, which the city manager (over my strenuous objection) had switched from being a general service to being a self-supporting "enterprise." In effect, the supposed $75 million deficit was just an accounting device used to reflect payments made from the general fund to the solid waste department to cover whatever expenses could not be funded from the solid waste fee.

The accountants called that $75 million figure a "retained earnings deficit." It never dawned on the prestigious CPA firm that "retained earnings" cannot be a deficit, since they could not have been "earnings" to begin with. They would have been losses.

It was actually $75 million in accumulated yearly deficits for one department. Not for the city as whole. And there was no negative bank account, no overdraft, no money owed to anyone. *It was an internal accounting device.*

And it was so confusing that the accounting standard was later reversed by the new CPA firm engaged by the city. Presto, no more $75 million deficit!

The whole episode—the whole financial emergency—was a chimera. In case my reader wants better proof, I can offer this simple figure. In four months of acting as mayor (November 1997 to April 1998), I managed to accumulate, in pure cash reserves, a total of $130 million! Just the sale of the property where the new Miami Heat arena was built pumped $37.5 million into the city's coffers.

In fact, Miami in 1997 and 1998 was on the verge of a building boom that would see its considerable tax base double in a decade. There was never anything like a fiscal emergency, which state law defines as two years in a row in which the budget deficit could not be covered from the sale of surplus assets. (By way of illustration, the Watson Island previously referred to could be sold probably for more than a billion dollars; not that we would ever want to privatize this precious, public resource in the middle of glorious Biscayne Bay...)

I made a big splash in New York during those post-Thanksgiving days of 1997. I met with Mayor Rudy Giuliani and former mayor Ed Koch. I made three presentations in one day to the three credit-rating agencies: Standard & Poor's, Moody's, and Fitch.

And I managed to sneak into Trump Tower for a fundraiser hosted by Donald Trump for none other than Jeb Bush.

I don't want to bore my reader with details. Suffice it to say that, thanks to Giuliani, we managed to get a last-minute invitation to this august event, held in the famous Round Room, which was split by a receiving line that cut the circle exactly in half. In the middle of the circle stood three people, all at least six feet tall.

The three were Jeb Bush, Trump, and his girlfriend du jour. (I don't remember her name and prefer not to look it up in newspaper accounts.) If I'm remembering correctly, she was the first of the three tall persons on the receiving line. She was a blond six-footer. That much I remember.

As I went to shake her hand, she exclaimed, with some excitement in her voice, "Are you the mayor of Miami?"

"Yes, I am!"

Then she quickly added, "I have been waiting to meet you, because I wanted to tell you that this guy [pointing to Trump] has been mean to me. He has been two-timing me."

I have no idea what she expected from me. I will tell you this: As soon as I got the chance to call my wife, Rita, in Miami, I blurted out the whole story to her, looking for some feminine insight. Rita said she understood: "The lady," she said, "probably figured you were a multimillionaire, reasonably good-looking, and young; plus, you appeared to her as a well-dressed, six-foot Latin man. What better foil to make Trump jealous?"

Parenthetically, I once came close to being a millionaire, when a

Russian group offered to buy my Brickell condominium for a humongous figure, so they could tear the entire building down and use it as parking for the building next to it, which is on the water's edge. Unfortunately, my fellow condo owners did not agree to the sale, and I never made a cool million.

Not that I am crying poverty. Thanks to the Save Our Homes legislation, my taxes remain low, since they are based on my modest purchase price of $199,000. I will discuss that tax advantage and how it affects new homebuyers later when I discuss the dearth of affordable housing in Miami-Dade.

Now back to Trump. This guy is a piece of work. There is no politician even remotely like him. There probably never will be—at least in the American presidency.

Donald Trump, when I met him a quarter century ago, seemed like the classic Hollywood playboy. One would never have cast him as a serious actor, let alone as a viable candidate for president. No one could have guessed that he would become a master in the use of social media.

No public figure in history has been able to communicate, in a fraction of a second, with thirty million followers at any time, by punching 140 characters into a computer. That thirty-million number gets compounded very quickly when the mainstream media inevitably comment (mostly unfavorably) on what Trump emotes. And another few million get to read his comments in the social media of others who retweet them.

And because he has social media and a slight majority of voters who lean towards the conservative side of the ideological spectrum, I would never underestimate his potential for coming back and being an effective leader.

Mario Cuomo once said that "campaigning is poetry and governing is prose." So far, Trump has been much better at campaigning than at governing.

The same was true, to a great extent, about the man I consider to be the second-most-charismatic politician I've ever met—after Robert Kennedy. His name is Maurice Ferré.

6

Maurice Ferré: Miami Royalty

can't think of anyone to compare Maurice Ferré to, other than the Kennedys. Like the Kennedys, he was born with a silver spoon in his mouth. His father, José Luis Ferré, was a very wealthy media magnate in Puerto Rico. You can think of him as Joseph Kennedy, the multimillionaire head of the Kennedy clan. Although he was much less visible than Joseph Kennedy, José Luis Ferré played a similar role in his charismatic son's rise to power as mayor of Miami.

Maurice Ferré landed in Miami with a millionaire's portfolio, a glamorous and rich wife (Mercedes), and looks that could make many a woman swoon. He never could succeed in business, but he started off with so much money that it would have taken a major catastrophe to lose it all.

Former television personality Ralph Renick used to say that "as a young man, Maurice Ferré came to Miami from Puerto Rico and made a small fortune…out of a large one." Never has a politician combined superlative charisma with an abysmal lack of business practicality like Ferré.

Thankfully for him, his wife, Mercedes, was the daughter of a very successful Venezuelan architect. When Ferré managed to squander his family fortune, Mercedes came to the rescue and assured the couple an old age of relative financial security, coupled with a vestige of power and glamour that was just everlasting. It helped that Mercedes was a Jackie Kennedy lookalike and that their kids were smart, good-looking, and successful.

In many ways besides good looks, Ferré was the Hispanic equivalent of JFK. He was rich, famous, and powerful. He had a summer house in New England. His wife, as previously mentioned, was glamorous and wealthy. He was supremely confident in every word he uttered and every political move he made.

Ferré had been mayor for a while when I arrived in Miami in 1975. At the time, he was the unquestioned BMOC (big man on campus), and that applied both to the political fraternity and the business establishment.

About the closest thing to his competitor for BMOC in Miami was Alvah Chapman, who was the chairman of the board of the company that owned the *Miami Herald*, named Knight Ridder. The newspaper chain had its headquarters in Miami, and that meant it was just about the biggest corporate presence in town, other than perhaps three Florida utilities— Florida Power & Light, BellSouth, and the Florida East Coast Railway.

Add one large bank with its headquarters here, called Southeast National, and you pretty much had the cream of the crop in one hand.

Alvah Chapman was not satisfied with being the informal leader of Miami's civic life. So he created a cabal that met secretly and even had the chutzpah to call themselves the Non-Group. The presidents of the aforementioned utilities and banks plus a developer or two, a couple of big-time lawyers, and some other wealthy entrepreneurs comprised this unusual secretive organization whose avowed purpose was to make sure that the politicians did the right thing.

It worked pretty well for about a decade, until the *Herald* itself exposed them and hinted that they were violating a state law that required total transparency in agencies that set government policy. That, of course, was nonsense, since the Non-Group had no elected officials and no tangible civil authority. But the revelation caused embarrassment—particularly when the newspaper itself published interviews with some members who denied the very existence of the group.

Excuse me, the Non-Group.

Anyhow, none of the Non-Group members rivaled Ferré in power or cachet; few, if any, rivaled him in wealth. Ferré's U.S. holdings included cement manufacturer Maule Industries and a handful of buildings in downtown Miami.

Wealth and power were just two of the three legs of the Ferré mystique. The third leg was charisma.

Analyzing Ferré's charisma begins, of necessity, with sheer photogenic good looks. The emphasis is on "photogenic." Ferré has a perfectly symmetrical face; it is boyishly round and thus has never suffered the fate of those of us whose profiles are not as pleasant.

I used to say about myself that on a really good day, I could look like Fernando Llamas from the front; but from a side view I resemble a tall, erect lizard. (Writing a feature story on me for *Tropic* magazine, a reporter named Guy Gugliotta once referred to me as being "pleasantly dog-faced.")

Ferré, by contrast, was good-looking from all angles, at all times. He also had a cherubic smile for every occasion—including when he was angry or sad. The best test of his ability to smile under fire came when Joe Carollo ambushed him in a press conference.

That was in 1983, during a runoff with yours truly.

Somehow, Carollo tricked Ferré into calling a press conference to announce the support that Carollo had promised to give. Poor Ferré went along with the ruse and showed up at the appointed time, only to find himself with tons of media and no Carollo.

Here, Ferré was a victim of his own best asset: his extraordinary self-confidence. Assuming that Carollo was just tardy, and wanting to keep the media from leaving, Ferré delved into a lengthy soliloquy about the virtues of the admittedly mercurial Carollo. This went on for a good fifteen or twenty minutes. Still Carollo did not appear.

Those present said that the wait took at least a half hour before Carollo sauntered in and sat down next to Ferré, who was quite visibly relieved.

But not for long.

After being introduced, Carollo immediately began to attack Ferré—explaining that he had never promised to endorse the mayor. "You all have been brought here on false pretenses," he said. "In fact, my reason to be here and agree to a press conference was precisely the opposite: to tell the world that his man is a divisive force and should not be reelected."

It was then that Ferré rose to what is worthy of an Academy Award for Best Dramatic Performance Under Fire. Suppressing his shock and anger, he gave what I call his best Mona Lisa smile. It was the sort of melancholic, empathetic, diffident smile of a superior being who finds himself in the midst of infantile humans and manages to not be too uncomfortable in their presence.

It was Maurice Ferré at his best. And, I should add, it did the trick, as the people who ended up embarrassed by this freak show were first Carollo and then yours truly. (I lost the election, which took place just a couple of days later, by a considerable margin.)

The next time Ferré and I faced each other was in 1985. By that time, I had lost three elections (two for commissioner, in 1979 and 1981, and one for mayor, in 1983). Even close friends of mine thought that I was really not meant for politics—that I was just another of those idealists who at best have an impact by offering ideas but never implementing them.

Every society has those kinds of theoretical political leaders. At the presidential level, there have been many great ones: Barry Goldwater and Daniel Patrick Moynihan come to mind. Before them was the golden-tongued Adlai Stevenson, whose eulogy to JFK is so often quoted.

Stevenson even had a great self-effacing quip to explain his inability to win the big one. It came out spontaneously during yet another failed run for the presidency. While Stevenson was giving a speech, a supporter yelled out, "Governor, all the thinking people are with you!" To which he replied, "Yes, but I need a majority."

I had a lot of thinking people with me in my various races. In my very first campaign, for city commissioner, I had a coterie of big names, including the elite in the Miami legal community—the Sandy D'Alembertes, Janet Renos, and Janet McAlileys.

The *Miami Herald*, in that first race, gave me a gushing endorsement; the editorial board said that I was the most qualified candidate on the entire ballot. It endorsed me "with singular enthusiasm."

By the time 1985 came around, the *Herald* had given up on me; it endorsed a banker named Raul Masvidal. (By this time, it had given up on Ferré also, though for different reasons.)

I defeated Maurice Ferré in 1985. But he didn't go away quietly into the night. Not even close.

He showed an uncanny ability to stay in the public eye soon after my election, when Mother Teresa visited. The occasion was a breakfast in support of the pro-life movement. The tables were adorned with red roses, which were the symbol of the movement.

As the incumbent mayor and a longtime activist in the movement, I was asked to introduce Mother Teresa to the breakfast crowd, a good 1,200 people. It would never even have entered my mind to use this saintly lady for a photo op.

Not so with Maurice Ferré. As the breakfast ended, there was a press opportunity, and here Ferré made his move. He obviously had planned it, for he had plucked a rose from one of the tables and worked his way to the edge of the press room, where I was having a quiet tête-a-tête with the famous missionary. I thought it only fair to introduce the former mayor, who had from time to time said positive things about the right-to-life movement.

Immediately, he fell to one knee and presented Mother Teresa with a red rose, as one might do when meeting a beauty queen, a pope, or a monarch. It was a bit odd, since this was a press opportunity, and I am sure Mother Teresa was not expecting such reverential homage, being the simple soul that she was.

All I know is that the next day, the front page of the *Miami Herald* carried the picture of Ferré kneeling and handing her the red rose. Later, when I met up with the former mayor, I mentioned how he had stolen the show that day. He answered glibly, "Suarez, you have to know when and how to handle photo ops."

You had to give it to him. He was a master at garnering attention.

Ferré's charisma was buttressed enormously by his self-confidence. Like all great politicians, he had an abiding level of self-esteem. Even as I write these lines, while he is in his early eighties and well past any electoral success, he has managed to have a voice in important policy-making bodies.

Premised on the strange cross-over endorsement of Republican Rick Scott in the 2010 gubernatorial campaign, Ferré (a lifelong Democrat) has landed on various transportation boards. The one that has most brought him into contact with Francis and me is the countywide MPO (Metropolitan Planning Organization), which oversees the funding of transportation projects.

It is here that Ferré has interacted with Francis, who also sits on the MPO as representative of the county's largest city: Miami. Both came on the MPO board at about the same time, and for a while it looked like

Ferré would control the narrative. He had strong, natural allies on the mostly Democratic board; he also seemed to connect with another wealthy politician, Miami Beach mayor Phil Levine.

Like Ferré, Levine is supremely confident and can be equally aggressive in his approach; unlike Ferré, Levine has a hard time not being abrasive.

For about a year, the two of them, plus Francis, dominated the proceedings of the MPO. Ultimately, Ferré and Levine ended up marginalized and Francis ended up pretty much in charge of the whole shebang.

Francis is a doer, not just a talker. But it helps him enormously to have extraordinary charisma, along the lines of Bill Clinton, John F. Kennedy, or Ronald Reagan.

That charisma, supported by my analytical powers and his own ability to grasp transportation and housing models, has enabled Francis to be a builder and not just a pretty face. In that he resembles the person who was the greatest municipal builder of all time: Robert Moses.

7

Francis the Power Broker

O ther than Franklin Roosevelt during the post-Depression era, also known as the New Deal era, there is no single American— and maybe no single human being in history—who built more public projects than Robert Moses of New York.

In Miami, during the first part of the second decade of the twenty-first century, the closest thing to Moses was Francis. And he did it with no executive power whatsoever, and very little actual authority. Moses, by contrast, was the chairman of five highway, parks, bridge, and housing authorities. It is said that the five agencies he headed were all equipped with an executive dining room and that each had a meal ready for him and his guests to eat at any time.

Francis had none of that. Yet he cobbled together a $69 million deal that allowed the once-abandoned railroad along the east coast of Florida to have a grand central station in downtown Miami. The project was not only the largest but the only privately funded passenger rail system to be built in the United States in the past hundred years.

That $69 million in public subsidies allowed Miami's downtown to become a rail transportation hub, whereas before it had been a mishmash of elevated highways that separated historic neighborhoods while making commuters depend on single-occupancy automobiles and expensive parking buildings.

Even more impressive than the grand-central-station compromise is what Francis cobbled together from disparate and disparaging parts. In achieving consensus on a mass transportation plan for the county, Francis realized two things that had eluded other policy makers.

One is that South Florida is laid out in a way that begs for a passenger railroad. The industrialist Henry Flagler, of course, had sensed that more than a century ago. As a thin peninsula, bordered by the sea on the east and the Everglades on the west, Miami needs just one north–south transit solution and a couple of east–west solutions.

Luckily for Francis and me, the north–south solution is already mostly in place, in the form of the Florida East Coast (FEC) railroad line that borders the I-95 corridor. The width of its right of way permits double tracking, which means the freight line can continue to operate while a passenger line is built comfortably alongside it.

Ironically, one of my first tasks as a Miami lawyer was to fight in court to keep the FEC freight line in place—since the city of Miami wanted to eliminate the last spur that connected the freight line to the Port of Miami.

I was hired out of law school by Miami's oldest law firm, Shutts & Bowen. One of my first assignments was to battle the city as it tried to turn the last chunk of rail into a park.

It would ultimately become the home of the Miami Heat.

That was 1975. Roll forward and we see, by the luck of the draw, the private owners of the rail line deciding—on their own—to build a passenger rail line that will connect Miami to Orlando, with stops in Fort Lauderdale and West Palm Beach. All we had to do was rent some access to this passenger line and our north–south transit issues would be resolved by the combination of the existing I-95 superhighway and a slower, at-grade commuter train using the FEC line.

Once Francis had cobbled together the $69 million grand central station, he directed his attention to the rest of the rail system. As good politicians do, he began by coming up with a catchy acronym.

Huddling together with our two transportation bureaucrats, whom Francis quickly dubbed his "angels," he piggybacked on the famous San Francisco BART (Bay Area Rapid Transit) system and came up with the slightly more presumptuous SMART (Strategic Miami Area Rapid Transit).

Within a few months of the grand-central-station victory, Francis somehow took over the county's MPO, schmoozed his way to the vice chairmanship of said MPO, convinced the county commission chairman to make him chairman of a governance committee, and otherwise cajoled and induced the fractious twenty-one-member MPO into agreeing on the elements of a $3.6 billion rail plan, now boasting the SMART title.

Never has anyone absorbed so much stupidity from so many public officials and turned it into so much smart planning.

In the meantime, even as he dressed up the plan with a fancy name and announced, consensus on its total cost and component parts, Francis blissfully ignored the funding battles.

In that he was taking a page from Robert Moses, whose tactic was precisely that. You announce the project, identify the start-up funding, work up a design, and get everyone committed to it.

Later, when the funding runs out, you remind the politicians that they were photographed approving not only the grandiose plan but even the beautiful design. And that they had all come to the ground-breaking and had been photographed with the proverbial shovel.

One way or another, the funding appears.

Moses in New York had big backers: the various mayors of New York City and governors of New York. People like Al Smith and Fiorello La Guardia and John Lindsay. Icons all.

We had Carlos Gimenez and Tomás Regalado. Not exactly icons.

But we did have a nice acronym (SMART). Francis somehow bamboozled all the policy makers into adopting the SMART plan. Never mind that they had no idea of how to fund it or build it. It sounded good.

And it would have been good, if the county mayor had exerted even a smidgeon of leadership. Instead, he delayed, deferred, deceived, and ultimately derailed the entire plan.

But let's go back to the early days, when we were young and in love with rail as the solution to the congestion woes of a city that had grown from sleepy resort town to bustling metropolis.

8

The Early Days of Miami's Mass Transit

Miami is a transportation anomaly in almost every respect. For many years it simply emulated Los Angeles, starting with a well-maintained highway grid that connects the urban core reasonably well. Because it is a subtropical region, there are no weather complications that affect our ground transportation.

Ordinarily, a well-planned, well-constructed highway grid, in an area blessed with mild weather, in a country where gasoline is cheap and automobiles are plentiful *and* cheap, should mean a fairly efficient system of ground transportation. But with cars and cheap gas comes congestion, and as a city grows denser, it needs at least a skeletal system of mass transportation. Such a system is needed, in particular, at the urban core, which is expectedly the largest workplace.

In Miami, we have such a working system that serves the downtown area; it is called Metromover and happens to be the only component of our mass transit system that works well. This is in great part because it is free, although some of my colleagues are constantly trying to charge a fare. More on that issue later on.

As Miami grew and expanded both horizontally and vertically, it became clear that we would need some form of mass transportation to connect downtown with the four corners of the metropolis, using either elevated or subterranean rail connectors. A typical system would have at least five spokes radiating out from the inner core: four spokes going to the four corners and one going right down the middle.

Three decades ago, Miami started building such a skeletal system. But the city fathers completed only two spokes, one connecting downtown to Dadeland Mall and another connecting downtown to the industrial city of Hialeah, which was headed by a classic strong mayor named Raúl Martínez.

Raúl Martínez reportedly forced the deviation of Miami's Metrorail (elevated) system to his working-class, predominantly Cuban city. It is said that after Havana, Hialeah has the highest concentration of Cubans.

And Raúl Martínez fits Hialeah like a glove.

9

Raúl Martínez, Hialeah Strongman

n the old days, Hialeah was a cauldron of corruption. Its epochal strongman mayor was named Henry Milander, and he ruled the city with blatantly unethical élan.

Former Florida senator and governor Bob Graham tells the story of how his father, Ernest Graham, got fed up with the corruption, which was affecting his dairy business in what later became the neighboring city of Miami Lakes. Ernest managed to get elected to the legislature and, as his first order of business, sponsored legislation eliminating the city's charter. It passed by a margin of 108–2.

Immediately after the vote abrogating the Hialeah charter, Ernest Graham sponsored legislation reconstituting the city's charter, with a brand-new slate of city officials. That also passed 108–2. And so the worst phase in Hialeah's history ended with a double bang, presaging the arrival of Cuban refugees, possessed of their own brand of small-town politics and their own strongman mayor, who ruled the city for a couple of decades.

His name is Raúl Martínez; he was the epitome of the new Hialeah.

Hialeah, more than Miami, is the stereotypical Cuban-American city, akin to Union City but much closer to the native *patria*. It is overwhelmingly Cuban, overwhelmingly suburban, overwhelmingly devoid of the tree canopy and boutique stores beloved by the mainstream media and academia. Hialeah is what the *New Yorker* magazine would consider an ethnic nightmare: It is full of people who have not read Henry David Thoreau.

In fact, the great majority of people who live in Hialeah would not like to live in or around Walden Pond. And the writers and editors of the *New Yorker* would have no idea why. It is not that they wouldn't like a bucolic, waterfront venue with amazing vegetation and vast, depopulated landscapes that prompt meditation. It is that they hardly have time for meditation—what with work and raising families and playing softball or soccer or packing up the family and going to the beach, which is an expedition in itself.

Hialeah is no different from another Miami neighborhood commonly referred to as Westchester, which is farther south but equally far from downtown and the beaches. It is no different from Flagami, which is also solidly middle class though a little bit closer to the urban core, a little bit older, and a little bit better landscaped.

It is not too different from the stereotype of Middle America that pervades the mainstream media. It is full of resilient, hardworking people who speak English with a regional accent, peppered by Spanish colloquialisms. Hialeah men go to the barbershop, not a hair salon. They are beefy, opinionated, and armed to the teeth.

And they love American politics.

If anything sets Hialeah apart from Middle America, it is the fact that Hialeah voters turn out for both local and national elections. Unlike the residents of Brickell, where I live, the citizens of Hialeah don't disdain local politicians as a class. They disdain only those they don't like, which in national politics means the Democrats. In state and local politics, the partisan lines are blurred and Hialeahans, like most Miamians, look to the person, not the party.

For many years, Raúl Martínez was a politician they liked—even if he was a registered Democrat. Mayor Martínez was the quintessential blunt and swaggering BMOC; he wore the title "strong mayor" well in a metropolis where the big-city mayor (Miami Mayor Maurice Ferré) was by charter a "weak mayor" and where the county mayor (Stephen Clark) was constitutionally just as weak—and acted even weaker.

Martínez was the Cuban equivalent of Lyndon Johnson. And he could work state and local legislators as well as Johnson. The result was that Hialeah ended up with one of two branches of Metrorail.

The other branch was dubbed the "Yuppie Train." It served the wealthy communities of South Dade.

I try very hard not to ascribe lesser motives to our public sector leaders. I try just as hard not to ascribe lesser motives to Miami's power players, including the media, the chambers of commerce, and the corporate leaders who control development and tourism entities as well as the campaign coffers of the politicians.

Yet the facts make it hard to resist the conclusion that the rich and powerful have hoodwinked the masses into dedicating resources in a way that favors the transportation needs of the rich and powerful, while trampling on the transportation needs of the middle class and the working class.

My reader should notice that I did not mention the poor, who in Miami are mostly the elderly and the recently arrived immigrants—many of whom are students either in public schools or at the mammoth Miami Dade College. Both of those classes of people are served fairly well by public transportation in comparison to the working-class commuter. They have highly reduced "golden passes" for Metrorail and Metrobus and, for the school-age kids, school buses. But none of that helps working-class and middle-class commuters, of whom there are more than a million.

In the section that follows, I'll describe in some detail the succession of ill-conceived (and maybe ill-intentioned) events and decisions that led Miami to a heinous form of "transportation apartheid."

10

Miami's Transportation Apartheid

I t all began with Metrorail (referred to by critics as "Metrofail"), and that was followed by mass transit fare increases and the invention of toll roads for existing highways, compounded by the sheer travesty of preferential "VIP lanes."

FDR was known for the "Four Freedoms." Miami should be known for the "Four Transportation Travesties." We failed by providing only two branches of rail service. Then we failed by having an aging bus fleet, mostly deprived of bus shelters, let alone any real-time, electronic-scheduling alerts. Then we increased bus and rail fares to $2.25 in each direction. Then, for the poor commuters who were not served by mass transit routes, we imposed tolls on roads already built with taxes already paid.

I have already alluded to the geographically devious way in which our county's planners chose to prioritize our county's modest initial efforts at building a mass transit system. There were only two links, and neither connected the main workplace (downtown) to the predominantly Black areas of the north or the predominantly working-class areas of the far southwest, west, or northeast.

And all the time the bureaucrats and their high-paid consultants were using every possible analytical tool to argue that we did not need, and could not afford, the additional rail lines that had been promised to the people of Miami-Dade.

The bureaucrats had one analytical tool to support their projections and proposals. They based their proposals on projections supported by ridership estimates. The problem is that those models are totally static. No consideration is given to the dynamics inherent in transportation economics.

While bureaucrats dithered and delayed, the private sector rail tycoons moved forward, using their own resources, and brought us a major rail connector. It took the name of "All Aboard."

All Aboard is the name of a rail connector that has been in the works since I arrived in Miami in 1975. It is an existing railroad track, owned by the Florida East Coast Railway (FEC). The FEC, which is now a publicly held company, has fought tooth and nail to keep a spur in place that connects its existing north–south freight line with the Port of Miami.

The seldom used FEC rail line thus connects North Florida (and Georgia and the Carolinas) not only to the Port of Miami and its substantial freight operation but also to downtown Miami and its substantial commuter activity. In other words, the rail line, if it could be double-tracked, could serve both passengers and freight.

And so it was decided to double-track the rail line. Bonus: The FEC's market studies had led it to conceive of initiating a passenger rail service from downtown Miami to Orlando (where Disney World is), providing additional stops in Fort Lauderdale and Palm Beach.

And thus it happened: In the past half decade, Miami went from being a rail transportation orphan to being the beneficiary of the only privately financed, owned, and operated passenger track being built in the nation. All we had to do was bargain for ourselves a "track access fee" for joint use of the passenger line, acquire some trains (or trolleys), and build a few little platforms where passengers could get on and off, much like they do at any bus stop.

County planners were not involved in the decision to build the All Aboard passenger rail that will connect Miami to Fort Lauderdale and Palm Beach. That was done by the FEC without consulting the public sector; the FEC owned the right of way and could finance the improvements with its own capital.

The rest of the All Aboard (now rebaptized as Brightline) connector, reaching from Palm Beach to Orlando, is mired in litigation and has apparently lost the hoped-for federal incentives that would have lowered the cost of capital substantially. Even so, because it would be a rail monopoly servicing a very desirable route (Miami to Orlando), it is pretty much guaranteed sufficient ridership.

Why do the FEC bigwigs think ridership is guaranteed? *Because ridership is a function, more than anything else, of viable alternatives.*

Transportation planners have made mass transit in our county (read: buses) so inefficient, so tardy, so unwelcoming, that it is a viable choice only for those who cannot afford to buy a car. You want to know how many people in our metropolis already have bought a car? *Try one and three-quarters of a million.*

In effect, the only people in our county who have no viable, efficient alternative to the automobile are the very poor, who don't own a car, and the working poor, who own one but cannot afford the insurance and gas.

Well, that was before our expressway authority started tolling motorists to use five perfectly good, elevated highways that crisscrossed the county, and before the state started tolling motorists to use the VIP lanes on the famous interstate connector known as I-95, which has served downtown Miami in a north–south direction for a few decades *at no cost.*

In sum, the FEC passenger line being built by a private company could provide a very efficient viable alternative to the increasingly crowded and increasingly expensive I-95 corridor. Traveling from Fort Lauderdale or Aventura to Miami could be made as pleasant and desirable as allowed by the setting of the lowest possible fares.

If we wanted to make this a wholly viable alternative, we would set the fares at zero and make I-95 almost irrelevant. To do so would require only that we imitate the model of what was accomplished by my son when he cobbled together the interlocal agreement that connected downtown to the existing tri-county rail line, called Tri-Rail.

It took a lot of consensus building, the use of tax-increment financing, and $69 million of public funding. But the most important component, the perpetual easement to use the line for a commuter train, cost barely 1.5 percent of the total amount – or a cool million dollars.

By way of comparison, a million dollars is less than what each of thirteen county commissioners is allotted for staff salaries each and every year.

Francis had made up his mind that the Tri-Rail trains, which entered Miami-Dade way west of downtown, should have a downtown destination.

It seemed like a simple proposition, as there happened to be a rail line from the current end of the line, in Hialeah, that traveled east to the previously mentioned north–south FEC line, which was about to be double-tracked for use by the Brightline trains.

City and county leaders all saw some wisdom in connecting Tri-Rail to downtown, even if its ridership was dismal. It should have been easy, due to the existing right of way and the fact that the last eight miles of passenger track were already being built.

Everyone relished the idea of a grand central station located right at Government Center, where Metrorail, Metromover, Tri-Rail, and Brightline would meet. It would be Miami's version of Union Station, if not quite the Big Apple's Grand Central.

But there was a little problem. The trains that served the government-run Tri-Rail and the ones that were being built by the privately owned FEC for its Brightline service to Orlando had totally different floor configurations. Handicapped passengers boarding one kind of train would be at different levels from the ones boarding the other kind of train.

The only feasible solution was to have the two kinds of tracks splitting vertically towards the end of the line and arriving at two different levels. That kind of station, plus the other improvements to the line, would cost close to $70 million.

And the FEC was not about to pay that from its own stockholders' pockets.

Luckily for all concerned, the area was part of a community redevelopment district, which used future tax increases to fund present capital improvements. The agency in question, called Southeast Overtown/Park West, was headed by another city commissioner (Keon Hardemon), and he was of like mind to Francis: He wanted the rail connection to go through his district, which had high rates of poverty.

With Francis doing his Kissinger-like shuttle diplomacy between city and county, and Hardemon doing his Martin Luther King Jr.–like negotiating on behalf of his district's impoverished citizens, the two crafted the nearly $70 million deal. What was most surprising about the deal was that the use of the fourteen miles of track that belonged to the FEC *was purchased, in perpetuity, for a mere million bucks.*

That was probably the best acquisition since the purchase of Long

Island from the Dutch or Louisiana from the French. But the kicker was just as good: In exchange for using tax-increment funds from the community redevelopment agency, Overtown residents would forever be given free passes to use Tri-Rail.

Never mind the constitutionality of that particular form of preferential treatment. What counts here is the value of that model. It reminds me of what was arguably my finest moment, three decades ago, when I convinced the federal government to fund our downtown Metromover system.

Those were the days of Ronald Reagan, when the federal agency in question, called UMTA (Urban Mass Transit Administration) was reluctant to fund an elevated double loop in what was still an embryonic downtown.

One of my first tests of leadership as mayor of Miami came in 1986, when UMTA decided to hold hearings in Miami to determine the wisdom of spending a quarter-billion dollars to build an elevated double loop (the previously mentioned Metromover) in downtown Miami. I had just been elected mayor of the city and had a good relationship with the mayor of the county, who was what you could call a hands-off politician. I was the opposite; even though my pay was only $5,000 a year, I was the ultimate micromanager.

I had read that UMTA was headed by a wonk named Ralph Stanley, and that he had ties to my alma mater at Harvard's Kennedy School. I also had read that his agency had crunched the numbers and, based on ridership estimates, calculated that each mile of the Metromover would cost about fourteen dollars per person riding the system.

Hell, a taxi at that time would cost about five bucks at most. And for a person walking, if the weather was fine, it would take no more than ten minutes to get from one end of downtown to the other. (At a brisk pace, probably just five minutes.)

If it wasn't hot as hell in Miami during daylight hours, or raining cats and dogs, walking was the obvious choice. If it was raining and someone had spare cash, perhaps the taxi ride would make sense.

I decided to follow my instincts, which told me that downtown Miami, in part because of the beauty of Biscayne Bay, in part because it was acquiring a critical mass of businesses, and in part because the government had chosen to place its main courthouse and its main government buildings there, would ultimately become a mini-city in itself. Even though the Brickell and Omni areas were not yet thriving office and residential districts, my intuition told me that they would be.

So I got approval from the county mayor and went to the UMTA hearings, armed with the kind of confidence you have when you are a thirty-six-year-old newly elected mayor who is just itching to beat the Feds with analytical models.

My argument was simple. I told the UMTA bigwigs that their denominator was accurate, meaning the cost of the system was incontrovertible. But, I argued, the numerator, representing ridership estimates, was off by at least a factor of ten. So the real numbers were a buck-forty per rider per mile, not fourteen bucks.

As I walked out of the hearing, a staffer asked me where I had gotten those estimates of ridership. I gestured like I was pulling them out of thin air—which was pretty accurate, as I was going on instinct.

You have to do that often in politics. If you're wrong, you are often kicked out of office by the voters. If you are right, you get to enjoy, thirty years later, reading the numbers that show (in this case) that the Metromover ferries eleven million passengers a year.

A big part of that is because it's free.

That was about twenty-five years ago. Roll forward to the present, and we still have only two branches of Metrorail and a downtown Metromover. The mass transit tree is bare, and the clear result is that fewer than about 5 percent of commuters here use mass transportation. The other 95 percent clog our highways and curse the day when the powers that be decided to install tolls that charge them for using highways built three decades ago with taxpayer dollars (mostly gas taxes and impact fees).

And what do our leaders do? Well, they talk about the problem endlessly and occasionally calculate what it would cost to complete at least five new branches. The current estimate is $3.6 billion. And there is no current plan to fund that amount.

That's right. Our county mayor and our commission chairman have no current plans to fund the $3.6 billion expansion from local funds. That, despite the fact that our county budget exceeds $8 billion and that in 2002, a decade and a half ago, a half-cent sales tax was imposed for the purpose of funding the much-needed expansion.

That tax produces $274 million a year—which would be enough to issue thirty-year bonds in excess of the $3.6 billion needed. Unfortunately, the special tax proceeds are instead used for maintenance and operations of the existing skeletal system.

And our leaders refuse to do anything about it. Enter the Suarez duo of commissioners.

11

The Battle to Fund SMART

The southern tip of the Florida peninsula is not rectangular; it is more like a semicircle that works its way south at the same time it heads west. Early on, the federal government saw fit to build a wide and elegant divided highway, the southernmost extension of the famous U.S. 1, diagonally along the semicircle, bordering the bay and providing straight-line access to downtown and to the affluent neighborhoods that lay immediately south.

This worked well for the better part of the twentieth century; eventually it dawned on the powerful residents along this stretch of U.S. 1 that a nice train along the existing right of way would nicely complement the highway. And so they finagled from the Feds enough funding to connect the bulk of my county commission district to downtown Miami.

Alongside the beautiful six-lane U.S. 1 (until recently known as Dixie Highway), the county politicians built the southern branch of the mass transit system.

But the Metrorail line reaches only from downtown to the previously mentioned Dadeland Mall, a stretch that covers a measly ten miles. Dadeland is a humongous shopping center, with enormous surface parking plus a rather ample parking building, for those who perhaps don't like to get wet as they walk from their car to Macy's and the other department stores on a rainy day.

Dixie Highway and the Metrorail line that abuts it more or less divide my district along economic lines. Those living north of the line are middle class. Those living south are either wealthy or upper middle class.

But no one really thinks of the Metrorail line as dividing those who live on the "right" side of the tracks from those who live on the "wrong" side. That phenomenon is worth exploring, and I will do so in the rest of this book. But here I want to emphasize that both sides of U.S. 1 are served well by the Metrorail line, short as it is. For the wealthy who live south of it, the Metrorail line provides a means by which the typically bilingual office workers can reach downtown and the domestic workers can travel from inner-city neighborhoods to stations close to the plush residential communities where they work, with names such as Gables by the Sea and Journey's End.

Hispanics and so-called Anglos (the name given to white non-Hispanics born here) from the southwest areas supported the funding of Metrorail. It serves both communities well, and no one really cares that one group (the Anglos) lives mostly on the south side.

There is little, if any, tension between the two groups.

That in itself is worth exploring, and I will in the next chapter. Here I want to emphasize that the two branches of our transit system serve either the privileged few (neighborhoods in my district abutting Dixie Highway) or the politically connected few (Hialeah residents who happen to live close to the famous Hialeah horse track).

To explain the former is easy: My district—spanning Pinecrest, Coral Gables, South Miami, Coconut Grove, Brickell, and Key Biscayne—is not only wealthy but full of influential media folks. Almost every publisher and editor of the *Miami Herald* over the past thirty years (including Alvah Chapman and David Lawrence Jr.) has lived in my district. The powerful auto magnate Ron Esserman lives there, as does Progressive Insurance heir Daniel Lewis, Related Group mega-builder Jorge Pérez, famous architect Bernardo Fort-Brescia (married to Laurinda Spear of Helms-Spear fame), and Facundo Bacardi, chairman of the board of the largest privately owned liquor company in the world.

At present, it is probably the district of its size (at a quarter-million people) with the greatest number of billionaires in the world, other than possibly Manhattan, London, Hong Kong, and Beverly Hills. When asked about what it's like to represent my district, I often quote a line by the congressman in the movie *Charlie Wilson's War*: "I represent the Second Congressional District in Texas; I get to say yes a lot!"

It was clear that my district would have at least a small branch of the rail system. Unfortunately for the rest of the twelve districts in the county, only Hialeah got a rail line—and a short one at that. The entire system, when I was elected in 2011, covered only twenty-five miles. That is scant coverage in a county of 2,400 square miles.

The fact that we even had a train is testament to the power of the Anglo elites, who lived in my district, and the Cubans who ran Hialeah, in the northwest area of the county. It was an unusual coalition, and it worked for about three decades, roughly from 1960 to 1990.

A little deeper explanation is worth giving.

12

The Changing Nature of Miami Demographics

Contrary to some national news reports, the assimilation of the many waves of Hispanic immigrants has happened with startling ease in Miami-Dade. In rough terms, we can consider the past half century as consisting of two waves: mostly Cubans in the first twenty-five years (1960 to 1985) and mostly Central Americans, Haitians, Colombians, and Venezuelans in the most recent twenty-five.

By current statistics, the two mostly Hispanic migrations—which include three generations of the first wave of Cubans after Castro, beginning in the early 1960s, and two generations of more recent arrivals—have led to 60 percent of the county's population. (African Americans and Haitians comprise about 20 percent, and Anglos also comprise 20 percent.)

But the numbers don't tell the whole story, because the assimilation includes a lot of mixing of other ethnicities with Cubans. In my own family, for example, we have descendants of Irish, Brazilian, Puerto Rican, and Cuban-Lebanese heritage. The culture thus forged is worth discussing.

It may be unique in the history of the United States. And it colors our politics, making for a very peculiar way in which public opinion is shaped. The media, in part due to narrow-mindedness and in part due to the unprecedented complexity of the phenomenon, mostly misunderstand or ignore it.

Cuban Americans are characterized as being classic, conservative Republicans, who would expectedly be against big government and every kind of tax that might feed it. But that is not an accurate characterization. In the past two decades, Cuban-American voters have supported a $3 billion capital improvement tax, a $1 billion school board bond, and an almost $1 billion bond issue for the public hospital.

In addition, they have approved the imposition of a half-cent sales tax to expand the mass transit system, as I mentioned.

The bonds earmarked for school, hospital, and capital improvements are perceived to have had their intended effect. Not so for the half-cent (*medio-centavo*) sales tax, which produces over a quarter-billion dollars a year in bondable revenues that have been diverted to operations rather than to capital improvements. During the sixteen years of the imposition, only one small link, connecting downtown to the airport, has been built.

The half-penny tax is thus highly unpopular, and any inkling of adding another half cent to the existing sales tax is met with virulent opposition. And the opposition is not based on ideology; it is bred of the frustration that Miami has no viable system of mass transportation, except lumbering buses that cost too much and take too long for the cross-county commute.

Thanks to the combined efforts of Francis and two county commission chairmen (Jean Monestime, 2015–16, and Esteban Bovo, 2017–18), plus myself, there came a time in the summer of 2017 when we seemed on the verge of actually funding a complete system of mass transportation.

Unfortunately for us, Mayor Gimenez suddenly did a flip-flop and decided that trains were passé. In one fell swoop, he went from being a supporter of the rail expansion to being an opponent. His argument? That we could not fund the expansion of the rail system—and besides, he said, "trains are obsolete, nineteenth-century technology."

I was baffled by this turnaround. So was everybody else. But I could see the silver lining. I am—as my kids like to say—the "silver-lining king."

Before I delve into that bizarre story, I need to set the stage by discussing what can only be described as a pincer movement by Miami's politicians, coached by Miami's bureaucrats, with the effect that Miami's working-class commuters were strangled and—in many cases—relegated to the class of the working poor.

Media pundits and academicians write endless articles—even entire books—about the ethnic forces that shape Miami politics (nowadays referred to as identity politics). Others try to apply the ideological parameters that tend to shape national elections, meaning Democrats versus Republicans.

Miami's politics include those variables but also have varied elements that are not susceptible to either ethnic or partisan analysis. There is the tension between the intelligentsia and the working class, between the inner-city dwellers and the suburbanites, between those on the beaches and those on the mainland, and between the urbanists and the libertarians.

It would take a better-trained social scientist than myself to analyze the mass transportation battles described here and assign weight to each of those divides. Here I package them into a simpler dichotomy: elites versus populists.

And, as my reader will see, Francis and I almost always end up on the side of the populists. It was not so with Mayor Gimenez.

13

The Mayor vs. SMART

Nothing better illustrates the tension between a bureaucratic mayor like Carlos Gimenez and a progressive, fiscal conservative like me than the battle to fund our mass transit system. In this battle, I was joined by every mayor in the county as well as by most of the county's legislative delegation.

Mayor Gimenez, on his side, had the entire bureaucracy. In Miami-Dade, that consists of no less than 4,283 managers. Yes, you read that right: *The county's top-heavy government, which has no marketing or research functions, which doesn't have to compete for clients, which hasn't changed its services in any significant way for fifty years, needs more than four thousand managers to function!*

The ridiculous county bureaucracy is not entirely Gimenez's fault, by any means. The county's accelerated growth and bloated salary structure were the creation of county managers during the last four decades of the twentieth century, before the county changed to a strong-mayor form of government.

The first executive mayor was the charismatic Alex Penelas, who was a good leader and progressive but certainly not a reform-minded fiscal conservative. Under Penelas, in 2002, the county's voters approved a sales tax surcharge of 0.5 percent for transportation. Under state law, the measure had to be approved by voters in a countywide referendum, the wording of which indicated that the funds would be used to add five corridors to the existing Metrorail skeleton, which consisted of only two branches.

For the succeeding fifteen years, the transit surtax produced close to a quarter-billion dollars a year. In that time, however, the county bureaucrats managed to fund only a 2.4-mile link between the existing Metrorail system and the airport. That cost about $500 million—equivalent to only two years' worth of the surtax revenues. For most of the other thirteen of those fifteen years, the county raided the funds and used the money for operations of its skeletal transit corridors and buses.

Altogether, they had misspent close to the $3.6 billion that the proposed new system is estimated to cost.

In the meantime, the county commission was struggling with priorities. Each and every commission district (except possibly mine, which was served by the Metrorail branch lying almost as a perfect spinal cord through various bedroom communities) was at the mercy of the automobile and the scant bus service, consisting of fewer than seven hundred buses. Each and every county commissioner wanted to prioritize his or her own district for the expanded rail service.

The battle to fund trains serving a particular district raged for about five years following my election in 2011, which coincided with Gimenez's election as mayor. Never mind that county bureaucrats *had not identified the funding for any corridor*. The battle for prioritizing any of the six districts raged.

Into that motley scene came Francis, who managed to get appointed to represent the city of Miami in the countywide agency that deals with federal transit funds (the previously mentioned MPO). He also managed to get selected by the twenty-one-member board as its vice chair, serving as the number-two person on a board where the chair position traditionally went to the chairman of the county commission.

Somehow, against all odds, Francis cobbled together a coalition of the six mayors on the board (representing Hialeah, Homestead, Miami, North Miami, Miami Gardens, and Miami Beach) plus most of my county commission colleagues. It wasn't easy initially, as former mayors Maurice Ferré and Phil Levine (from Miami Beach) began a bizarre dance as malcontents who spent their time on the board either pontificating about (Ferré) or trashing (Levine) our admittedly unfunded but at least consensual efforts to advance a transportation plan.

Francis and I spent two years and one election cycle (2015–16) working on Gimenez to lead the funding effort. At one point, in mid-2016, when

I still had some leverage as a potential challenger to him in the upcoming reelection, Gimenez actually gave us a timetable for his funding plan. He said he would announce the plan in two weeks. But it never happened; instead the mayor simply announced that the rail expansion would not happen at all.

We were not idle during all this time. Knowing that Gimenez's style of governing was reactive rather than proactive, I floated a three-point funding plan. The initiative consisted of returning the half-penny surtax to its proper use, recovering some portion of the auto-tag renewal fees our county sent to Tallahassee, and extracting from the highway tolling authority (MDX) a goodly part of its excess revenues.

Gimenez didn't support any of the three points but criticized, emphatically, the auto-tag idea. Unbelievably, he said that if our county received a goodly portion of its auto-tag renewal fees ($167 million per year), *other counties would want to do the same thing*!

Which, of course, was precisely the idea. As Gimenez was the leader of the state's largest and most industrialized county, it was incumbent on him to seek a fair share of monies sent to the state. But, of course, it was not the mayor's idea, and that was that. He had to throw cold water on it.

But we never expected that he was going to throw cold water on the whole shebang. In the end, in what has to be the most shocking *volte-face* by a big-county mayor in history, he simply gave up on the whole rail plan and announced, as I said earlier, that trains were a nineteenth-century technology and that he would support a funding plan only for dedicated lanes for buses (called BRT, for "Bus Rapid Transit").

In the meantime, I continued my battle with the trustees of the half-cent sales surtax.

14

Battling the County's Transit Agency

A s mentioned before, the effort to fund five new rail lines began in 2002 with the passage of a half-cent sales surtax. It was evident to all at that time that Miami's skeletal Metrorail system needed at least four or five more branches. Led by Miami-Dade's charismatic mayor at the time, Alex Penelas, the voters approved the half-penny imposition for the sole purpose of expanding rail service.

In charge of managing this new tax, which produced a cool quarter-billion dollars a year, was the Citizens' Independent Transportation Trust (CITT). The emphasis should have been on the "I," for "independent." The board—or, more correctly, the trust that ran this agency—should have functioned independently of the county bureaucracy. Instead, it acted as a stepchild to the county's transit administrators, who used it as a piggy bank when lean years came, beginning with the 2008 recession.

It took me four years on the county commission to engage in hostilities with the CITT board, and fully six years to win my first battle. Before I delve into that battle, I need to explain what happens when bureaucrats instead of the representatives of the people are in charge of budgets.

In Miami-Dade, during my tenure, the majority of the elected decision-makers were bureaucrats. The mayor, Carlos Gimenez, was the ultimate bureaucrat. He had started his career as a firefighter in the city, had worked his way up the civil service ladder to fire chief, and from there had somehow been named city manager by none other than the infamous Joe Carollo.

We'll get back to Gimenez in a little while, when we discuss the aftereffects of the mayor's sudden attempt to derail the rapid transit plan.

As I write this, on the county commission, which is composed of thirteen members, there are two school administrators, one retired county administrator, one nonprofit administrator, one retired cop, one retired marine, and two former legislators. The dean of the commission has been elected seven times, for a tenure spanning close to three decades. His wife is a high-level county administrator.

Another commissioner is married to a woman who owns a business that has been linked to county contracts. One commissioner has a food truck that apparently caters to park employees. The wife of the chairman of the commission (himself a former legislator) works for U.S. senator Marco Rubio.

So there are only two commissioners who don't derive at least half of their family income from government or government-supported agencies.

As many as six of the thirteen receive some form of government pension.

Only four of us have private-sector jobs without which we could not feed our families. It is difficult, under these circumstances, to convince our colleagues that municipal government is too big, its managers too well compensated, and its pensions totally out of sync with the private sector.

Even worse, almost all of our colleagues are convinced that we need 4,283 managers to supervise twenty-four thousand rank-and-file employees, most of whom do nothing particularly complicated or innovative. Even though the county has only nine essential services (police, fire, parks, public works, solid waste, water and sewer, corrections, libraries, and mass transit) and none of those have undergone technological breakthroughs in half a century, our workforce is saturated with computer technicians, lawyers, finance/budget analysts, communications gurus, and all kinds of "community advocacy" and "community relations" staff. Not to mention human resources administrators to do the bean counting for a payroll that has no less than a thousand job titles!

I know New York is worse in terms of bureaucracy. I am guessing Chicago and Los Angeles are too. But this is still beyond the pale in terms of layers of bureaucratic fat.

After seven years of the CITT's existence, the only real transit link completed with the half-penny surtax was a 2.4-mile track connecting downtown to the airport, as I mentioned. That was but a minnow compared to the whale that the county needed: a bit more than eighty miles of new rail extended over five new corridors.

Things got worse after 2008. Using the 2008 recession as the excuse, the county divested the surtax fund of about $100 million a year, equivalent to 40 percent of its funding capacity. I made two forays into the thicket of the entity that managed this money, the aforementioned CITT. The CITT had fifteen board members: thirteen appointed by the individual county commissioners, one by the county mayor, and one by the county's League of Cities.

My first attempt, in 2015, was not well organized. I simply asked to speak at a board meeting, found a sponsor to put the item on the agenda, and made my pitch. I lost 9–4.

Two years later, I did serious planning. I visited or called a majority of the board members. I also put together a position paper, with charts of bonding capacity and county budget comparisons showing that we had long passed the point where property taxes were declining; in fact, I explained, our real estate taxes had gone up by half a billion dollars in just five years since the low point, which was in 2012.

The climax of the effort depended on being able to recruit a dozen elected officials, of diverse ethnicities and geographic representation, to support the effort. This was not easy by any means. It meant taking mayors from small cities and state representatives out to lunch, offering implicit promises of support in their next campaigns, and writing endless (and often fruitless) analytical memos that offset the barrage of misinformation coming from the county bureaucrats.

A typical exchange with a legislator went like this:

"Commissioner, the director of the trust [an amiable but otherwise clueless fellow named Charles Scurr] says that if the county does not receive one hundred million dollars of the surtax money this year, bus and Metrorail service will have to be cut back," the legislator would say.

"My representative," I would respond, "it is not the trust's responsibility to bail out the county's transportation system. That approach was an emergency measure, first established in 2009, when the Great Recession occurred and real estate taxes took a hard hit. But since that low point, tax revenues have increased by more than five hundred million dollars; all I propose is returning one-tenth of that, or fifty million dollars, back to the trust for its intended purposes."

The legislator would usually ask for a breakdown of the commitments already made and that the bureaucrats insisted could not be taken away. Memo after memo would flow to the legislators (and mayors), each insisting that the trust could, indeed, fund at least half of the $3.6 billion needed for the six rail corridors.

But often the legislators and mayors were swayed by the bureaucrats and confused by the numbers. "Brief me on the numbers again," they would ask. Finally, I simplified my answer: "Listen, [so-and-so mayor], the numbers are not that complicated. The trust receives a quarter-billion dollars a year, of which about one hundred million dollars are bonded out and fifty million dollars are pledged to the cities. That leaves one hundred million dollars to issue bonds for the new rail lines."

The math was actually quite simple, but the bureaucrats added arcane terminology like "debt–service coverage ratios" and "bondable capacity." When the politicians asked simple questions, the bureaucrats would give complicated answers.

I almost hit the roof when CITT director Scurr was asked what the cost per mile was for the six corridors of the SMART plan. He seemed troubled by the question and stammered, in a very serious tone, that it was between one hundred million and two hundred million dollars per mile. The next day I called him into my office and put the question to him in private. Before he could answer, I said, "Charles, what is so hard about dividing $3.6 billion dollars by sixty miles? What do you get?"

Believe it or not, he answered, "Five hundred million dollars." To which I responded, with some vehemence, "No, Charles, it is not five hundred million dollars; it is sixty million dollars!"

Another bureaucrat, who managed our highway authority (better known as the agency that drove our working class crazy with ubiquitous tolls) waxed poetic about his enormous "debt–service coverage ratio" of 1.9. It was a meeting of the countywide transportation organization, and it was not the time or place to chastise him.

But afterward, I wish I had. I wish I had said, "Sir, the extra ninety percent in revenues that you are storing in your coffers could be funding an extra ninety percent in capital projects. And, by the way, none of the underwriters that you rely on for funding need such high reserves. Instead of being proud of those reserves, you should be embarrassed that when you went out in the market to sell the muni [municipal] bonds, you didn't think to make the underwriters compete to see which one gave you the lowest debt–service coverage ratio."

And I would have added, "By the way, there is almost no risk involved for the underwriters. These are backed by investment banks, and those are backed by the Federal Reserve, which since 2008 has issued securities worth three trillion dollars, or thirty percent of the entire money supply of the nation, at a little over one percent! Do you seriously think that they will not compete for countywide authority bonds, paying tax-free interest rates of 4-5%, whose revenues have been growing with every new toll you place on highways that will last forever, due to our great weather?"

And then the coup de grâce: "As added security, our government has bailed out the companies that bail out the investment bankers. Yes, I refer to AIG, which—believe it or not—is a company that insures risky investments. In effect, sir, we have taken what was previously a 'public consumer good' [highways] and privatized it, by charging users for something already paid for with taxes, *so that we can allow the very wealthy to earn tax-free, risk-free interest...*"

Privately, I did my best to educate the legislators, mayors, and commissioners throughout the county of the travesty that had been perpetrated on the county's taxpayers. Put simply, the half-cent sales surtax had been imposed, abused, and misapplied. Monies intended for the construction of five or six additional rail corridors had been squandered for over a decade.

It was a clear case of breach of fiduciary duty, and almost everyone in government was going along with it. But my private in-your-face lobbying combined with the sheer frustration of decent, motivated public officials worked. The quantitative confusion gave way to a moral suasion that impelled a score of public officials to follow, if not lead.

In the end, no fewer than twelve legislators and mayors agreed to support my efforts, either in person or in writing. And I made sure they had front-row seats (as well as parking in my spot next to county hall, in the case of a legislator who arrived late from the courthouse).

How we did that was simple logistics. The day of the vote, my staff was assigned to grab enough front-row seats in the audience to accommodate the public officials as they arrived. It helped that the CITT board meeting was really two meetings: The first was an executive committee meeting, and the second involved the whole board. Most CITT board members, perhaps because they sensed a tectonic shift in the functioning of their board, attended both meetings.

The first round of public officials turned out to be all mayors, including the most important one, Miami's Tomás Regalado. I had him "batting cleanup"—that is, going fourth. The first three were representatives from the south end: Cutler Bay, Palmetto Bay, and Pinecrest (the latter represented by its former mayor, Cindy Lerner, whom I called my "pit bull").

The deliberations of the executive committee were marred by legal confusion, which arose from wording of the resolution introduced by my appointee, a rookie board member named Melissa Dynan. Thankfully, the executive committee did not vote and left the matter to the entire board, which met at six p.m. This allowed a slew of state representatives and city commissioners to attend.

I will spare my reader the confusion of the debate. What became clear to a majority of the board members was that they had a fiduciary duty to the electors, and the fiduciary duty was to use the surtax funds for expansion of the rail system. No ifs, ands, or buts.

In the end, they voted 7–5 in favor of our proposal. Somehow, we overcame the eminent prophets of doom sent by the mayor—including the budget and finance directors. For a week after that, we basked in the glow of a major victory and braced for the backlash, which we anticipated would be a memorandum showing all the basic services that would have to be reduced.

The last thing we expected was what the mayor did. I called it the Monday-morning ambush.

Without so much as a heads-up, let alone a formal consultation with the leaders of the state legislative delegation, the county commission, or the transportation trust, the mayor simply announced that the transit plan was dead. He said that trains were nineteenth-century technology and that all we would get was $500 million worth of buses that would use express lanes on our highways.

It was an amazing show of hubris, chutzpah, or what Cubans call *gandinga*. *Herald* columnist Fabiola Santiago compared Gimenez to Marie Antoinette: "Let them ride buses" if they don't have a train, Santiago penned.

Never have so many people, including allies and enemies alike, been shocked by one man's stupidity. In twenty-four hours, Gimenez turned the tide against himself in such a drastic way that it seemed possible he might not last the four-year term.

Talk of a recall began in earnest.

15

The Aftermath of the Transit Ambush

The mayor's shocking turnaround created all kinds of political waves. The mainstream media were surprised but, for the most part, still subdued.

I cranked up the social media to make up for the nonchalance of the mainstream media. Using Santiago's Marie Antoinette comparison as a launching pad, I blasted Gimenez at every opportunity, which riled up other private citizens on social media.

Critics on social media were very rough on the mayor. Frankly, I incited some of the harshest commentary, by pouncing on the mayor's rationale that trains were nineteenth-century technology. I immediately tweeted: "So is electricity; and the wheel was invented circa 3,500 B.C."

On one highly watched program on Channel 10 by well-respected journalists Michael Putney and Glenna Milberg, the questions were mildly worded but the body language was unmistakably harsh. My staff commented on the puzzled, disbelieving look on Putney's typically demure face as he questioned Gimenez on how he could go back on a voter-approved referendum that had given rise to the funding source.

Channel 6, as well as the three Spanish television stations, introduced the mayor's surprising abandonment of the otherwise agreed-on rail plan by playing his campaign ads of just nine months before; in those ads, the mayor explicitly promised to complete the five rail corridors.

We noticed the mayor's popularity quickly dropping to all-time lows.

He had never been particularly popular, but he had never been particularly unpopular either. As the successor of a recalled mayor, even a plodding bureaucrat was a refreshing improvement.

But that favorable image quickly dissolved. Now Gimenez's arrogance was tantamount to Marie Antoinette's, and his drab, aging appearance and monotone speech combined to make him an excellent foil for his opponents.

My reader might ask, what opponents could a lame-duck politician have? The answer is that almost all politicians want to have a legacy of some sort. Gimenez had managed to alienate each and every stakeholder in the field of public transportation, plus every environmental group, plus most of the legislators and mayors. So we were mystified by his hubris.

Most high-level politicians, if they are not planning to run for another office after their term ends, will support family members or allies in lower-level elections.

Gimenez did not have much of a network of successors. His own family members were problematic, to put it mildly. And he really didn't have allies. As he was nearing the end of his tenure, his custom of supporting ill-chosen candidates reached a crescendo. He chose to support not only the bête noire of Miami politics (Joe Carollo) but also the Rasputin of Miami, Alex Díaz de la Portilla ("DLP").

DLP deserves at least a short chapter in my book. But before we go there, let me assure my reader that Gimenez did not prevail with DLP. As I was writing this book, the primary election took place; DLP lost by more than thirty points to the candidate who was supported by almost all people of good faith.

And those people include Francis, myself, and the writers at the *Miami Herald*.

16

The DLP Brothers

There are three DLP brothers. There is the nerdy Ivy League grad, who seems totally ill suited to politics. There is the Clark Kent lookalike, who seems perfectly suited to politics. And then there is Alex DLP, the lovable rogue.

If I had to compare Alex Díaz de la Portilla to a national figure, it would probably be former New York congressman Adam Clayton Powell Jr. Like Powell, DLP is incapable of playing by the book. Yet it's hard not to like him.

Alex DLP is one of those politicians who go through life without acknowledging any legal limits. He flouts the law whenever he can get away with it. For many years in the legislature, he got away with it.

Each reelection to the Florida House of Representatives, DLP would be charged with ten or twenty finance-reporting violations. He would never plead guilty, never pay the fine, and never accept the punishment meted out by the state elections commission, which was mostly toothless.

Alex DLP's business dealings were also cloudy, to put it mildly. And his romantic adventures were quite turbulent. He got married once, and his divorce was expectedly bitter, but the lingering custody fight was not about children; it was about a dog.

When the judge ordered him to give his ex-wife custody of the dog, Alex refused and was consequently held in contempt of court. Somehow, he beat the rap and never complied with the court order.

Miguel Díaz de la Portilla, Alex's older brother, had all the tools. He is smart, amazingly good-looking, and ethical. My son and I supported him twice—first when he won a seat in the state senate and again later, when he lost the same seat in an unexpected upset. I have to think by that time the family name had lost some of its luster.

It's a shame, really. Miguel deserved better. But the family name had left him in a lurch. His senate district was reapportioned such that his opponent, a Democrat, had the numerical advantage. The voters chose a totally uncharismatic Harvard Law grad over Clark Kent. It was an interesting moment in Miami-Dade County politics, in which the county went from majority Republican legislators to majority Democrats.

There was a qualitative and a quantitative factor at play here. The quantitative factor was evident: Miami-Dade now had two hundred thousand more Democrats than Republicans. Qualitatively, the old appeal of Republicans to family, faith, and "force" (my collective term for support of military, guns, and strict law enforcement) no longer worked.

Henceforth, all politicians had to put forth some sort of positive plan to govern, including economic growth, protection of the environment, and full funding of health care, education, and transportation services.

Note that I mentioned the environment ahead of health care and education. Polls in the past decade put the environment as a very high priority for voters. The issue can be the proverbial "third rail" for a politician. If a politician's record is not absolutely pro-environment, he or she is seen as a pariah, a bad person, a polluter.

The pro-environment label took on a special urgency for politicians in South Florida, since at this time in our history the issue of protecting the environment appeared as a single, preeminent priority: sea level rise.

I am a scientist at heart. An engineer, really. That means I am a practical scientist first and a theoretical scientist second. Either way, I look carefully at numbers.

Sea levels are relatively easy to measure. High tides leave marks on seawalls and other vertical surfaces. And, if we in Miami want more precise data, we happen to have an NOAA (National Oceanic and Atmospheric Administration) center right on our doorstep, on the causeway that connects Miami to Key Biscayne.

Measurements taken there show that over the past fifteen years, the level of our coastal waters has risen to heights that are truly problematic. Miami was not just part of a worldwide phenomenon; it was ground zero for it.

If forecasts could be believed, Miami could be underwater by midcentury.

By pure coincidence, I had some governmental authority to delve into the most popular of the environmental causes in these parts. I was a member of the South Florida Regional Planning Council, a tri-county agency charged with reviewing large-scale developments with a view to assuring that one county's overdevelopment would not hurt the quality of life in neighboring counties.

It was there that I came face-to-face not only with sea level rise but also with a related phenomenon: saltwater intrusion.

17

Sink or Swim

As one of thirteen county commissioners, with no executive power, I was not really in a position to enact much by way of policy. However, I was helped by some timely appointments to a regional board. My appointment was serendipitous.

As it happened, I was often appointed to outside boards because no one else on the county commission wanted to serve on the various outside boards whose ex officio membership required appointment of a county commissioner.

These outside board appointments somewhat made up for my lack of inside clout. In two out of three battles for the chairmanship of the county commission, I not only lost but was left out of the winning coalition. In effect, I was a "back-bencher" during my entire nine-year tenure on the commission. Only once was I ever appointed chairman of a committee, and the committee was not considered all that important.

But that didn't keep me from having an appreciable impact on policy. Being appointed to outside boards gave me justification to use my staff as support for tangential initiatives such as those derived from my membership on such boards. Two prominent examples were the Children's Trust and the South Florida Regional Planning Council (SFRPC).

It was through my membership in the SFRPC that I became conversant with the issue of sea level rise. Sea level is a complex scientific phenomenon. It makes politicians wear a scientific hat.

Science and politics don't mix too well in general. At the municipal level, they don't mix at all. County commissioners just don't get elected on the basis of their knowledge of science.

Yet we county commissioners are often pressed into service as scientists. On the issue of rising sea levels, we are at the proverbial front lines of the war on salt water.

For a few years now, many a journalist and scientist has written that Miami is ground zero for sea level rise. A *New Yorker* story in 2016 went so far as to suggest that Miami's coastal levels were rising at ten times the national norm.

Holy moly! How can that be? Does the ocean have a lump or bump as its waves roll around the tip of the Florida peninsula, as if some enormous sea monster were swimming under the surface and lifting it?

Actually, there is a lump or a bump. But now I am getting ahead of the story, which begins when I made the mistake of explaining, during a commission meeting, the three most important variables that affect sea levels. I had not spoken much on the issue, but foolishly thought that an occasional foray into marine geology might help us in grappling with transcendent (and borderline apocalyptic) issues, such as whether we should change our building codes to require residences and hotels next to the bay to be built on stilts. Or to prohibit them entirely.

There is such a clamor in the environmental community, and in academia, on this issue that any self-respecting public official feels compelled to speak out on it. Sometimes the clamor reaches hysteria, as during a recent commission meeting when a young lady testified wearing a diving helmet to stress the danger we were facing.

So I foolishly dove into the discussion, saying, "Perhaps it's useful to state the three factors that affect sea levels. One is thermal expansion of the water with temperature rise; the other is melting of the ice caps, which adds to the volume of water; the third is tectonic plate movements, which affect the depth of the ocean floor."

I could hear a commissioner on my right mumbling, "OK, Harvard, we know you are smart," or something to that effect.

The one on the left was more disarming. He leaned over and whispered, "So, just how bad is it?" I thought for a minute how to keep it simple. Then I responded, "Well, if you assume the hundred-year trend, we are talking three millimeters per year." Millimeters evidently did not quite register with him, for he inquired, "Well, how much is that?" So I kept it even simpler: "If you assume it continues at that pace for a hundred years, you have about a third of a meter."

This did not satisfy him; *clearly, he had no grasp of the entire metric system.* Humbly but insistently, he posed his third question: "How much is that?" This time I finally gave in: "Well, that is just about a foot."

He pondered that for a few seconds and exclaimed, as if he had just experienced a eureka moment, "I have to move!"

Worldwide measurements of sea levels are not uniform, as one might expect. Besides the volcanic changes that affect the depth of the sea bottom in a particular location, there are anomalies in certain regions. It turns out, as I mentioned, that there is a lump in the sea right near Miami's shore. It is a lump caused by the Gulf Stream, a huge current of warm water about ninety miles wide. That huge current was measured and thus confirmed, to a great extent, by none other than Benjamin Franklin.

Good old Ben was assigned to be the ambassador from the fledgling republic of the United States to Gay Paree, of all places. (In those days, France was our biggest ally and Britain our worst enemy.)

Anyhow, what happens is that the Gulf Stream's waters snake around the Florida peninsula and head north, always keeping pretty close to the shore (about thirty miles off it). When the huge, warm current passes New England and gets close to the ice cap, the melting ice there causes the salty water to sink; this is simply a case of the ocean water, like any other fluid, dividing itself into heavier water below and lighter water above.

That movement, in turn, slows down the current and—under Bernoulli's law—causes the current to rise about a foot higher than normal. This rise, in turn, causes the sea next to Miami also to rise an exaggerated amount, giving the impression that the entire ocean is spilling over Miami Beach onto the mainland.

How long this will happen is anyone's guess. Whether the trend will reverse itself soon is also a guessing game. But at least it explains why Miami's sea level–rise measurements, which are taken from the NOAA facility in Virginia Key, are so precipitously high (and why the *New Yorker* article was not too far off in its dire predictions, which were based on recent, rather than long-term trends).

All of this should not be that difficult to analyze, if you think about it.

Sea levels are basically a function of sea depth and water volume. And water volume is basically a function of temperature, which has a direct effect (heat increases volume) and an indirect effect (heat melts the northern and southern ice caps). Yet even my staff, provided with every possible teaching aid imaginable, could not grasp it.

The experience of one summer intern was illustrative. This young lady had earned a master's degree from the Rosenstiel School of Marine and Atmospheric Science, a branch of the University of Miami. This was the best of our local university programs on environmental sciences—arguably the best in the world on weather phenomena affecting the Miami region.

So I tasked her with producing a study on what appeared to be an exponential rise in the level of Miami's seas. And I provided her with the best available sources: data provided by the regional stations of the NOAA, located at Key Biscayne and Key West, plus analysis of that data provided by Brian McNoldy, who taught at Rosenstiel.

The draft she produced was almost unreadable. She obviously couldn't write worth a lick, so I assigned her to a related project, which was to simply publicize our efforts to transform the famous Calle Ocho from a one-way to a two-way "neat street" that would serve both the merchants and the residents of Little Havana.

Now, you have to understand that she wasn't expected to produce any in-depth analysis or any drawings. Those already had been provided by an urban planning entity called PlusUrbia. The PlusUrbia team had envisioned a gorgeous, workable, livable streetscape with two lanes of auto traffic, flanked by two dedicated lanes of trolleys.

All the intern had to do was produce some social media postings announcing and touting this gorgeous redesign of Calle Ocho.

Instead, she wrote a memo in which she suggested that Calle Ocho had to be raised some ten feet or more, due to expected sea level rise. This was a totally extracurricular diversion on her part. So I decided to call her out in the middle of a staff meeting,

The conversation went more or less as follows.

"Amy," I said, "where did you get the impression that you were supposed to be analyzing sea level rise on Calle Ocho?"

"Well," she promptly answered, "you have tasked me with being up to speed on our county's sea level rise issues, and I figured I should include that analysis in the Calle Ocho streetscape redevelopment."

"But, Amy," I stammered, "aside from the fact that it was not part of your task, and just out of curiosity, why do you think that Calle Ocho is threatened with sea level rise?"

She was firm in her conviction but weak in her analysis: "All of Miami is threatened by sea level rise, and Little Havana should not have its streetscape redesigned without this being part of the analysis."

"OK," I said, "let's assume that I wanted that analysis built into what was supposed to be a simple media dissemination of the renderings. What metrics make you think that sea level rise in Little Havana poses an imminent danger?" Before she answered, I gave her metrics to work with.

"Amy, don't you know that Calle Ocho is about ten feet above sea level? And don't you know that the last hundred years have seen a rise in sea level at a very precise rate of three millimeters per year? If that is the case going forward, when do you calculate that Calle Ocho will be underwater?"

"Oh, sir," she answered, "I can't calculate that."

To which I snapped, "What do you mean you can't calculate that? The math is simple: If you assume three millimeters a year increase in sea level, how many years will it take to reach ten feet above sea level?"

She had no clue, so I helped her. "It's equivalent to one foot every hundred years, which means it would take a thousand years to reach ten feet."

And so it went. No one seemed to have a handle on Miami's peculiar conditions. The fact remained that there was a unique factor at play in Miami, which merited further analysis. Somehow, we had to figure out why our area was experiencing an accelerated rate of sea level rise.

I tried to explain that in some position papers, but no one listened— least of all the bureaucrats. I take that back: The politicians, gathered in Miami Beach for the mayors' conference, took even less notice of these nuances.

Perhaps no single event exemplifies the problem of having democratically elected laypeople deciding environmental policy. In 2017 in Miami Beach, a host of mayors gathered to discuss, among other things, the threat of the rising sea.

The two protagonists in this curious affair were the diminutive mayor of Miami Beach, Phil Levine, and the gargantuan mayor of New York, Bill de Blasio. One was rich and absorbed in the one-dimensional politics of Miami Beach, an island city that has but two main roads, stretches perhaps ten blocks, and contains no more than two hundred thousand people.

The other city is an empire. New York is to Miami Beach as Goliath was to David. It is King Kong to Miami Beach's lovely actress in skimpy attire. If waves were to engulf New York, the economic losses would be in the trillions of dollars. When a tidal wave hits Miami Beach, it can get by with a few emergency pumps.

New York is a different story.

In 2017, both cities came together to embrace in a ritual to Poseidon, the god of the sea. And, as with everything else important, it happened in Miami.

18

Phil Levine: Quintessential Beach Mayor

The summer of 2017 saw the final act of Miami Beach's flamboyant multimillionaire mayor, Phil Levine.

In many ways, Miami Beach is the tropical version of Manhattan: It is an island that everyone wants to visit; it has expensive hotels, ostentatious stars and starlets, and mayors who do their best to outshine and impress both their millionaire residents and their well-heeled visitors.

Levine ended a four-year reign of turmoil when he hosted the 2017 mayors' conference. Those four years were a veritable roller coaster of bungled deals, populist rhetoric, and inconsistent policies. He and I rubbed elbows when we both ended up as members of a select subcommittee whose task it was to plan a mass transit link between Miami and Miami Beach. Mayor Levine's election had presaged a wholesale reform of Miami Beach politics. And, as always, it had an ethnic flavor. The incumbent was an affable, Cuban-born, earthy lady named Matti Herrera Bower. She had great instincts, but scant analytical skills.

One time, when I had just been appointed to a committee overseeing the efforts to build Baylink, the rail connector between downtown Miami and Miami Beach, I scheduled a meeting with the Miami Beach city manager. This fellow, named Jimmy Morales, puts the lie to the idea that bureaucrats are all overpaid and unimaginative. Morales, a Harvard Law School graduate, could actually make more money in the private sector.

But he loves public service and is very good at it. He has survived two mayoral transitions in Miami Beach. On this day, he was about to find out who would be his next mayor. By pure coincidence, we had scheduled the meeting for the very day of the vote; the incumbent mayor, Herrera Bower, termed out as mayor but was on the ballot as a commission candidate. Chances were high that she would not be elected.

But she was still, technically at least, mayor. And she insisted on attending my meeting with City Manager Morales. The problem was that she and I were technically members of the same Baylink committee, and under Florida's Sunshine Law could not meet in private. To comply with the law, we would have had to post advance notices of the meeting.

This was not part of the plan. I knew she wasn't going to win and, frankly, did not really need any input from her. She was the lamest of lame ducks.

So I had my staff explain that to her staff and headed over the causeway to the beach. By pure coincidence, I had wanted to discuss some complicated legal matter with the county attorney, Bob Cuevas, and for the first time (and the last time ever, as it would turn out) invited him to join me on the trek across the bay.

He accepted. And that was a good thing, as my reader shall see.

I started the meeting with the manager, and soon thereafter Mayor Herrera Bower's staffer showed up. I explained that the Sunshine Law prevented us from discussing matters that were pending regarding the Baylink committee, but she insisted on staying.

Wanting to get things moving, I explained to the manager, county attorney, and others present that I had previously met with Herrera Bower and that her main concern—which I thought was warranted—was that any train crossing Miami Beach streets should not have enormous, mixed-use terminal stops. She wanted just simple platforms, no more commercial development.

That had always made sense to me, which I stated at the meeting. Just as I was finishing saying that, the mayor walked in and sat down. I recounted the prior conversation I had had with her, and again restated that the two of us could not meet on this issue without proper public notice.

To this she replied that she "would just listen." At this, I asked the county attorney if that would be proper, and he had to advise us that it would not.

But she didn't budge. Not wanting a confrontation, and not wanting to waste an opportunity to meet with the city manager of an important neighboring city, I put on the table a totally different topic: the completion of the new Miami Beach convention center.

The mayor snapped, "Why are you interested in this? It doesn't concern the county." I quickly but calmly replied, "Yes it does, Mayor. The new convention center is funded with bed tax monies that we have to approve." Then I added, "By the way, I agree with your views on the convention center hotel."

This mollified her somewhat. But the in-depth analysis I had hoped for was not to happen on that day. And it was frustrating to think that the lady would not wait until the end of the day to hear the election tallies, which ultimately showed that she was out of office and irrelevant to any further discussion of Baylink.

Such are the ways of Miami politicians. They have big egos.

It reminds me of the Winston Churchill saying about a rival, to the effect that "he is modest, and he has much to be modest about." Except that our pols down here are not very modest.

Roll forward to the Miami Beach mayors' conference and quintessential Miami Beach politician Mayor Levine. As I write this book, he is still in office, and has announced that he will not be running for reelection.

Miami Beach was too small a stage for Levine. You just knew he would run for governor. And you knew that he would tout his efforts to keep Miami Beach streets dry, using three traditional tools: pumps, seawalls, and higher-level streets.

It should be noted that raising streets has fallen out of favor. And increasing the height of seawalls should also be disfavored, particularly where "living shorelines" can be enhanced, as has been done in Miami Beach. Levine would have done well to study the use of natural barriers to contain the ocean, as has been done in places like the Netherlands.

Inland canals are a different story.

My wife and I spend our summers in a rented condo in Miami Beach. A seawall that keeps the inland canal from spilling onto the streets during storms is making our lives miserable, as it has forced the beach's mainline,

Collins Avenue, to be a narrow divided-lane highway with only one lane in each direction. When I leave my summer rental place, I have to head north for five blocks and then maneuver a U-turn to head south and cross the bay on the only causeway that offers easy transit to my downtown office.

But Mayor Levine's worst moment was not his battle with the rising waters—whether from canals or the ocean itself. It was in the area of his city's rapid transit. It was there that he clashed initially with the county and ultimately with his own constituents.

19

Baylink

esides Levine and myself, there were three other members of the Baylink committee: county commissioner Bruno Barreiro, whose district covered most of South Beach, and the mayors of Miami (Regalado) and the county (Gimenez).

From the start, the bureaucrats tried to run the show. Counting on initial funding of $300,000, the first thing the bureaucrats did was hire consultants. And, of course, the first thing the consultants did was spend it on studies, beginning with rehashing/updating a ten-year-old study by a prior consultant.

I did my best to thwart the bureaucrats. In the first meeting of the committee, I insisted that we name a chairperson so that the meetings would be headed by the elected officials rather than by the bureaucrats.

Figuring that the mayor of the county had the most standing of the five committee members, I nominated Gimenez for chair. No one reacted, so I tapped Regalado under the table and he realized my motion needed a second, which he gracefully offered.

Nominating Gimenez for chair was a big mistake. I must have forgotten that he was the ultimate bureaucrat. That trait came back to hamper the committee's functioning later on. Initially, at least, it helped to give Gimenez a little extra standing.

I say initially, because that first meeting of the Baylink committee almost deteriorated into a bureaucratic disaster. Gimenez was actually helpful here in his role as chairman of the committee.

Here's how it went.

A consultant got up there to analyze the proposed rapid transit link. It was assumed that we would be using at-grade rail in Miami Beach and elevated light rail as the trains crossed the causeway from downtown Miami to South Beach. None of this was exactly rocket science. Boston has mixed elevated and at-grade rail. New Orleans and Colombia do too. Miami used to have at-grade streetcars in downtown, for God's sake!

So the consultant proceeded to estimate the cost of what she considered the three components of the link, beginning with a proposed new, elevated loop that would transport people on the Miami side of the bay. But, lo and behold, instead of using the existing (and very successful) Peoplemover, she proceeded to estimate the cost of a new elevated guideway that would connect to the cross-bay rail link.

Immediately I broke in: "Mr. Chairman," I practically shouted, "are we not going to use the existing light rail system in downtown Miami?" The consultant (incredibly) answered, "Well, this analysis is based on not using existing infrastructure." And she proceeded on her merry way to estimate the cost of the loop on the mainland side of Baylink, which was already being served by not one but two loops of the Peoplemover.

Thankfully, Gimenez broke in: "Now wait a minute; you have not answered the commissioner's very logical question. You are not seriously saying that we will be duplicating the infrastructure that already exists on this side of the bay?"

The question answered itself. The consultant wised up and proceeded to analyze the cross-bay component of Baylink.

That was the last, and only, time I ever heard Gimenez think for himself and not assume the bureaucratic view of things. But the consensus on the Baylink committee did not last. Soon, Mayor Levine went rogue.

I should have known it would happen. Right from the start, Levine had been uncomfortable sitting on a five-person committee where he had to play second fiddle to the mayor of the county (third fiddle if you count the mayor of Miami, though that was less of an issue, since Regalado was not fluent enough in English for Levine to feel overshadowed).

Gimenez certainly was playing first fiddle, and he seemed particularly bold with his newfound chairmanship of this board. It should be kept in mind that this was a subcommittee of the MPO, of which Gimenez was not even a member. Now he found himself (thanks to me) the chair of a multijurisdictional committee empowered with planning authority over three municipal entities plus the state of Florida, which was there in an administrative capacity.

At the second meeting, the fireworks began. By then Levine had lost all patience for this slow-moving process. He quickly realized that the purpose of the committee was to satisfy all federal planning and design norms, so as to have the project eligible for federal funds. A National Environmental Policy Act (NEPA) study had to be performed, a process with a two-year timetable.

For Levine, this was way too long. He wanted to start on the part of the connector that would be entirely within his city. It was envisioned as a simple train or streetcar, at grade, which would connect Fifth Street in South Beach with the convention center, located a mile and a half north. Using innovative technology, a simple streetcar, rolling at grade and using power lines also at grade, could be quickly designed and installed.

Note that I said "innovative technology" for what otherwise appears to be very conventional streetcar technology, such as used in Boston and New Orleans. The innovation came from a power system that would become live only when the train was above it. When there was no train, there would be no complete circuit and thus no electricity flow. Thus, one could dispense with unsightly overhead cables while not having to worry about the proverbial ground-level "third rail" that could kill pedestrians, bikers, and drivers crossing over the at-grade power line.

You could hardly blame the mayor of Miami Beach for wanting to move quickly. A simple streetcar connecting his city's south side to the convention center would reduce traffic enormously. It would allow the hotels in South Beach to lure conventioneers in the vicinity of the convention center by offering transport to the famous watering holes and restaurants in South Beach. It would also allow employees to transfer from a grand central (multimodal) depot in South Beach to the quaint Miami Beach streetcar. Henceforth, at least South Beach would not be dependent on automobiles or unsightly, lumbering buses.

Plus, I presume that Levine wanted to end the horrible dependency on mammoth parking structures in what was becoming the most valuable beachfront real estate in the world. (By way of illustration, a single condominium on the thirty-second block of Collins had recently sold for a spectacular $39 million!) Levine probably figured that the elimination of parking structures, coupled with the new phenomenon of ridesharing (such as Uber and Lyft), would ultimately mean the parking spaces would be replaced by boutique shops and restaurants.

Miami Beach would complete its transformation from sleepy winter resort to bustling year-round convention attraction and permanent residence for the rich and beautiful.

For a while, Levine accepted a compromise in his eagerness to begin building the intra-city streetcar. I cobbled together the compromise during a Baylink committee meeting, specifying six parameters that would assure compatibility between the three branches of the system: the existing Miami loop (Metromover), the elevated cross-bay connector, and the Miami Beach streetcar. (Among the principal elements were that the tracks and technology had to be the same and that there had to be a single operator for the whole system. This would assure seamlessness, or—as the bureaucrats now call it—"one-seat" mass transit.)

The compromise held for a while, but Levine was restless to begin accepting bids for his intra-city streetcar. This despite the fact that we were just then negotiating with the Feds to be allowed to use the streetcar ridership in the funding application for the entire system.

For once, the bureaucrats came up with a brilliant idea. It was called the Program of Interlocking Projects (POPS). When it was announced to the committee, I turned to Levine and said, "From here on I will call you 'Pops.'"

I doubt that he was amused. It was his last time attending Baylink committee meetings. For that matter, it was the last time that committee met.

Soon after that, Levine was pressed by his colleagues into having town hall meetings to discuss not only the cross-bay component of Baylink but the intra-city streetcar. Nearly half of the residents opposed the cross-bay component, and the other half opposed the streetcar. That was around the time that the convention center hotel plan stalled, and with it the hoped-for funding source for the intra-city streetcar.

It would be up to other mayors to restart the alliance with the county with a view to enabling the Miami Beach component of Baylink. On the county side, we settled on a cross-bay extension of the Metromover, which would not involve Miami Beach officials in any important way.

We would fund it, build it, and leave the passengers at the Fifth Street entrance to the beach, where the city could decide if and how to transport them from there.

In the meantime, I suspect the city will expand its version of trolleys-on-wheels, of which at this writing it had four in operation, charging nothing; they're used with great acceptance by tourists and locals alike. (At last notice, the trolley fleet had grown to fourteen and is ferrying about four million riders a year.)

Of course, this did not solve the problem of the hotel workers, the construction workers, and the delivery and repair people who had to commute from across the bay.

That would be up to the county. And the county was still run by 4,283 bureaucrats and a bureaucrat-in-chief.

Could we possibly live with that for another three years?

I suspect by this time my reader must be wondering why I blame so many of our problems on the bureaucrats. This is not to pass the buck; the buck stops with the elected officials.

The problem is that the elected officials have allowed themselves to be dominated, in both analysis and vision, by the appointed administrators.

In Miami-Dade County, the imbalance of persuasive power is magnified by some peculiar features of civic society, including the inordinate credibility that the media give the bureaucrats.

This whole theme is worth discussing in some depth.

20

Bureaucrats vs. the People

L ocal government suffers most from having the wrong people make the most money for doing the least difficult tasks. Whereas a rookie street cop makes $45,000 a year for having to chase and investigate the bad guys, the director of something called "community advocacy" makes perhaps $150,000 for holding "Kumbaya"-like forums on police–community relations.

Starting engineers in Miami's Water and Sewer Department make $50,000 a year and can design a system that pumps and filters millions of gallons of water a day. The director, Lester Sola, makes five times that amount and his prior job was to supervise the Division of Elections.

Sola is a marvelous human being, as bureaucrats go. But not being an engineer or a scientist hurts. Recently we were discussing water flows in the system, and he did not know what "CCF" stands for in his department's billings to the residents. Because I know that a cubic foot contains about 7.5 gallons of water, I was quickly able to decipher that acronym as referring to *centum* cubic feet—that is, hundreds of cubic feet.

The lack of actual technical expertise on the part of department heads is just one example of bad management. As we shall see in this chapter, the utter lack of efficiency in Miami-Dade County's government and its related agencies is beyond the pale. Here I want to relate a story of one of the county agencies, which is actually an autonomous trust, like the previously mentioned transportation trust.

Besides being a county commissioner, I serve on the Children's Trust, which is an independent agency that administers preschool and other children's programs. Its executive director is a bright enough guy; he was formerly a public-school principal.

The trust is managed by a volunteer board, whose current chair is a very caring lady named Laurie Weiss.

As far as I can tell, neither Weiss nor the bureaucrat who runs the trust, James Haj, has ever voiced an original idea on how to make this agency more effective in helping kids become productive, healthy adults.

Let me modify that. From what I have seen during twelve months of service on the board, neither they nor any other bureaucrat in this agency has ever thought outside the box. The paid employees are probably afraid to.

As for the chair and other board members, they are the classic case of a board that is controlled by the paid employees and hired consultants who tell them how to evaluate the worth of programs funded by the trust, and by the media that give the trust a report card with either critical or laudatory articles.

I had just been appointed to the Children's Trust when I ran into trouble for questioning certain priorities. Here I was, a veteran with a combined fifteen years of service in government and thirteen political campaigns (not to mention forty-two years of law practice) doing something as simple as putting a matter on the agenda for discussion, and I found myself accosted by bureaucrats as if I had committed a mortal sin.

As mentioned, the Children's Trust is an independent board charged with allocating a healthy amount of real estate tax revenues (over $120 million a year) to various programs that help children get the right level of education, physical and mental health care, and mentoring when parents are not up to the task of parenting. As the lone county commissioner on its thirty-member board and by far the best-known person on the board, I expected no problem in having my items placed on the agenda.

I also expected the board chair, whose father was the venerable Jay Weiss and a good friend of mine for many years, to be amenable to my initiatives. After all, I had just finished creating an unprecedented alliance of the county, school board, and Children's Trust that collaborated to employ 1,500 youngsters in summer jobs—a program that did not exist before I pushed it through as chairman of the county's Economic Prosperity Committee.

Laurie Weiss herself had told me that the program was earning plaudits as a national model.

Well, I found out the hard way that the simple procedural act of putting an item on the agenda would be a Herculean task.

It all started on the way to a board meeting, when I instructed an aide to arrive ahead of me and let me know the preferred procedure for placing an item on the agenda. His initial response floored me: A bureaucrat told him that board members were not allowed to put items on the board agenda!

"What do you mean?" I asked him. "I am the person with the legally imposed fiduciary duty of managing this agency, setting its priorities, making sure we accomplish the goals of the legislation that enables us to tax citizens to the tune of over $100 million per year, and using that wisely to help children in need. How can I not be allowed to put an item on the agenda?"

My poor, flustered aide spent a good day negotiating with the staff of the Children's Trust, who were presumably negotiating with Weiss, the board chair. He told me he had a backup plan. I said I didn't need a backup plan. He said, "Let me tell you about it before you take a different approach."

"OK," I said. "Just for fun, what is your backup plan?" He delved into it with relish. "We get you appointed to the bylaws committee, and then you change the bylaws to allow a board member to put items on the agenda."

I almost fired him right then and there.

Realizing that this board was totally controlled by staff and by a passive chair, I tried a novel approach. I would have what in Florida is called a "sunshine meeting."

I never expected to have to go rogue just to comply with the law—or to advance the cause of the very children whom I had been appointed to serve on this trust's board.

Under Florida's Sunshine Law, no two members of a government or quasi-government board, such as the Children's Trust, can meet to discuss pertinent matters without doing it "in the sunshine." Even casual conversations on the general goals of an agency are forbidden, unless the general public is advised via an ad in a newspaper of general circulation.

In effect, the media have a front-row seat to any serious, substantive discussion by members of government boards. Add in the power of the media to investigate government activities and the tendency of the bureaucrats (as well as some elected officials) to leak negative stuff about public officials, and the media have a field day for influencing public policy. They have front-row seats as well as backstage access, while the politician who obeys the Sunshine Law is thrust onto the stage with nary an opportunity to practice lines with fellow actors.

I will discuss that more at length a little bit later. Here I want to explain how and why the Children's Trust bureaucrats sought to control the agenda.

It all began when I prepared the notice for a sunshine meeting. As soon as the executive director of the trust found out about it, he tried to convince me not to have the meeting. That was followed by putting pressure on me to hold the meeting at the trust offices.

"No way," I responded. The sunshine meeting was to be at one of my county offices, which just happened to be in a poor area of my otherwise affluent district.

My young staffer did not see why I insisted on that. Later, it became clear to him that I was securing what in politics is often called the "home-court advantage" (mentioned most notably in the movie *The American President*).

The person who controls the setting of a meeting has a distinct advantage. He or she does not have to wait in the reception area until being invited to come into the meeting area. He or she gets to decide where everybody sits and, essentially, when the meeting begins.

More important, in the case of my Coconut Grove field office, I got to display all the sketches done by my architect-in-residence (JC Garrido). This collection of drawings is so large that it does not fit at my downtown office. And it is truly spectacular.

That is why I often schedule meetings in the Grove office; it is my way of displaying our vision for Miami-Dade. In this case, it worked particularly well, as the superintendent (the flamboyant Alberto Carvalho) seemed very impressed with what he was seeing.

Imagine sitting at the head of a large conference table, in an open, rectangular office that measures perhaps thirty feet by forty feet and is filled practically wall-to-wall with gorgeous renderings of public spaces and sunken or elevated highways, museums, pools, arches, and whatnot.

But I am getting ahead of myself. I have not yet explained the degree of difficulty in getting this meeting scheduled—over the objection of the very bureaucrats that control the board of the trust, whose members are technically their bosses.

You see, the bureaucrats don't have to deal with the Sunshine Law. They can talk to board members anytime they want—about anything they want. Unlike them, when I convened the sunshine meeting, I was forbidden by law from outlining the specific measure we wished to discuss. For that reason, I had to rely on sheer persuasive power to obtain from other board members commitments to attend.

Thankfully, all but one of the five board members that I invited readily agreed. One did not, and she joined the behind-the-scenes chorus of trust bureaucrats (joined presumably by the chair) who tried to dissuade me from having the sunshine meeting.

The irony of the whole thing is that the item I wanted to put on the board agenda was really just an "urging," which is bureaucratese for a recommendation to the legislature to pass a particular bill. The bill I was recommending was one that would apply greater resources (manpower and money) to the after-school initiative that I had been promoting with my own campaign funds.

In other words, my initiative was not controversial. It was "motherhood and apple pie" stuff. For the trust, it was "revenue-neutral," meaning it did not take any funding from existing programs.

It was a win-win, a no-brainer.

But for the bureaucrats, and even for some members of the trust (including, apparently, the chairwoman), it was a rogue operation by a newly appointed member of the board. Neither its merits nor the proven track record of its sponsor mattered.

It was rogue, and rogue is wrong, by definition.

Ultimately, I won the battle, but the trust won the procedural war. I had my sunshine meeting, at my office, and had an exceptionally good response not only from the board members initially invited but also from the chairwoman herself, who appeared in person.

And yet their obstructionism made me realize that the trust board, as presently constituted, was not going to be an agent for the kind of change we needed to foster in the short run. My tenure on the trust would be just two years; and trying to get this agency to move in a radically new direction would not be worth the effort, particularly since the trust manages most of its $120 million fairly efficiently.

Let me explain.

The Children's Trust was an almost exclusive creation of former *Miami Herald* publisher David Lawrence Jr. It was part of a national early-childhood movement that sought to ensure that preschool children would have educational, nutritional, and health-care nurturing prior to entering the first grade. Americans of all persuasions are convinced that poor kids should start school on an even playing field with kids from more affluent families.

Let me illustrate with some statistics. In our metropolitan school system, which is demographically typical of that of most American cities, three-quarters of all kids receive either free or reduced-charge lunch. What that says is that from first grade, at least, there is already a lifeline for poor and lower-middle-class children. It provides nutrition, health care, and every advanced educational tool imaginable.

For seven or eight hours in each workday, during nine months of the year, the kids of Miami from ages six to eighteen are safe, protected, fed, and educated. However, up until a few years ago, many kids from birth to six years of age were bereft of nutrition, protection, and education.

As Lawrence himself preaches with the zeal that characterizes this extraordinary man, modern neuroscience tells us that as much as 80 percent of all learning is done by age two. Children who are lacking in nutrition, health care, and any kind of nurturing before reaching school age will begin first grade seriously impaired.

The Children's Trust has pretty much evened the playing field for children in Miami. At last look, there was no waiting list for prekindergarten programs. As far as government can solve the problem of growing up poor, we in Miami have fulfilled the early-childhood part of the problem.

That observation calls for a digression that brings me back in time to 1992, when I was active with the U.S. Conference of Mayors. At the time, the percentage of poor and working-class children who had access to preschool care was minimal.

Kids who came into the school system from disadvantaged homes were almost doomed to academic failure; many lacked proper nutrition, and a goodly portion did not have sufficient cognitive skills to absorb the lessons of formal schooling. By the time they started kindergarten, they were already behind the intellectual curve of their more affluent peers.

They became part of the so-called "underclass," which inherits and passes on a generational legacy of poverty combined with educational deficiency. Even without considering the dearth of two-parent homes and the pervasive crime of many inner-city neighborhoods, the elements of societal failure for these kids were established from the earliest age.

About a half century ago, the only liberal voice to warn America of the impending doom was that of U.S. Senator Daniel Patrick Moynihan. As the first prophet to discuss openly the dangers of the disintegrating family, he was pilloried by his fellow Democrats.

Some even called him a racist.

It was not a good time to voice what we, the big-city mayors, knew: that the family was the essential unit of society—the foundation on which a society is built. Conservatives had been saying that for many years, but their recipe was more discipline, more religion, more of what was called "law and order."

Most big-city mayors in the late eighties were liberal Democrats. (I was about the only independent at the entire mayors' conference, and the only one who had supported Bush the elder.) But ideology, or party affiliation, is not all that important when you are a big-city mayor. What counts is how your city grows, whether you have high unemployment, whether you attract the sports franchises and the great educational institutions.

And whether you can keep the peace.

In a prior decade, when Lyndon Johnson was president, the inner cities were the cauldron of a particularly volatile mixture of elements: anti–Vietnam War protests and racial unrest. At the peak of the demonstrations and urban civil disturbances, a reporter asked Johnson, "Mr. President, things could not get much worse, could they?"

"Oh yes," said LBJ. "I could be a mayor!"

The mayors of America in the sixties, seventies, and eighties were clearly the front lines of society's governing army. We lived and worked in the trenches.

By the time I was elected, in the mid-eighties, things were still not easy in the inner cities of America. White flight had reached a crescendo; entire communities were devastated by racial strife, lack of opportunity, educational apartheid, and the feeling that the upper classes were simply moving to the suburbs to escape the "ghettoes."

To me, it was not a matter of ideology. I think like an engineer. I look at the parameters of the equation before me. And the parameters indicated that we needed to do three things in Miami: one, take care of the middle-class bedroom communities, which mostly entailed keeping taxes low and police protection high; two, take care of the underclass, which entailed getting our fair share of federal grants for community development, housing, and education; and three, improve Miami's image as a city that welcomed foreign capital and immigrant populations who were willing to abide by the American code of work, tolerance, and ethical behavior.

These goals required a mix of Democratic compassion and Republican efficiency. And they required that all kids reaching school age be on an even playing field.

I felt at ease among Democratic mayors at the U.S. conference. I also would have felt at ease among Republican mayors, most of whom represented suburban municipalities that were whiter, wealthier, and more conservative.

To me, then and now, results and fairness are what counts. Almost every time, in every human situation, fairness comes when you give the most innocent in our society a fair opportunity to succeed. To me in the eighties, that meant what is now called early-childhood intervention— what I had growing up in a stable family with educated parents who gave me the opportunity to be educated.

It was easy for me to support the goals of the U.S. Conference of Mayors. But before I narrate that interesting chapter, including what ended up being some lively interaction with the mayor of Boston regarding then-president George H. W. Bush, let me digress for a moment to describe my roller-coaster relationship with David Lawrence Jr.

21

In Praise of David Lawrence Jr.

I have previously mentioned this former publisher of the *Miami Herald* (our principal and only English daily) and given credit to him for our early-childhood initiative. Lawrence was unusual in two ways.

He not only stayed in Miami after his tenure as publisher but remained active—though somewhat behind the scenes. Well, not really too much behind the scenes; let's just say behind the curtain.

After launching the Children's Trust, Lawrence took an office in the same building complex, which also housed United Way and the Early Childhood Initiative, a separate nonprofit institution. It was a nice, powerful, well-funded troika, and Lawrence sat astride them like the proverbial Colossus.

Lawrence is a classic bleeding-heart liberal. Because he hangs around with other liberals, he occasionally falls into the traps that characterize the knee-jerk liberals of our time. In matters of foreign policy, classic knee-jerk liberals have a really hard time with the idea of war.

They also suffer from a trait that is absolutely verboten for a leader: They are pessimistic about things. They are particularly pessimistic about the use of force.

Lawrence was the *Herald* publisher when George Bush the elder obtained congressional approval to repel the Iraqis from Kuwait. The result was the Gulf War, and it involved a coalition of over thirty nations.

That war was justified under both international and domestic law.

It entailed the use of overwhelming force against a tyrant, who had committed all kinds of atrocities against both neighbors and his own countrymen. It was strategically sound and morally justified.

The morning that the war started, Lawrence and I were sitting next to each other at an early-morning community breakfast. He leaned over to give me the news that the invasion had started just minutes before. Then he followed with a prediction: "This is going to be a long, drawn-out process."

"No, it won't," I quickly replied. "It will be over in days."

And it was.

Would Lawrence have reacted differently if the commander-in-chief had been a fellow Democrat? Probably not. My guess is that Lawrence was surrounded by media and academic elites, and they almost universally hate having to fight and almost universally tend to be pessimistic about the fate of modern civilization.

Combine abject pessimism with hatred of war and you have every reason to think that the world's lone superpower, supported by almost every secondary power, would have trouble winning a war even against a single country that lacked the latest military technology.

Yet Lawrence is not by any means the classic knee-jerk liberal; nor is he an elitist, as a matter of practice. Perhaps it's because he has a deep faith in God; whatever it is, Lawrence believes that good people can make a difference.

He certainly believes *he* can make a difference. Towards the end of my tenure, in the early nineties, there was a marked drop in the support that the local Catholic Church was able to give its handful of inner-city schools. Holy Redeemer in Liberty City was the first to close down. Pretty soon, it seemed that St. Francis Xavier, in Overtown, and Corpus Christi, in Wynwood, were also on the brink.

I turned to Lawrence for help. And he became a whirlwind of fundraising activity, using both personal and institutional resources. Writing editorials and making phone calls, he raised about a quarter-million dollars for each of the two parishes. Much of the money, including the single biggest contribution, came from Jewish donors.

Lawrence and I had a falling-out during my brief mayoralty of 1997–98. It is not worth rehashing here; suffice it to say that with him at the helm, the *Herald* bought into Joe Carollo's dysfunctional view of the world and his accusatory ways, which led naïve prosecutors to set traps for law-abiding folks and even more naïve journalists to believe that Miami was on the brink of bankruptcy and that Joe Carollo was the shining knight that could rescue the city.

That all ended—thankfully—in four short years, when Carollo was ousted after a reign of terror that included the aforementioned night in jail and the indictment of his chosen chief and city manager, Donald Warshaw. In between, the city almost erupted into a full-blown rebellion when Carollo's police force arrested four hundred mostly peaceful demonstrators who were objecting to the forcible seizure, at gunpoint, of a young exile named Elián González.

I myself, standing peacefully on a sidewalk, was nearly arrested by a field force that had been ordered to clear not only streets but sidewalks of peaceful demonstrators.

Roll forward to the present, almost two decades later, and Lawrence and I find ourselves in every kind of alliance, including one to prevent Carollo from winning a commission seat. Lawrence has opened up at a judicial reception to tell me that this man is "destructive" and "insidious."

Well, we knew that. In fact, my own campaign to oust the man had started way back in 1987. As noted earlier, I called it the ABC campaign, for "Anybody but Carollo."

It was only when Carollo almost single-handedly destroyed the suburban city of Doral (which now happened to be the new *Herald* headquarters) that it dawned on Lawrence and other *Herald* elites that this man was a dangerous demagogue.

Part of the problem, I think, is that the *Herald* never quite understood the transformation that Miami underwent during my eight years as mayor (1985 to 1993). The writers' habit of sensationalizing controversy and negative outcomes would expectedly blind them to the amazing progress we made in my three terms. While they acknowledged that I had been a popular and ethical leader, they remembered a couple of isolated incidents—actually, not even a couple. Just one, which I treat in other chapters.

By the time I left office, in 1993, I was an influential leader on the national scene. Because I was independent, neither party totally embraced me, but presidents and governors of both parties worked closely with me, with the result that Miami went from cultural wasteland to being home to a magnificent performing arts center and a site of the renowned International Book Fair. We went from having no downtown nightlife to having the largest and most successful specialty shopping center (Bayside), from having a single, disgruntled professional sports team to having new franchises in Major League Baseball, the National Basketball Association, and professional hockey.

Miami, in short, went from "Miami vice" to "Miami nice." Whereas in prior civil disturbances, occurring in 1968 and 1980, Miami had lost lives and entire neighborhoods to fire, in 1989 I contained the rioting at enormous risk to my own life and followed that with lawsuits to bring single-member districts to the county, the city, and the school board.

Miami, during my tenure, had three successive Black police chiefs. Whereas in the decade before me there had not been a single unit of affordable housing built by the city, in my eight years, we built 1,500 units plus two police substations and eleven mini-stations. Other mayors saw all this and respected me—particularly the gaining of professional franchises in both basketball and baseball.

I tried my best to use Miami's renaissance as clout to accomplish important societal goals within the U.S. Conference of Mayors. One, in particular, dealt with making preschool childcare affordable to all.

Ironically, where I (and the other mayors) did not succeed in the early nineties, David Lawrence Jr. succeeded in the late nineties, as we shall see in the next chapter.

22

Democratic Mayors vs. the Republican President

I was always a fairly active member of the U.S. Conference of Mayors. The organization had a well-staffed Washington, D.C., office, which supplied me with materials for testimony whenever I wanted to testify before the U.S. Congress.

The leader of the U.S. mayors' conference was typically a well-known and respected Democratic mayor. In 1992, it was Raymond Flynn, the flamboyant Boston heir to the line that was made famous by James Michael Curley of the book *The Last Hurrah*.

Curley reigned as mayor of Boston much before my time, but I suspect, from what I have read, that he was a lot like Mayor Flynn: earthy, jovial, and effective as a leader in great part because he was comfortable in his own skin. Being Irish in Boston is very much like being Cuban in Miami: You don't have to apologize for your style.

In Miami, for example, we kiss women as a greeting pretty much after the first time we meet them. We also hug the men, pretty much about the same time in a relationship—which is to say, immediately. Of course, the custom also works in reverse: You can withhold a kiss or a hug if the person, after the first couple of meetings, turns out to be obnoxious. This sends a message...

The custom of kissing and hugging practical strangers sets us Latinos apart from what I recently read about the British, whose functionaries even in the nineteenth century were shocked to see American presidents and society folks shaking hands with ordinary citizens. I suspect it was different for the Irish, and certainly for Irish Americans, who are warm to you right off the bat.

So it was with Mayor Flynn. The good mayor, in 1992, was touting an initiative of the mayors' conference that would derail about $11 billion in federal transportation funds towards early-childhood programs.

Flynn's staff had calculated that with the $11 billion (most of which was going to wasteful programs, such as the "Bridge to Nowhere" that became famous in Sarah Palin's run for vice president) earmarked for transportation projects, the entire demand for early-childhood programs could be funded.

Thereafter, argued the mayors (in a unanimously approved resolution), every needy child would be able to enroll free in preschool programs that would provide nutrition, health services and pre-primary education. To the extent possible during working hours, America's children would be treated equally by society. As a result, it was argued, our inner-city kids would begin kindergarten and first grade on an even playing field with their wealthier suburban counterparts.

This was Flynn's plan, but Flynn could not present it to President George H. W. Bush because the president would not give him an appointment. So he called me, knowing that I had supported Bush in 1988 and presumably had a tight relationship with the "prez."

Unfortunately, I had lost all access to the president, due to my rather open (and some would argue, intemperate) criticism of his failure to help the inner cities. After the successful Gulf War, which Bush had prosecuted magnificently well, the president's poll numbers had shot up to about 88 percent. It was the kind of political capital that should be invested—we all thought.

Let me clarify that. As is depicted in the movie *The American President*, when you have high poll numbers, you have to invest the political capital to get things done. If you don't, you will soon find yourself in a downward cycle of popularity, and chances are, you won't be able to accomplish anything.

Mayor Flynn knew that Bush was riding a wave of popular support; he also figured that Bush might want to invest that political capital. But he could not get an appointment, despite being the chairman of the nation's most powerful municipal organization—the United States Conference of Mayors.

Realizing that he was being stonewalled by the administration, which was Republican, and thinking it was because he as well as the great majority of big-city mayors were Democrats, Flynn turned to me. "You are close to President Bush; can you get us an appointment?" he asked. I said I would try.

The conversation took place in a van, as we were being herded someplace in Washington, D.C. So Flynn had time to expand on another interesting insight, which illustrates, once again, his folksy Irish ways.

He was musing about the refusal of Bush to meet with us and said, "Suarez, it is evident that this man does not understand the 'mother factor' in politics." So I asked him to explain, and he did: "Suppose the president invites a bunch of mayors to meet with him. Even if we are from the opposing party and don't particularly like what he says to us, we cannot come out of the meeting at the White House and just lay into the man. You want to know why? Because my mother would kill me. She would say, 'You can't go to the president's house and come out, after he shows you respect by inviting you, and blast the man. It just isn't right to do that.'"

He was right, of course, though one never knows what some other member of the delegation might do. I once led a delegation of Haitian Americans to a meeting with Bush when he was vice president. Afterward, we were all fairly complimentary of the vice president—except for one member of the delegation. This fellow, named Roger Biamby, was very critical of the vice president, which was a little embarrassing, since our arguments in favor of Haitian immigration had been well received...

In any case, I was by now pretty distant from Bush and had no luck getting an appointment for Flynn and his cohorts. I actually got to confront the president when Jeb Bush invited me to a reception at which those who had donated $2,000 or more would have a photo op. He told me the $2,000 minimum would be waived for me—which was a good thing, as I had not learned the art of fundraising too well, had no political action committee, and had no funds of my own for such an occasion.

As I was posing with the president for a photo that I did not need—since I already had the one that counted, which is the one in which we are sitting in a tête-a-tête at the White House—I put the question to him. I was blunt: "Mr. President, I have been trying to get us, the leadership of the Conference of Mayors, a meeting with you, but we are being ignored." He gave me a quizzical look, as if saying, "Suarez, you have been criticizing me publicly for some time; the fact that previously you were my campaign co-chairman for the Southeast region of the U.S. does not mean a darn thing now, when I must stand for reelection."

Or, more simply: "What have you done for me lately?"

I am convinced that was not the George H. W. Bush I had supported in 1988. That was not the "compassionate conservative" I knew. In my mind, what had happened was evident: His advisors had convinced him that he was on top of the world. Invincible. Above and beyond FDR and JFK and even Abraham Lincoln.

It doesn't work that way for us mortals. What actually happens is quite the opposite. And that brings me to a second digression, involving a trading partner of Miami that has probably the closest cultural resemblance to Miami in the entire western hemisphere.

I'm referring to Argentina.

We all know that Miami is an international city. It is clearly the gateway to Latin America. In many ways the mayor of Miami is treated like a head of state when visiting Latin American countries. We've been called the "capital of Latin America," and there is a lot of conceit in that phrase, but also a lot of truth.

23

The Mayor of Miami as an International Figure

once heard Andy Young, when he was mayor of Atlanta, refer to Miami mayor Maurice Ferré (my predecessor) as an international icon. "When I grow up," Young said, "I want to be Maurice Ferré."

We all did. Every mayor of every major American city had to at least try to emulate in his or her city the enormous international profile that Ferré had built up for Miami during his six terms as mayor.

To do so, we engaged in a totally asymmetrical game of home-and-away "trade missions." Let me elaborate.

As everyone knows, the classic international "junket" (presumably meaning a legitimate trip abroad but suspiciously being more like an excuse to take your spouse to Europe at government expense) is a prerogative of members of the U.S. Congress. You start by heading a committee with international functions—which can be either military or commercial. Then you arrange to be invited to Paris or Cairo or Moscow by the foreign head of state.

Mayors of cities like Miami (and counties like Miami-Dade) are not, by formal definition, involved in either foreign trade or international diplomacy. But in many ways, when serving in the capacity of such diplomats, we have more of an international profile than any member of Congress, including any senators not named Kennedy.

At least in Latin America.

The media are always ready to pounce on you if you abuse that role, by spending all kinds of money on what is the municipal equivalent of a congressional junket: a trade mission.

Of course, if you don't do these missions, the media criticize you just as fiercely, saying that you have failed to promote your city's well-deserved and much-needed international image.

If it wasn't for that, you could probably be an excellent mayor of Miami or Miami-Dade without doing a single trade mission. Let me tell you why.

Miami is so well located, has such an attractive climate, and is so multilingual and multiethnic that anyone who's anyone, or is married to anyone, or is the college-age son or daughter of anyone, wants to come here. And I mean not once every few years, but at least once a year.

Preferably for one or two weeks. And if the kids are young, with a stop in Disney World.

Nevertheless, it is de rigueur to go on trade missions, so my approach is to make them count. I don't like to travel, and I am not much for ceremony, so trade missions are not my cup of tea. But it is definitely part of the job description for the mayor of Miami.

So, being the perfectionist that I am, I try to be the best at it; often, I do meet interesting international figures. So it was in Argentina in 1991.

I went on a trade mission to Argentina in late 1991, as the elder Bush was getting his horses ready for a reelection bid that, by all rights, should have been a walk in the park.

As I said, when you travel as the mayor of Miami, you are treated like royalty. In most countries, they waive all customs and simply stamp your passport on the plane or in a plush VIP room, where they ply you with libations. Receptions are held in your honor, and gifts are given that often exceed in value the little trinkets that we bring.

A word on the trinkets that we bring. When I was elected mayor in 1985, the city had two main gifts: a huge, illustrated tome of National Audubon Society pictures of birds and a paperweight with the city seal.

Neither of these gifts made any sense. The bird book was enormous and a bother to carry when giving it—and probably an even bigger bother to carry when receiving it. And it was probably expensive, though I never found out, since I canceled all future orders.

The paperweight was useless and dangerous. Who used paperweights anymore in the late eighties, when society was moving towards a paperless economy? Plus the darn things weighed a ton and could really hurt your foot if they fell off the desk. Foreign leaders, on receiving one, would look at it as attentively as their manners would allow and then pass it carefully to their aide, hoping not to be asked what they would do with it, for fear of embarrassing me, the giver.

I quickly replaced the bird book and paperweight with two items. One, for visiting dignitaries, was a small but beautiful beach towel with a painting of a Miami Beach scene. It cost us about five bucks, was light, and was a big hit with the foreign dignitaries.

The other was even better, if you rate it based on value divided by price. I had cufflinks made from our lapel pins, to imitate ones given out by the president with the presidential seal. With box and everything, we got them for a mere $2.40!

And the foreign dignitaries loved them.

The cost of our trinkets was insignificant compared to the cost of trade missions as most politicians do them. I was determined that mine should cost the city exactly what the city could afford: zero dollars.

So I had strict requirements. The first and most important was that *a trade mission must include fifty private-sector participants, who would pay their own way.* The reason for this was quite simple: Our travel agent, when arranging overseas travel for fifty passengers, would throw in one free airfare and one hotel room, which went to me.

The second requirement was that the city would not pay for any receptions in the host country. The U.S. ambassador was good for one lavish reception in every country, particularly in Latin America, where the mayor of Miami is a big deal. Another reception would usually be sponsored by an international bank with offices in Miami. A third reception might be hosted by a major company in the host country that wished to do business in Miami.

Then the trip would be dressed up with all kinds of official meetings, arranged by the U.S. State Department through the U.S. ambassador and the congressional liaison. There would be a few receptions hosted by the embassy as well as U.S. companies abroad, plus the local dignitaries. If at all possible, I'd meet the head of state or a handful of ministers.

If the junket was to Paris or to Madrid, Spain, I'd get feted by the mayor, who in those cities is next in power to the president, if not next in line to *be* the president.

A formal affair with the mayor of Paris is particularly impressive. The luncheon or dinner is staged in a formal dining room in city hall, which is in a regal building called Ile De France, which literally means the "island of France." The most visible tapestry shows the creation of the French Republic, with the iconic Marquis de Lafayette mixing the colors of the city with the emperor's colors to create the tricolor flag of France.

The interesting (and scary) thing is that on the tapestry, Lafayette, as the municipal authority, stands on a higher step than the emperor.

Another impressive setting is the U.S. embassy in Argentina, which is a very large and ornate building, with a central staircase reminiscent of the one just described in Paris. Here the U.S. ambassador hosted a reception for me and my Miami delegation. We stood in line and greeted at least two hundred guests; what helped enormously was that I was flanked by the archbishop of Buenos Aires and the ambassador, so I could talk government and religion in equal parts during what seemed like a two-hour receiving line.

As mayor of Miami from 1985 to 1993, I went on about a dozen trade missions, plus a couple of diplomatic ones. On each of those, I did not spend one penny of public funds.

I could not justify it.

Besides Argentina, two of my most memorable trade/diplomatic missions were to the Far East (Hong Kong, Taipei, Tokyo) and to Jerusalem.

These are worth a short chapter.

24

Memorable Trade Missions

The trade mission to Hong Kong was totally sponsored by Swire Properties; the one to Venezuela by Banco Consolidado and the Cisneros Group; the one to Chile by Banco de Chile.

In Buenos Aires, Argentina, we had the U.S. ambassador's lavish reception plus some others given by banks and international entities. I was a big enough deal to even rate ringing the closing bell in the Argentinian stock market. And the city's mayor invited us to a musical performance at the famous opera hall Teatro Colón, where I was seated in the president's own booth and was saluted by the symphony maestro at the beginning of the performance.

The mayor of Buenos Aires is equivalent, in rank, to a governor. He was not able to join us for the Teatro Colón performance, and so he sent his intergovernmental relations director. This particular intergovernmental relations director just happened to be a very attractive woman, and she was wearing a very attractive dress that day as she escorted my wife and me to our seats in the presidential box.

All I remember of the dress (and all my wife allows me to remember) is that it was made of leather and had a zipper that went all the way down the front. That certainly made it a practical piece of clothing, if the idea was to get rid of it quickly.

I can only suppose…

Being offered the presidential box at the famous Teatro Colón is an example of what I meant when I said our home-and-away trade missions are asymmetrical. When Miami mayors go overseas, the country inviting us lavishes every kind of fancy meal on us and plies us with gifts and fancy receptions.

When they visit us, we give them, at best, some Cuban pastries and cafecito at city hall. Foreign dignitaries seem to accept the idea that when they visit us, the best we can do is show them the bay from the balcony at Miami City Hall, which (I should add) is the historic seaport for the Pan American Clipper hydroplanes.

It has a lot of history, even if not a palace possessed of rich tapestries.

When we go abroad, we expect to meet with the heads of state.

So it was when I went to Argentina, but then-president Carlos Menem was not able to grant me an appointment. As a consolation prize, his brother hosted us, and he was the sitting senate president, which in Argentina's government was just about the second-most powerful official. There, Senator Eduardo Menem made a startling pronouncement about what President Bush needed to do.

The exchange went like this:

"Mayor Suarez," he said, "I understand that you were a big Bush supporter. What are his chances for reelection? May I assume he is a shoo-in?"

"No, Senator Menem," I answered. "The president has had very favorable numbers since the successful prosecution of the Gulf War. However, he does not seem interested in helping the city mayors in our efforts to improve the lives of our poorest constituents." Then I told him the story of Mayor Flynn's childcare initiative and of the president's unwillingness to meet with us.

He quickly retorted, "Well, then he is violating an important norm of politics, which is that you cannot sit on your political capital. It will not stay in place, if you don't invest it. You must invest your political capital."

It reminded me of the scene in the movie *The American President* when a political advisor, played by Michael J. Fox, tells the president that he should "take his high poll numbers for a spin" with some aggressive legislative initiatives.

Mayor Flynn's childcare initiative took place back in 1991–92 and we were never able, at the national level, to provide a guaranteed early-childhood network. But at least in Miami-Dade, we did have the Children's Trust, and it did just about meet the entire demand for those eligible for preschool combined with an existing federal program called Head Start.

Yet in Miami, in the second decade of the twenty-first century, we needed more than early-childhood intervention. We needed after-school programs for pre-adolescents that would stimulate their curiosity, their physical fitness, their self-confidence, and their minds.

In subsequent chapters, I will describe what Francis and I were able to accomplish in our efforts to fund universal after-school opportunities for the portion of our 350,000 public school children whose families could not afford to provide them.

Now let me get back to the role that well-connected Miami mayors can occasionally play overseas.

25

A Visit to Jerusalem of Gold

led a delegation to Israel when I was mayor. It wasn't strictly a trade mission, nor was it a diplomatic mission. I wasn't representing a country or even a city. But in a sense, I was representing more than that.

I was representing a nation—the nation of my birth. Let me explain.

In Miami, there is a rather large and powerful Cuban-Jewish community. The Cuban Jews, or "Jubans," were desirous of participating in the magnificent effort of creating a forest in Israel, otherwise a fairly arid land.

It is called the Jewish National Fund and it boasts millions of trees carefully planted and nourished into adulthood. So it made sense for exiled Cubans, who are part of a diaspora with its principal concentration in Miami, to plant a green banner in Israel.

As the first Cuban-born mayor of Miami, I was a symbol for these people, who are a diaspora within a diaspora. Not to mention that I am pretty sure I have some Jewish ancestry, given the similarity of my last name to the classic Jewish last name Schwartz.

When approached about leading the delegation to Israel to plant a banner, I immediately said yes. It was particularly interesting to join that group and share the spotlight with Alex Daoud, then the mayor of Miami Beach.

Alex Daoud (whose last name is an Arabic version of David) was and is a classic, made-in-Miami marvel of a man. He is big, boisterous, and prone to ethical lapses; ultimately, he ended up spending time in jail for accepting bribes in exchange for official favors.

He has written a pretty salacious book about his lapses and about his encounters with lobbyists, the media, prosecutors, and other politicians. His only mention of me in it is favorable; it deals with an exhibition boxing match that he and I staged to raise money for an inner-city gym, with ourselves as the fighters.

I will spare my reader the details of that clownish but well-intentioned event. Let's just say that I survived an encounter with someone who outweighed me by about sixty pounds and who was an experienced amateur boxer. (He did hit me one time a little too hard, and I almost fell, which would have been quite embarrassing…but thankfully, Daoud immediately embraced me in what in boxing is called a "clinch." It gave the impression that he was trying to protect himself by slowing down the action.)

I guess I owe him one there.

The trip to Israel is a different story. There were moments on that trip in which Daoud, as mayor of Miami Beach (with its large Jewish population) eclipsed me totally. One is worth recounting.

The flight to Israel was uneventful except for two moments, both taking place towards the very end. One was the playing of the melody "Jerusalem of Gold" as the plane landed in Tel Aviv. That was special.

On the plane, Daoud was being his usual garrulous self. He looked very disheveled; he'd probably had a few drinks that made him even noisier than was customary. He also flirted with the ladies.

As we were ready to land, it was evident that Daoud had not had a very restful flight: His collar was up over his jacket as he went into the bathroom. He looked like he had been sleepless, tossing and turning in what was probably an uncomfortable seat for a man standing six-foot-four and weighing a good 250 pounds.

Somehow, between that last bathroom stop and the landing, he cleaned up, shaved, straightened his shirt collar, and exited so far in advance of the rest of us that when I walked out of the plane, he was already doing his political act.

Hard to believe, but there he was, conducting the Israeli band that was welcoming us on the tarmac! Daoud had gone from sleepy, unkempt visiting dignitary to band leader extraordinaire in less than five minutes.

The rest of our visit was more standard fare, though the term really does not apply to visiting Jerusalem. As always, I was not able to stay too long abroad, and when my hosts found out about that, they offered me a personal guide and half-day tour of the city.

As I finished the tour, I offered the guide some compensation, since I had found out that he was a volunteer, not a paid employee of the government. He turned it down, saying, "We here in Israel just want you to get the full flavor of what this country has to offer, so that you can communicate it to the rest of the world."

Indeed.

By pure coincidence, I was able to meet up, while in Jerusalem, with another well known Miami resident, the inimitable Jorge Mas Canosa.

26

Jorge Mas Canosa
in Jerusalem

My visit to the Holy Land was made that much more memorable by the coincidence that another well-known Miamian was in town. We ran into each other in the lobby of the King David Hotel. I was startled to see there, in the flesh, the inimitable Jorge Mas Canosa.

Mas Canosa was, for about three decades, the most powerful Cuban-born figure in the United States. At the height of his power, he commanded almost as much media attention as Fidel Castro.

My first encounter with him, after my mayoral election in 1985, was at the Caribbean Conference in Miami. The conference highlighted—like no other event—Miami's geopolitical importance. It regularly drew heads of state from almost every Caribbean country, plus at least one or two from Central America.

That first year of my mayoralty, the conference was particularly well attended. We had the usual slate of Caribbean prime ministers plus the presidents of the Dominican Republic (Joaquín Balaguer) and El Salvador (José Napoleón Duarte). Both were very deferential to me: Balaguer made an official visit to Miami City Hall, and Duarte asked to see me after one of the events, which I had left a bit on the early side. When told I had left, he asked if I was far away and was told that I lived close to the downtown hotel where the event was being held.

The man said he would wait for me. Sure enough, I got in my car and drove to the InterContinental Hotel from my house in north Coconut

Grove. (At that time it was only a five-minute drive.) That was my first unexpected, memorable experience in international affairs. I greatly admired Duarte; he had been tortured by radicals of both the right and the left. He had been a prominent sponsor and signatory to the Esquipulas II peace agreement, which settled once and for all the Central American insurgencies of the time.

My fondness for Duarte was also enhanced by personal considerations: He had studied engineering at University of Notre Dame, and I had studied engineering at Villanova University. We were similar in many ways.

The very next day, we hosted President Balaguer at city hall. My wife, Rita, acted as hostess, and she established an excellent rapport with the president from the moment he arrived curbside at our quaint little city hall.

Rita and the president were chattering away in Spanish the whole time, as if they were lifelong friends. (I am pretty sure they were discussing my wife's favorite charity, Amor en Acción, which involved trips by my daughters as high schoolers to Haiti and the Dominican Republic, where they helped build schools and infirmaries.)

Duarte's and Balaguer's courtesies to me as mayor of Miami exemplify the importance that Miami has in this hemisphere. At this particular conference, an American vice president also visited. It was none other than George H. W. Bush, and he was looking for some Hispanic support in his bid for the presidency. Bush arrived for a welcoming speech on the very first day of the conference, where we hosted him at a cocktail reception.

The logistics of this reception were quite unusual. It was held in a roped-off area in the middle of the InterContinental Hotel lobby. My only official task there was to present a gift to Bush; sure enough, this was my first experience with the enormous book of the National Audubon Society's bird pictures. It was handed to me by someone from the protocol office of the mayor; I dutifully handed it to the vice president, who didn't know what to do with it, as his Secret Service agents were standing outside the roped-off area.

For a second the vice president seemed flustered; the damn thing was so heavy and unwieldy that you could not thumb through it while standing up. But this was a man of great diplomatic experience, and he soon managed to ditch the huge bird book and not miss a beat. As for myself, I made a mental note to eliminate all further purchases of the book;

for good measure, I decided right then to eliminate the Office of Protocol. Henceforth, one of my handful of staffers would handle such duties.

After the bird-book incident, I noticed the presence of Jorge Mas Canosa, along with his closest deputy, my good friend Francisco "Pepe" Hernández. Pepe signaled to me to come over for a second and asked me to get Mas Canosa into the roped-off area.

Up to that point, it had not occurred to me that I had such powers. So I acted on instinct and lifted the rope for Jorge and Pepe to walk in; soon after that I introduced Mas Canosa to the vice president of the United States.

It's funny now, thinking about it. How do you introduce a Cuban exile leader to the vice president? At the time, Mas Canosa's chairmanship of the Cuban American National Foundation (CANF) did not have any kind of ring to it. At that time, in 1985, the CANF was struggling to get its feet in place in the halls of Congress and the White House. (It was aided, in that effort, by a prominent attorney, Barney Barnett, who modeled the CANF's lobbying activities after those of the formidable American Israel Public Affairs Committee, or AIPAC.)

Through the good offices of Miami mega-developer Armando Codina, the Bush family and the CANF would establish a much closer relationship. Codina astutely brought Jeb Bush into his real estate firm, which sealed his already existing relationship with the vice president. By 1988, when it came time for Bush to run for the presidency, the ties between Codina and the Bushes were quite strong.

And that brings me back to my serendipitous meeting with Mas Canosa in the lobby of the King David. After meeting briefly in the lobby, we agreed to go for a walk later on by ourselves. I wanted to discuss the upcoming presidential election; and being alone with Mas Canosa in a faraway spot would be ideal for a tête-a-tête.

We agreed to meet in the lobby at ten p.m. and go for a walk. Barely a quarter-century after this memorable walk with this remarkable leader, I realize how special that moment was. Mas Canosa was the Cubans' golden-tongued orator, a modern version of the Cuban patriot José Martí. Like Martí, he was accused of harboring hopes of being the president of Cuba in its post-Castro phase. Like Martí, he never had the chance to see his country liberated.

The main topic that night was the upcoming presidential election. Mas Canosa, being totally nonpartisan, was well able to support a Democratic candidate, but the Democratic field that year was weak, whereas the Republicans had two very strong candidates: U.S. senator Robert Dole and Vice President George H. W. Bush.

My pitch to him was as follows: If we let nature take its course, the bulk of Miami's Cuban-Americans will stand solidly behind Bush—because, among other reasons, Armando Codina will shepherd them. If, on the other hand, we negotiate at least a little bit with Dole, we will have some bargaining power. If Dole looks likely to win the nomination, early alliances could give us enormous access.

As the saying goes, "Money talks in politics, and early money shouts."

I rattled off the names of a handful of well-heeled politicians and big-money contributors who were willing to woo Dole as well as Bush, and willing to stay put until a collective decision could be made later, as we got closer to the primaries.

It was the "Jerusalem Plan," and it was well conceived and baked. If Jorge Mas Canosa signed on, it would be the icing on the cake.

And he did, which kept the plan in place for about three days. As soon as I got back to Miami, given what is probably a tragic flaw in my personality—what many advisors and friends tell me is my down-home naïveté—I felt compelled to disclose the plan to the opposition: mega-developer Armando Codina. I must have thought it would be good to set the rules for a fair fight.

But there are no such rules in politics. Codina promptly called everyone whom I could possibly have in my alliance and dissuaded every single one from continuing their participation. For all I know, he had the vice president call each one. I know this: Soon after the crash of my Jerusalem Plan, all those folks in my short-lived alliance had invitations to an elite reception at the official residence of the vice president of the United States.

All except me, of course.

All I got was a visit from Elizabeth Dole, who was then the secretary of transportation—someone whose help we needed badly in Miami, given our faltering system of mass transit. Soon after her visit, I was invited to meet with her senator husband. In between, I was treated to lunch in the Senate cafeteria by their strongest ally, the powerful New York Senator Alfonse D'Amato.

I assumed the lunch invite was so that D'Amato could work me over. It was. But the whole thing backfired; D'Amato's staff informed me that he was bringing a union leader to join us for lunch. The guy evidently did not like Bush, and both he and Senator D'Amato had a field day insulting Bush over lunch, hoping the character attacks would convince me.

Bush, they insisted, was a weakling—an effete Yalie who would not stand up to the Soviets or do much to liberate Cuba, and so on.

It was a turn-off. I had been invited to meet with the vice president at the White House that very afternoon. The usual twenty-minute appointment had been converted into a forty-minute appointment, and it was a very compelling courtship.

The high point was when the vice president turned to me and, in his humblest and most sincere (almost pleading) voice, said, "Mayor, I really need your endorsement for the presidency of the United States."

Let me say this. Such a statement, if spoken by a candidate who did not share my centrist ideology, would have had almost no effect. But coming from a man who was moderately progressive and compassionate, a fiscal conservative, pro-life, and ethical to a fault—not to mention a breath away from being the most powerful person in the world, it was very effective.

Particularly considering I had come to this county as an exile and lived in this city (Washington, D.C.) just twenty-four years before, and each time I had driven down Pennsylvania Avenue, I wondered what it was like to be invited there to share views with the president.

A few years later, in 1989, Bush sent me in a presidential delegation to monitor the post– Omar Torrijos elections in Panama.

That quasi-diplomatic mission and one to Kuwait in the immediate aftermath of the Gulf War were perhaps the highlights of my short-lived extracurricular foreign-policy career.

27

A Presidential Delegation to Panama

t finally happened in Panama, after decades of strongmen like Omar Torrijos and Manuel Noriega: In 1989, Panama held a free, ostensibly democratic election.

Panama is sort of a home away from home for me and my wife, much like the Dominican Republic. It feels so much like the land of our birth.

Let me say something about that. Cubans, like Dominicans and Panamanians, are very lively, very musical, and very lighthearted. And all three countries are tropical, with fertile soil and lush vegetation. In Cuba as a youngster, I could smell the fruits hanging from the trees.

Parenthetically, I should clarify that Cuban soil is special. It is thought that Cuba was never covered by ice during the last Ice Age. There was little or no erosion as the seas receded back into their current configuration. So the level of fertility is spectacular. Fruits like mangos and guavas fill trees to the point that they fall, unplucked and uneaten, covering the ground like a blanket of sweet-smelling nectar.

In parts of Santo Domingo and Panama, you can smell that sort of tropical-fruit saturation. When you combine that with a happy people, devoid of any racial prejudices or complexes, who have a strong admiration for the United States, you have what Cuba was all about: a tropical paradise, anchored to the technology and democratic roots of the United States.

Cubans, like Panamanians and Dominicans, understand that we're not as good at democracy as North Americans. But one could argue that we are happier. It has always been my hope to blend those traits into a well-governed city, in which the essential values of tolerance, strong family bonds, a strong work ethic, and the rule of law bind the people together in a way that allows all but the very weak or very corrupt to prosper.

My ties to Panama go back to my college days at Villanova, where there was a large contingent of Panamanian students who wanted a top-notch engineering education. They came to my rescue when Bush invited me to be part of a delegation observing the first democratic elections since the Omar Torrijos era.

The idea that I could represent the nation that had inspired Alexis de Tocqueville's treatise on democracy was an inspiration in itself. The idea that it would be a way to support fledgling democratic efforts in a nation so similar to my country of birth made it even more special.

Imbued with what later turned out to be a slightly exaggerated sense of mission, I accepted President Bush's invitation to be part of the presidential delegation to Panama. I was picked up in a C-32, which is a modified Boeing 757 used for high-level cabinet members and members of Congress. Inside it has a very elegant seating arrangement for those in what ordinarily would be first class. In this case, there were four of us: Senators Bob Graham and Connie Mack from Florida, Senator John McCain of Arizona, and yours truly.

It was a high honor. Other dignitaries, including various congressmen (John Murtha of Pennsylvania and Larry Smith of Florida), were seated in a separate compartment, in regular seats. So were former U.S. senator Richard Stone and former ambassador to Panama Jack Vaughn. The delegation also included some State Department bigwigs. One, who was not so big, briefed us as we arrived at the U.S. military base in Panama.

"Ladies and gentlemen, distinguished members of this presidential delegation," he said in a somewhat solemn and subdued tone, "the president thanks you for your service. However, you should know that the Noriega-installed government does not accept you as official observers. And we cannot guarantee your safety. You have been issued White House IDs, which hopefully the government and its military will acknowledge. But there are no guarantees..."

As he was saying this, I worked out in my mind what I would do. Having dressed in a classic guayabera that is typical in Central America, I figured I could ditch my White House ID if things got hot, act as if I was mentally challenged, and use this as a disguise to avoid being arrested or molested in any way.

I even practiced a little speech. I would say, "I lost my way, but I know I can find my way to where my mom is…" My "mom," in this case, would be the U.S. embassy, where I would seek asylum.

Noriega was beginning to sound a bit too much like Fidel Castro, and I was not looking forward to an interrogation cell—and even less a permanent jail.

Right about then the diminutive State Department official delivered his coup de grâce: "The president has appointed Congressman Murtha as chair of this delegation and asks that you channel all your media comments through him."

That was a laugh! First, he told us the U.S. government could not protect us. Then he added insult to injury by saying that our comments to the media had to be channeled through a congressman who didn't even speak the language of the country whose election we were supposed to be monitoring.

What a joke. When he said that, I was sitting right next to Senator McCain; I glanced at him to see what his reaction was to this bit of indignity. Below the level of the table, where only I could see it, he gestured in a manner that is internationally recognized as what my very religious sister calls "engaging in self-sex."

At that moment, McCain became my hero. Well, he already was, but from that moment forward, we were joined at the hip.

Except that he went off to do his electoral monitoring with Senator Mack plus some State Department escorts, whereas I snuck away with my Panamanian friends, who had all kinds of mobile phones, a very powerful jeep, and serious contacts on the U.S. air force base.

I figured those friends were my best bet to not only observe the election close-up but make a quick getaway if things got hot.

It also freed me to finagle a meeting with the archbishop of Panama, the very wise and worldly Marcos McGrath, who was a Notre Dame graduate and a member of the order that runs that university. (Most people think it's the Jesuits, but it's actually the Congregation of Holy Cross.)

The meeting with McGrath was enlightening. Here was a true

cleric-diplomat, a man with the courage to promote democratic change and the sensitivity to understand that Panamanians had to be the main actors in their own deliverance from dictatorship. Using lay leaders in each of his church's parishes, he had formulated a plan to reveal true election returns to the world, so as to frustrate the likely electoral fraud by the sitting Noriega puppet government.

Here's how the plan worked. Polls taken before the election indicated that the voters in Panama's electoral districts had fairly homogeneous views. With that in mind, and to assure objectivity in the selection of precincts to be monitored, McGrath used random numbers to pick some fifty electoral precincts. The list of those was delivered to a handful of foreign embassies in a sealed diplomatic pouch the night before the election.

Immediately after the polls closed in each of the fifty chosen precincts, the lay observers called in the results, which were then tabulated to provide fairly accurate estimates of the nationwide results. Archbishop McGrath had a messenger deliver to me a copy of the tabulated results.

It showed the opposition party winning by a substantial margin (about 67–33). Because the precincts had been randomly preselected, and their names provided to major embassies in secret, there was no intimation of any bias in the sample.

Two days later, when the Noriega-controlled electoral council had finagled an opposite result, the world community had proof of the fraud.

I myself was able to corroborate, with my own eyes, the election results of a single but populous precinct, which was in a very poor area, called San Miguelito. Three vivid experiences stick in my mind from that day as an electoral monitor.

One was seeing a Panamanian election worker calmly breastfeeding her baby while doing her job. Another happened when a frustrated voter, whose name did not appear in the voter rolls, appealed to me for help. Without skipping a beat, I went to one of the supervisors, and a new ballot was improvised, with the proper voter ID put in by hand; and the voter was able to submit her ballot.

The third and final vivid episode was at the end of the day. A crowd of no less than two hundred residents stood up on the hill above the electoral schoolhouse for at least an hour and a half, waiting until the votes were counted. They would not leave until they knew that, at least in this one little corner of Panama, democracy had been served!

And so it was. As the sun set, close to eight p.m. in that poor schoolhouse on that hill in Panama, the poll worker rushed out and yelled the results; and the people on the hill above the school, who had waited all day, yelled and cheered that the opposition had won.

And for that one day, in that poor barrio, the citizen was king.

28

A Briefing at the White House

After arriving in Miami from Panama, I was told that the same C-32 airplane would pick me up in Miami for a visit to the White House. There, our delegation would meet with President Bush.

It was impressive, of course, but also a bit comedic. The twenty or so delegation members were ushered into a rather imposing conference room and told that the president would be with us in a few minutes. Besides the three U.S. senators previously mentioned (McCain, Graham, and Mack) and former senator Richard Stone, there were some high-level administration officials.

Two of those merit mention: John Sununu, who was chief of staff, and Brent Scowcroft, who was the president's national security advisor. I ended up sitting next to Sununu, and next to him was Scowcroft.

While we were congregating, good old Richard Stone became my mentor in this affair: He assumed the role of introducing me to everyone who had not been on the flight with us, including Sununu and Scowcroft. To each high-level entrant into the room, he would proudly present "my friend, Mayor Suarez of Miami."

But then Stone disappeared, and I assumed he went to his assigned seat. I also assumed we were about to begin; and thus my gaze was directed to the door that connected this room to the president's office. Suddenly, from the other end of the room, a man entered and approached me. I was startled by the man's sudden appearance, through the wrong door, and I struggled to connect the rather familiar face with the man's name.

But I could not. So I simply introduced myself: "I am Xavier Suarez, mayor of Miami, sir." And the man answered, "And I am Dan Quayle, Vice President of the United States."

So much for protocol.

Soon after that, in walked the president from the other end. He assumed his seat at the middle of the conference table, across from Quayle.

And we began the briefing.

Chances are that this was the last time I will ever have sat at a briefing table with the president of the United States. I guess I realized that at the time, because I remember a couple of things in some detail.

Each delegate, including me, spoke briefly. The funniest exchange was when former ambassador Jack Vaughn prefaced his remarks by saying, "Mr. President, the other members of the delegation were sent to precincts in Panama City; I wasn't so lucky. I was sent into 'bush country.'"

He had barely finished the phrase when Sununu quipped, "We don't use that expression around here anymore!"

Everyone laughed. But then things got hot again, as Bush asked one of the career officers what he thought of the opposition candidate in Panama, Guillermo Endara. Now, it was pretty clear that Endara was a bit of a bon vivant, a man who would never have been accused of great smarts or leadership qualities. He was rotund, well into "the Third Age," and married to a twenty-nine-year-old, who allegedly kept him busy in the private quarters of the presidential palace.

Panamanians are very quick to apply nicknames to their leaders. Endara was "the one who smiles"; Ricardo Arias, one of his vice presidents, was "the one who thinks"; and his other vice president, Billy Ford, was "the one who talks."

The career officer, no doubt mindful of the low esteem that everyone had for the jolly Endara, expressed some doubt as to his ability to govern.

This angered me, and I jumped in: "Mr. President," I said, "I don't think it's our role to evaluate the capacity of Endara to govern. Our task was to evaluate the fairness of the elections, and it is clear that the Panamanian people have elected the person they want, and by a large margin, if the figures produced by Archbishop McGrath are any indication."

Senator Stone chimed in: "Let me add this," he said. "I lost my reelection to the Senate because I voted to give Panama its canal, in the hope that democracy would follow. It is important that we put our country's weight behind that objective, without the slightest hesitation."

At one point, there was discussion of the failings of the U.S. commander at the Panama base; this man had allowed a U.S. soldier to be grievously assaulted by Noriega henchmen, who had also molested his wife. When this was being discussed, I whispered to Sununu, "My contacts in the U.S. military in Panama tell me that there is a total lack of morale and respect for this commander." To which Sununu discreetly pointed to the notebook on which Scowcroft was scribbling, as if to say that the matter would be quickly resolved.

And it was. Within a short time thereafter, the commander was fired.

Perhaps because of our advice, and more likely based on the polling numbers captured by Archbishop McGrath, the United States ultimately intervened and restored the democratically elected president, Guillermo Endara.

The mainstream media helped a lot. *Time* magazine ran a cover story that described atrocities committed by the Noriega regime's so-called dignity battalions. The most poignant picture, featured on the cover, was of Vice President-Elect Billy Ford wearing a bloody guayabera. (Later it appeared that the blood was not his, but from some of the opposition activists that he had embraced...)

The restoration of democracy in Panama, orchestrated almost entirely by the United States, illustrated once again what a benevolent superpower could do. Whether this model of regime change can be emulated in places like Iran, North Korea, or my own native Cuba is a matter for further debate.

Closer to home, and given the limitations of my legislative role as a county commissioner, I used my wiles to reform our educational system. In working-class neighborhoods, the missing piece in the educational puzzle is the time between the last school bell (between three and three-thirty p.m.) and the end of the working day, when some parental supervision generally is available.

After-school programs were seen as essential to provide what the superintendent called "envelopes of safety."

29

Envelopes of Safety

As I said, in Miami-Dade, we are doing quite well for our preschoolers.

We are still sorely lacking, however, in middle school, which focuses on the last three years of what used to be elementary school. Kids in Miami (and I reckon in most major cities) lose their innocence during early adolescence, and the process speeds up enormously when they are surrounded by young adults who have peer control of the educational environment.

You can see the change in the kids' faces. In fifth grade, they are attentive and serious but willing to smile when they hear a funny story; and they are respectful of authority. As soon as they reach middle school, both their attention span and respect for authority wane; teachers no longer act *in loco parentis,* meaning as representatives of parental authority.

(In many cases, *one parent is absent to begin with.* One time we surveyed a neighborhood right smack in Miami's inner city; more than 90 percent of the children were living with one parent only!)

Very quickly, the role models change from parents and teachers to the students' slightly older peers, plus sports and entertainment figures. Many continue to read from the schoolbooks and do their homework. But too many, unfortunately, also put a quick end to conventional learning, conventional dress, and conventional speech.

Then three p.m. arrives and they go home. When they get home, their parent(s) is/are too often at work or just missing in action. The auntie or grandmother provides some parenting but very little help with homework and very little discipline.

The only solution (other than to somehow reverse what seems like an irreversible trend towards single-parent families) is to keep kids in school with every kind of extracurricular activity, from martial arts to dance to STEM subjects (science, technology, engineering, and math). These kinds of extracurricular activities are things that kids in the more affluent suburbs are getting; they are used for both remedial purposes and for advance placement in colleges.

Poor kids don't have that. There is no Volvo mom or SUV dad to take them to a private tutor, ballet, or karate. They start falling behind their suburban peers, and by the time they reach senior year in high school, only a small percentage are ready for college. The others either go into the service or get a job in security or making French fries.

They also miss school a lot more than their wealthier peers. They don't have the incentive of a fun extracurricular activity to overcome the slight nasal congestion or fever or simple laziness that can get you out of school.

When they miss school, they not only get behind in their studies; they might become permanently handicapped in subjects like math and science, which rely on cumulative learning techniques. You miss one lesson in geometry or algebra and you might never catch up, since you might never understand what is being taught, even if you try hard.

(It obviously helps to have a tutor or parent to help a kid who gets sick catch up on those kinds of subjects. But a goodly number of minority kids don't have that kind of adult around. Hence the need for after-school tutoring and coaching.)

Knowing these things, I had managed, with private funds, to start three after-school programs—envelopes of safety. They reached maybe three hundred kids in two schools. That is one-tenth of 1 percent of the public schoolchildren in our county. The Children's Trust already provided twenty-five thousand slots and various nonprofits an unascertained number. That totaled a little less than 10 percent.

So my initiative sought to expand the extracurricular activities substantially, keeping the schools open well past the closing bell. Thanks to the superintendent's support, the schools did not charge rent, utilities, or for supervision and security. This meant the space cost nothing, which meant if the legislature wanted to, it could require recipients of scholarships (called Bright Futures Scholars) to staff the after-school programs.

All the trust had to do was lend its support and its experience funding such programs.

That, I soon realized, wasted too much energy. Knowing how much public money is wasted by local government, I decided to focus on that as well as on any new money that came along.

By now I am sure you get the picture. Even a small bureaucracy like that of the Children's Trust is resistant to change.

In a big bureaucracy like the county's, the resistance is fed by many factors. The managers (bureaucrats) are one of them. The media comprise another, as we shall see later on, when I devote a chapter to the bizarre alliance formed, at the local level, between media and bureaucrats.

Another important factor is that we don't have the best and brightest in the legislative bodies that manage municipal governments.

Some people blame that on "single-member" districts; that is to say, small, somewhat gerrymandered districts created by judicial fiat to permit the election of a proportionate percentage of minorities to the county commission and various city councils.

Others blame it on the lack of fair compensation paid to the elected council members and commissioners. In the county, which manages an $8 billion-plus bureaucracy, the salary is $500 per month. On a typical month, I spend at least one hundred hours on county business, which works out to five dollars an hour!

Whatever the reason, the level of informed deliberation, reasoned debate, and effective governance is unquestionably abysmal.

And there are days when sitting on the commission feels like playing Trivial Pursuit. Let me illustrate with an example.

30

Commission Follies:
The Day of the Socks

At almost every commission meeting, we celebrate some kind of event that involves football helmets, baseball caps, T-shirts, or lapel pins.

Let me set the stage, which is ostentatious enough. I'm referring to the county commission chambers, located in a separate structure from the main building. It sits like an elevated octagon of proportions generous enough to have a press room and hallway leading to an auditorium that can seat about five hundred. In the back, above the enraptured audience, is a multimedia room that films and provides sound and light for a raised semicircular dais where the thirteen commissioners hold court.

In this august setting take place ten to twenty commission and committee meetings each month. Most of the time, nothing important is decided. Twice a year, in September, a budget is approved. In most other months, the only important matters discussed concern union contracts, procurement, and an occasional bit of legislation involving the county's master plan. Planning decisions are often accompanied by zoning changes.

Why planning and zoning are not combined into a single legislative decision is beyond me. And why we must constantly be changing both is even more incomprehensible.

But planning, zoning, budgeting, and procurement all have a raison d'être. Eighty percent of what we do has absolutely none. It is either purely ceremonial or involves resolutions by which we tell the world how to behave.

(Those resolutions are called "urgings," and they are usually directed at the federal or state legislatures, as I mentioned earlier; sometimes they are directed at foreign governments, but we won't go into those. They are divisive enough as is without my dwelling on them.)

But let's get to the fun part—the ceremonial items. On this day, as I write these lines, the big-ticket item is some very colorful socks, in blue and orange, featuring some sort of feathered pelican figure.

I don't remember what they symbolize and really didn't mind the item's being brought up in the ceremonial part of the agenda, perhaps as a way to lighten the mood on a tense commission day. Except there was no tense agenda today. And, I should add, there was the additional aggravation that the commissioner in question *insisted that we put on the socks.*

I thought she was kidding, until I saw on top of my desk, inside the wrapper originally containing the psychedelic pelican socks, the discarded socks of the commissioner who sat next to me.

There were actually some heavy-duty ecological items on the agenda on the day of socks. It was the year 2017, as I began my second, complete, four-year term.

The year 2017 also brought with it another important scientific discovery. It came to my attention as I read my college alumni magazine. It happened that the alumni news from Villanova's engineering department contained an interesting report on research being done on permafrost, which sounds complicated but is not really that difficult for laypeople to grasp.

31

Villanova, Global Warming, and Mexico

The article in my alumni magazine was about the effects of global warming. The analysis was centered on the effects of layers of frozen earth, called permafrost, as it melts.

The article reflected a study in its incipient stages. It offered few conclusions. But it did have some preliminary findings, and they were mostly positive.

The gist of the findings is that the melting of the permafrost soil creates a layer of very moist and rich peat moss (called sphagnum) which absorbs carbon dioxide in much greater quantities than dry, frozen soil. The study will seek to determine whether the effect will be quantitatively significant in retarding atmospheric concentrations of this greenhouse gas.

While Villanova is studying what could be a favorable result of melting permafrost, farther north there are studies that seek to determine what happens when the carbon-rich soil, formerly frozen, is now exposed to light, microbes, and flowing rivers that bring silt to the sea bottom.

As far as global warming, the key measurement being studied by most scientists is the concentration, in parts per million, of carbon dioxide in the atmosphere. The consensus on that is that there was an increase, during the last part of the Industrial Revolution, from 280 parts per million to 400 parts per million. That is a rather worrisome increase of almost 43 percent and seems almost perfectly correlated to the steady warming trend that has been witnessed over the past hundred years.

The warming trend of global temperatures has added about one degree Centigrade to global temperatures during the past century. During that same time span, the ocean levels have risen about one foot. Almost everyone agrees on that. And yet the past fifteen years have seen an almost exponential increase in sea level rise in these parts, while global temperatures have remained almost flat.

So the correlations are not as straightforward as they might seem.

Furthermore, the relationship between carbon dioxide and global temperatures is very complex. It belongs to an area of science called "chaoplexity," due to its combination of unpredictable, chaotic events with the sheer complexity of the variables at work. Focusing on carbon dioxide by itself can lead to false conclusions, since water vapor concentrations (clouds) have more of a trapping ("greenhouse") effect on heat. And methane is a factor, too, though it has only one-tenth the effect of carbon dioxide.

Once again, we are confronted with a policy question that begs for sober, scientific analysis. Instead, we get hysteria versus skepticism; and the back-and-forth charges of bias are covered by the media more than the cautionary statements of the few truly impartial scientists out there.

For me, as would be true of any self-respecting politician, the way to start educating myself about all of this was finding a good book on global warming. Thankfully, I had access to a great public library in Miami-Dade, and found a good primer on climate change, written by Harvard ecology professor Michael McElroy.

But my interest in science—and ecology in particular—goes way back to my college days. I majored in mechanical engineering at Villanova, as I mentioned, with an emphasis on energy conversion. Later, when completing a master's degree in public policy at the Harvard Kennedy School, I landed a summer internship at the Environmental Protection Agency (EPA).

The EPA team must have read my résumé carefully, for they immediately assigned me to review what are called "New Source Performance Standards" for new fossil-fuel plants. These were heady days at the EPA, as the Clean Air Act of 1963 had just been passed and the agency was tasked with determining how to implement it.

The act sought to hold the line on new emissions of toxic substances such as nitrogen, sulfur, carbon monoxide, and lead-containing particulates that cause the kinds of gaseous concentrations that lead to smog in Los Angeles and to breathing difficulties for the residents of Mexico City.

My summer internship at the EPA resulted in a bonus for me, as my boss asked me, when the summer ended, to continue my analysis of fossil-fuel power plants. When I explained that I had to go back to Boston to complete my studies, he said, "Oh, but we can pay you to continue working part-time for us while you study."

That was a hell of a good deal for me, and it put me at the level of my Kennedy School classmates, many of whom were midcareer and were on sabbaticals from various jobs. More important, it gave me experience with complicated models of air pollution, which later in life allowed me to obtain a consulting gig in the area of environmental science. That gig is worth recounting here.

This particular engagement was courtesy of a celebrated Florida environmentalist named Joe Browder. Browder called me one day and asked if I was available to consult on the awful air pollution in Mexico City, most of which was caused by emissions from the enormous bus fleet, which was powered by diesel engines.

Three clients would split my retainer. The principal one was the manufacturer of the engines, which were built by General Motors but were now owned by Detroit Diesel, a company that GM sold to famous race car driver and engine oil producer Roger Penske. The two other clients were the German manufacturer of the alternative fuel methanol and the British manufacturer of the additive that was needed to retrofit the diesel engines so they could be powered by the much cleaner methanol.

Before going any further, let me explain just how bad pollution can be in places like Mexico City. I was still mayor of Miami when a group of U.S. mayors decided to meet with our Mexican counterparts to discuss pollution issues. The venue was Mexico City.

I arrived on the morning of the meeting and was ushered by shuttle straight to the hotel where the meeting was being held. One of my few physical deficiencies is nasal congestion, and this was aggravated to the nth degree on that particular day. Mexico was experiencing extreme atmospheric "inversion," which is a fancy name for lack of air movement.

The lack of any breeze, coupled with the endemic air pollution of the city, meant that the pollution index was around four hundred, or about 40 percent beyond what is considered dangerous for humans.

During the entire trip from the airport to the hotel, I was draining nasal fluid. As I got to the hotel and our municipal hosts were escorting me into the mayoral forum, I had to rush to the bathroom.

And then the crisis was compounded: There was no tissue anywhere! Every other suffering guest of the hotel had wiped out the supply of paper towels and toilet tissue.

Americans do well to contain air pollution. The problem is that there are 188 substances listed by the EPA as hazardous to humans' health. Carbon dioxide is the opposite of toxic: It is the stuff of life for plants, without which the earth would be barren and lifeless.

But even this salutary effect has its limits, when its concentration in the atmosphere is not accompanied by sufficient vegetation.

Politicians should study the matter and not be swayed by ideological slogans and their party's talking points. It is not easy terrain for those who shy away from science.

And local politicians are definitely in that group.

Municipal bureaucrats are not much better. Up until now, they have made their living by complicating much simpler sciences than our planet's ecology. Like microorganisms, which feed on hydrocarbons, our bureaucrats have fed on finance and budget models that require little more than multiplication and addition, plus an occasional compounding equation, of the kind an iPhone or tablet can perform with ease.

By complicating simple equations and linear systems, the bureaucrats have created for themselves what I call a quasi-profession. It has allowed them to become the "one-percenters" of the public sector. Unfortunately, the media buy into the notion that the bureaucrats are exceptionally prepared, uniquely objective, and more than deserving of their enormous salaries and pension benefits.

To the media, those in the managerial class *deserve to be* the one-percenters in government—perhaps even more than the multimillionaires deserve to be the one-percenters in the business world.

Furthermore, most journalists are convinced that streamlining government bureaucracy inevitably means cutting services. That is so far from the truth that it is truly comical.

The irony is that in their own media enterprises, as well as in other private-sector ones, corporate CEOs respond quickly and effectively to any downturn in revenues by simply reducing the number of upper-level managers. (The *Miami Herald* has done precisely that many times during the last couple of decades.)

The same should happen in government but does not. To the contrary, every time there is an economic downturn, the bureaucrats convince the politicians to reduce the rank-and-file, while keeping their own salaries and benefits intact.

And so municipal governments continue lumbering on with top-heavy, inefficient, and complex structures where simpler ones would work better, could employ more entry-level individuals, and could serve the public more comprehensively.

Let's expand a little on the problem of the one-percenters in government.

32

One Percenters in Local Government

I have often pondered the logic of what should be an unholy alliance between the high-paid bureaucrats and the media. I have given this issue much thought and derived some theories on my own—in part because political scientists in academia don't seem interested in this phenomenon.

I have no statistics to prove my points. My analysis is anecdotal. Perhaps the phenomenon is peculiar to Miami, where one newspaper controls the print media as a monopoly and can easily expand its reach by consorting with the municipal government managers.

The mainstream media treat the bureaucrats as if they were, by definition, more ethical than the politicians. I suppose they have concluded that high-level managers have fewer reasons to seek bribes, given that they make a couple of hundred thousand bucks a year, while the commissioners make $6,000 annually.

Bureaucrats also have less reason to speak with a forked tongue, as many politicians tend to do. Like the British, who sound smarter than Americans because of their sophisticated accent, bureaucrats as a rule sound more knowledgeable than most politicians.

But that is partly by their own devising; they have invented a sophisticated-sounding language to describe fairly simple concepts. They don't need to speak with a forked tongue, since *the language they have invented is already skewed* to their preferences and objectives.

In effect, bureaucrats have created their own science of governing and have convinced the media that it is a solid science, rather than an artificial concoction, full of strange lingo and plagued with acronyms that pop up like weeds no matter how well you take care of your lawn.

At the root of the problem (if you'll excuse the continuing metaphor) is a built-in belief on the part of most journalists that many high-paid public employees are essential to the delivery of governmental services.

That notion is particularly erroneous when applied to local governments. Let me cut to the chase and explain the reasons.

Local governments, by law and custom, deliver services that are so standard, so tried and tested, that they don't require much creativeness or formal education. Two exceptions are police and teachers, and ironically their rank and file are not particularly well compensated.

Tasks related to public works, parks, solid waste, water and sewers, and firefighting can be performed by able-bodied men and women who can be counted on to be prompt, disciplined, and sober. The same goes for communication-related activities, such as are performed by civilian dispatch employees in the police department, who are not sworn police officers.

In the old days, before computers, a host of clerical employees were needed to keep track of the hundreds of thousands of properties and of their sales, which determine the appraised market price that local governments tax in order to provide police, fire, public works, parks, public health, and solid and liquid waste disposal services. The same was true for the water and sewer utility, which requires that every home and business be logged, monitored, and invoiced for its use of water.

All of those clerical employees have now been replaced by computerized data storage and processing systems. If a person sells his or her home, the property appraiser gets the sale information automatically from the clerk, calculates the documentary stamps paid, and records the new purchase price. The data input is all computerized and requires almost no human involvement. The same is true for each water user; the meter reads the amount of water used each quarter, assumes that the same amount was disposed in wastewater, and charges automatically for both by multiplying the rate set by the county commission times the amount used.

A computer cranks out both the real estate tax and the water and sewer fees. The home or business owner receives the invoices and pays them.

Those who don't pay have an automatic lien placed on their property, without the need to prove anything to a judge or jury.

Let's compare this model to one used in a private enterprise. My reader will see that there is no comparison.

In the private sector, a company must first determine what the demand for a product is. This is done by either market analysis or trial-and-error, as when someone simply buys a food truck and goes to work sites, hoping to sell food.

If you're involved in private enterprise, once you determine what product to make and what price to sell it for, you have to make it efficiently or face being undercut by your competitors. You must try to hire only the number of employees needed, pay them only a competitive wage, and hope that the market doesn't shift suddenly and leave you with a shelf full of obsolete widgets. Then, after you sell your product (or your service as an engineer, an architect, a lawyer, an accountant, a physical therapist, or the like), there is often the question of whether you will get paid.

Retail consumers pay up front; commercial buyers typically pay only a deposit and agree to pay the rest over time. After you deliver the goods or perform the service, the battle to close the deal begins. Often, the client balks at paying the entire amount owed or goes bankrupt. Collecting the contract price often leads to a lawsuit or some other form of dispute resolution.

In contrast to the private sector, municipal government creates its own demand, sets its own price of supply, and enforces collection by imposing automatic liens on the property of the consumer of governmental service. And there is no simple way to measure if the services rendered by government are worth the cost of the taxes paid by the citizenry.

For example, there is no absolute standard for how quickly a rescue truck should be able to respond to a fire alarm or an emergency medical call. Fire departments throughout the nation compete with one another as to response time. In the past couple of decades, a consensus has been reached that four minutes is a good response time.

Premised on that consensus and on the kind of vehicle they use to respond to emergencies, the various departments seek budget approval for enough vehicles, operated by enough firefighters, to meet that four-minute goal. But there is no magic to the four-minute goal, and no scientific basis for the kind of vehicle used—in most cases an enormous, expensive "mother of all ambulances." Since each of those contraptions costs close to a quarter of a million dollars, and since firefighters work in round-the-clock shifts (twenty-four hours), followed by forty-eight hours off (unlike with other businesses that have an eight-hour workday), meeting the four-minute standard is an expensive proposition.

If the rescue-vehicle service industry were market-driven, the entire model of service delivery described above would fall apart, as it would be proven totally uncompetitive.

Here's what would happen.

Firefighters (particularly the EMT ones) would work in two shifts of eight to ten hours each. They would drive small rescue vehicles equipped with a basic life-support system and a couple of fire extinguishers, as needed to quell kitchen fires. Such small vehicles, manned by one or two firefighters, would be constantly on patrol during daylight hours. From one a.m. to seven a.m., only a skeleton crew would be on patrol, and they would double as public service aides, arresting drunk drivers and otherwise deterring the minimal crime that occurs during those hours.

The cost of running a fire department would drop probably to half of what it is now. The cost of insurance for the general public would also drop, as the response time for small fires and medical emergencies would be reduced to a fraction of what it is now.

Those at the high echelons of the bureaucracy may not be innovative, out-of-the-box thinkers, but they sure know how to hide their secrets behind the wizard's curtain. They also know how to engage (and effectively bamboozle) the media by providing ready access to the information they want published, while giving the impression that their analytical models are extremely sophisticated.

Information is power, and the bureaucrats often seem to lavish it on the journalists in greater measure and in a more in-depth form than what they offer to a commissioner's staff.

I also have to admit that the journalists who cover us are, in the main, more competent than our staff. (This is what we lawyers call "an admission against interest.") I don't really have an explanation for that; it is certainly not the result of better compensation, as I am fairly sure that most commissioners pay their legislative aides more than what a newspaper reporter typically earns.

I know this: Because they are smarter, because they devote more time to salient issues, or because they are buddy-buddy with the bureaucrats, the print journalists are generally ahead of the commissioners in accessing the flow of municipal information.

Part of the explanation for the *Herald*'s investigative excellence is that Miami is not the typical city as far as print media is concerned. Let me explain.

In the old days, journalism used to be a hybrid industry composed of print and broadcast outlets, which included radio and television.

That has changed mainly at the national level, where cable television competes with traditional networks, and print media is now an interstate phenomenon, thanks to the internet. And there is a third, major form of media, which is social media.

Miami's media world has all of those interacting components, except that the print media is monolithic, consisting mainly of the *Miami Herald*.

33

Media in Miami

Miami, like the rest of America, suffers from a totally uneven form of democracy, by which public opinion is shaped as much by the mainstream media as any other organized group. The difference is that in Miami, the mainstream print media is mostly driven by one medium: the sole English daily, the *Miami Herald*.

It should be added that the *Herald* has a Spanish equivalent, *El Nuevo Herald*. Because of interlocking editorial boards and a common publisher and operational apparatus, the two newspapers are really one bilingual medium.

All other media, including television stations and weekly newspapers, don't compare to the *Herald* in terms of clout.

My son and I are quite mindful of that. We don't exactly cater to the *Herald*, but we don't mess with the newsprint monolith either. Both of us learned that lesson when I picked and lost a major fight with the *Herald* in 1997 and 1998.

Suffice it to say, my battle with the *Herald* almost two decades ago was totally one-sided. In Spanish we have a saying for that kind of lopsided fight: We say it is *león contra mono amarrado*, which, loosely translated, means "lion versus a monkey with its arms tied behind its back."

In print media, the saying is: "Never fight someone who buys ink by the barrels." Boy, did I mess up on that! By the time the fight ended, the *Herald* had a Pulitzer and I was put out of office by a peculiar court decision that ignored a runoff election in which I won both at the polls and in absentee ballots.

Now, almost two decades later, my son and I are about the only two Miami politicians who are well regarded by both the mainstream media and the blogs. We have accomplished that by returning phone calls and by being straight with all journalists, all the time.

In dealing with reporters from the *Herald*, it helps enormously that often they are way ahead of the news and thus very useful in crafting public policy. When they see a matter coming up on the commission agenda, they inquire as to our views, as well as those of other commissioners who are willing to state their views. The public discussion that ensues often helps to overcome the impediment of the Sunshine Law, which, as mentioned, doesn't allow us to discuss matters directly with our colleagues.

The local Spanish media are also very thorough, though often one has to provide them with the necessary documents, since they don't have reporters assigned to city and county on a 24/7 basis, as the *Herald* does. They are also different from the *Herald* in that they don't treat all politicians as adversaries—only the ones they don't like or don't agree with.

Almost always, they like and agree with Francis and me. And the relationship and flow of information grows over time, without the need to leak negative stuff about our political opponents. That probably sets us apart from most other politicians, who spend a great deal of political capital bad-mouthing their rivals.

The *Herald* is the leader, but it's by no means the only medium that feasts on the negative acts and omissions of Miami's elected officials. With scandalous news, such as misdeeds by a commissioner or an employee, other news outlets, such as the *New Times*, can beat the *Herald* to the punch. Occasionally a blogger does.

Often, the leaker is a bureaucrat who feels slighted or persecuted by a politician.

Here's a recent example. One of my colleagues on the county commission—J. C. Zapata, who has since retired—was applying to enter the Harvard Kennedy School to earn a master's in public administration. Knowing that I already had a master's degree in public policy from there, he asked me to write him a recommendation.

I readily agreed, and even went a step further. I called my former professor, the renowned Graham Allison, who is an advisor to presidents and a well-published author on international affairs. I explained that

Zapata was articulate, bilingual, smart, and Colombian American, which gave him a special niche in studies of Latin American issues, such as the negotiations with the guerillas still wreaking havoc in Colombia.

So far so good. And even better when Zapata was accepted to the program and I was able to take some credit for the admission. Except for one little thing, which later came out in the paper.

It turns out that Zapata paid an entire year's tuition (about $30,000) from county funds, using the argument that it was "continuing education." Well, that was clearly unethical. It did not embarrass me, but it embarrassed all of us in county government.

The airing of dirty linen, the chain of revelation, in this case was triggered by a disgruntled employee and probably expedited by the administration itself, since Zapata was a strong critic of the mayor and of the bureaucracy.

Thus it was that the bureaucrats got even with Zapata. And in the process, I lost an ally in the battle to streamline Miami-Dade County. Furthermore, I suspect that whichever bureaucrat leaked the news is now that much more connected to the newspaper than before, and the reporter involved is now that much more responsive to any news tip from the bureaucrat.

Bureaucrats: 1, commissioners: 0.

Any elected official who tackles the bloated bureaucracy of Miami-Dade County has to be ready for retaliation. And the battle is unceasing, mostly unrewarding, and maybe futile.

It really hurts that the main and only daily English print publication seems wholly unaware of how inefficient county government is.

It is surprising, since its reporters are excellent at covering the news. That is to say, they write very well about the small picture. But neither the reporters nor the editorialists grasp the big picture.

These are almost all intelligent and well-meaning people. They have great investigative resources. And they can hire accountants or consult them for free. So it begs the question, why don't mainstream newspapers understand that big-city local governments are cheating the taxpayer by as much as 30 to 40 percent of their entire budget?

Other than having the common, awful trait of emphasizing bad news, the *Herald* is a top-notch newspaper.

It is particularly good at uncovering official corruption, for which it has earned many Pulitzer Prizes. Despite the competition of social media, which has caused it to reduce its reporting staff, it is still a better investigator of public corruption than the state prosecutor or U.S. attorney.

In covering local governments, it strikes a very convincing pose: protecting the environment, combating official corruption, and supporting spending for infrastructure, including traditional (parks, schools, transit, utilities, airports, and seaports) and nontraditional (arts, sports, and convention) facilities.

But now here's the big difference in management styles between the monopolistic newspaper and local government: Whenever the *Herald* has a bad year or a cluster of bad years, it does what every competitive business does—it reduces its upper management or cuts managers' salaries, or both. For some reason, it doesn't advocate that for county and city governments.

I think the reason is twofold. One is that the *Herald* writers are convinced that managing a county with a $9 billion budget is inherently complicated and requires an enormous number of well-paid managers. The second reason is related but more sinister: It is precisely the bureaucrats who have made county management an incomprehensible black box, full of esoteric terms, acronyms, and mathematical models.

Let me give some examples.

There are no limits to the ability of the bureaucracy to invent new terms. I came back to local government after a thirteen-year absence; it was a shock to my semantic senses.

Let's take some areas of government, beginning with land-use planning and zoning.

What used to be an objection to a zoning change had suddenly become a "warrant." What used to be a letter of support for a zoning change was now a "waiver."

The zoning code for the city of Miami, which I had become familiar with, had now been changed to "Miami-21." Under the old code, "R" stood for "residential," "B" for "business," "C" for "commercial," and "I" for "industrial." All of those simple and logical classifications were gone—replaced by a totally incomprehensible new set of terms.

The county's planning code is just bizarre. An "EAR" is not something you hear with but a long-range estimate or report on development needs in an area. But that is what the planning code is supposed to be; so an EAR (Evaluation and Appraisal Report) is a sort of preliminary planning tool *that has no present legal validity whatsoever.*

One could argue that planning and zoning codes are inherently complicated and deserve technical terms. But the use of fancy new terms and acronyms to make them less intelligible to the layperson extends to even the most mundane activities.

In procurement, there is the negotiating term "best and final offer." The acronym is BAFO, but when spoken, it sounds like "baffle"—and thus becomes a self-fulfilling prophecy, as both commissioners and audience are baffled about what is being discussed.

No one seems to care whether or not an acronym is already in use. For example, we have PAC to refer to the performing arts center and a political action committee. Closely resembling that is PACT, which is either a common word for a deal or stands for the organization People Acting for Community Together.

To hear a transportation briefing and have any chance of understanding it, you must know that the CITT (Citizens' Independent Transportation Trust) manages the funds earmarked for the PTP (People's Transportation Plan), which is typically approved by the BCC (board of county commissioners) and the TPO (formerly the MPO, or Metropolitan Planning Organization), which uses FTA (Federal Transportation Authority) monies or FDOT (state department of transportation) and DOT (federal department of transportation) funds to build the SMART (Strategic Miami Area Rapid Transit) plan. And we can apply for federal funds for all of them under a new initiative called POPS, which stands for Program of Interrelated Projects. (Or maybe it's Project of Interrelated Programs. Only one or two people know which it is, and they won't tell if you get the name backward.)

I actually am happy about the SMART acronym, since it was developed by my son as a member of the TPO and since it was unanimously approved as a concrete summary of our transportation priorities. Believe it or not, that took six years, and at the end of the six years, we did not have funding for it; we had funding only to do the "PDE," or planning, development, and engineering study.

What's important is that we do have a SMART plan, and it is easy for me to explain, using the five fingers of my hand.

It takes a *Herald* reporter perhaps a day or two of reading the SMART plan and interviewing transportation managers to understand the terms mentioned above. The reporters are employed by the newspaper, based on basic intelligence and writing ability; they are then assigned some area of government and generally kept on it until they can cover it in depth.

Few, if any, commissioners have a complete grasp of those terms. And almost none of them, or their staff, understand the actual financing models. It is in the area of budget and finance that the gulf is greatest between bureaucrats and public officials. And that is where the media fill the void.

The media are not always equipped to grasp the underlying reality described by the models. Their control of information, including the mathematical models that describe that information, can lead to anomalous (and unfair) results in their evaluation of the political leaders.

Such was the case in the media's condemnation of the prior mayor of Miami-Dade, versus its tolerance of Mayor Gimenez in 2020.

34

The Recall of "Carlos I" as Mayor

The main difference between Miami-Dade's mayor in 2020, dubbed "Carlos II" by bloggers (Gimenez), and its former mayor, "Carlos I" (Alvarez) is that one supported the new Marlins baseball stadium and one did not. As much as I try to differentiate the two administrations, I cannot do so in terms of big issues, except for that one.

And in stadium funding, as a general category, the advantage, as far as I can tell, went to Alvarez, who voted to fund one stadium, whereas Gimenez voted to fund two equally bad deals for sports franchises.

Let me elaborate.

Before Carlos Gimenez came on the scene, Miami-Dade had experienced what everyone assumed was the worst case of inept bureaucracy known to man. Having only recently changed its charter to embrace a strong-mayor form of government, the county had endured a comedy of errors by its chief executive, Alvarez, who became mayor after a fairly distinguished career as the county's top cop. Alvarez had the ultimate tin ear. His worst gaffe was supporting the use of public funds to build a $600 million baseball stadium.

County residents started referring to the two successive mayors as Carlos I and Carlos II. Carlos I (Alvarez) was an affable supercop who got his kicks working out with weights. After he was retired by the voters via the largest municipal recall in the country's history, he actually won a bodybuilding contest in the sixty-and-older category.

Alvarez rose through the bureaucracy the hard way. It is not easy being a cop in Miami. Gimenez, by contrast, rose through the bureaucracy as a firefighter, which for about three decades now really has been a middle-level skilled position involving emergency medical training and an understanding of chemical fires and toxic spills.

There is not much by way of actually fighting fires. The World Trade Center tragedy (9/11) is a unique incident in a city that has vast rows of high-rises, many of which were built in the midcentury and are not equipped with sprinkler systems. The tragedy of 9/11 was greatly compounded by a combination of the heroism of the first responders and the uniqueness of the fire, which was fueled by outside combustible material rather than by the contents of the building.

In Gimenez's experience as a firefighter, what he mostly did was pencil pushing. And he was well rewarded for it, ascending to fire chief and city manager in a system so badly designed that he could retire as a fifty-year-old and take home a pension in the range of $130,000 a year.

On top of that, Gimenez has a separate pension of the cash kind—like an IRA or a 401(k). It is provided for in state law with a view to supplementing counties in Florida where salaries are low; since pensions are based on a percentage of an employee's last three years of salary, they can be quite meager in counties where a first responder might never make more than $40,000 a year. The legislature thus imposed a 1 percent tax on life and car insurance policies to fund this "supplementary pension fund."

In Miami and Miami-Dade, high-level firefighters can take home a cool $300,000 in cash upon retirement. That goes on top of a perpetual yearly income of $130,00. Retire as a high-ranking firefighter and you are an instant millionaire.

Mayor Gimenez is convinced that he deserves that. He is the proverbial guy who "was born on third base and thinks he hit a triple." He thinks that because he wore a uniform for thirty years, was chief of a fire department, was city manager, and then became the elected chief executive of a county with almost three million people and a $9 billion budget, he is big-time.

Since he earns so much, he defends the entire class of managers who earn salaries well in excess of $100,000 a year for doing mostly ministerial tasks, with no risk whatsoever of being fired and a fat pension awaiting them if they just behave nicely. He is a classic bureaucratic elitist.

Unfortunately, most of the media buy whatever the pampered managerial class sells them.

The weekly newspapers and magazines are often more technical in their coverage and more critical of the bureaucratic class. Because they don't need to sell negative news as much, they don't feed as much on negative leaks, which bureaucrats are always ready to dish out—particularly against elected officials who stand in their way.

As such, the weeklies can be an enlightening, in-depth, offset to the sole news daily.

35

Miami's Weeklies

n-depth articles or episodic, detailed coverage of an issue is done better by a weekly called *Miami Today*, particularly if the topic is transportation, or one called *The Miami Times*, if the topic is of special interest to the African-American community.

Regional issues are covered well by a chain of fourteen local weeklies published under the banner of Community Newspapers.

Those are all worthy publications, and each has a niche that it controls. The *Miami Herald* is our newspaper of record, the place where important local news typically first appears, the medium that sets the tone for the big policy discussions. A handful of its reporters cover local and state news, and its editors (as well as the publisher) are privy to information not often available to a simple county commissioner.

That is true even when the information is created by the county mayor, who has a habit of confiding only in the commission chairman and perhaps the committee chairman with jurisdiction over the matter at hand.

Somehow, by leaks, by computer wizardry, or by pure institutional wisdom, it is more often than not a *Miami Herald* reporter who gets the scoop on a major county news bit.

Add to that the previously mentioned handicap that an honest commissioner has, as prescribed by the Sunshine Law. It is easier for a reporter to predict a future commission vote, by simply asking each commissioner his or her views, than for a commissioner to know, given the fact that it is illegal to ask a colleague about views outside of a sunshine meeting.

The handicap is so great that when I was elected in 2011, I started scheduling frequent sunshine meetings, to the point that I must have shocked everyone. I don't think the entire county commission during the prior four-year term had scheduled as many as I did during my first year.

I don't want to guess why I had to revolutionize the whole custom of having sunshine meetings; cynics would say that it was simply because I obeyed the law. Others might point out that I had a lot of initiatives whose impact was outside my district, and that therefore needed to be screened by the district commissioner in question rather than being able to go straight to committee.

I have never been one to bother much about finding out reasons for things I can't control. My prior governmental experience was as mayor and de facto chairman of a five-member city commission. As such, I didn't give preliminaries much attention. I worked up the legislation I wanted and presented it to my colleagues in open session, after the numbers were crunched by a city manager who was generally in sync with me.

Occasionally, I would get pushback on the dais from one or more of my four commission colleagues. But most of the time, they simply followed my lead.

Sometimes, I *got way ahead of my colleagues* in negotiating a big deal—such as building an arena with which to seek an NBA franchise. This was a big fish for Miami, and I had to figure out how to reel it in—with or without the support of my colleagues.

The last and biggest hurdle that the NBA put before us was the requirement of 4,500 parking spaces, all of which had to be within 750 feet of the arena to be built. (We had already convinced the NBA that we had the funds to build a fifteen-thousand-seat arena, on a site that the city owned. The cost, a little over $50 million, would be financed mostly by existing "bed taxes," which are supplemental sales taxes on hotel rooms and restaurants in hotels.)

The financing was pretty much under control. But the parking was a tough nut to crack, and we had to do some creative accounting. Which we did, with help from the city manager, who happened to be a big basketball buff, as his son was a great local Division III college player (and later a coach at Barry University).

The layout of the 4,500 parking places had been concocted and delivered to the NBA, but it had not been put to a vote of the commission. This irked a crusty, old, longtime commissioner named J. L. Plummer, and he let me have it during a commission meeting.

"Mr. Mayor," he intoned in a raspy Southern accent, "I understand that you have, on your own, submitted a plan of 4,500 parking spaces to the NBA without consulting us or putting it to a vote."

"Yes, Commissioner," I meekly responded, "and I wish I had been able to get preapproval from you all. However, the requirement was thrust on us suddenly, and it became an emergency item. You can reverse my decision, of course, but before you do, please meet with the manager and see if his analysis satisfies you."

I knew, of course, that Plummer had a good friend in the construction business who thought he had a good shot at winning the bid for the $50 million arena. I knew that Plummer was grandstanding.

In the end, the commission unanimously endorsed the plan and we got the franchise.

As mayor of Miami, I found that the saying "I would rather seek forgiveness than permission" worked well.

Here in the county it was different. There were twelve other commissioners, and they were elected from single-member districts. They knew their turf, and they protected it.

But commissioners were not the problem as much as the high-paid managers were. These folks had two, and only two, objectives: to please the mayor and to maintain the status quo.

Most of the time, the two objectives were perfectly aligned. The reason for that synchronicity was crystal clear: The mayor himself was a bureaucrat, born and bred.

As I said before, getting the county bureaucracy to move aggressively was a Herculean task. And so for most of my nine years on the commission, I often focused my efforts on some other agency. Such was the case with the school system, which happens to be the fourth largest in the nation, with about 350,000 K–12 students.

36

Father and Son at the High Court of Education

have previously referred to the "envelopes of safety," or after-school programs, that I managed to fund using artful combinations of school district, county, and Children's Trust resources.

Here I want to offer a vignette of how I tried to expand the handful of such programs to the entire county.

It is a Wednesday and I am at a school board meeting in Miami. Our school system is the fourth largest in the country, with a third of a million students, as I said above. Most American cities don't have that many people.

On this occasion, I am scheduled to make a presentation on an initiative that I have concocted and implemented, as a pilot program, single-handedly. The initiative seeks to provide after-school instruction and coaching to inner-city kids.

The idea is to keep them from going home at three p.m., when there is often no one else at home—except perhaps an eighty-year-old grandparent who is often bedridden or sitting in a rocking chair, unable to do much beyond perhaps some cooking or light gardening.

I call the initiative "envelopes of safety" based on something the school superintendent, Alberto Carvalho, said when a stray bullet penetrated a portable classroom in Coconut Grove, which has now become gentrified but still has pockets of poverty and of the violence that accompanies it.

My initiative is no longer purely speculative. It is a working, thriving, successful program at Frances S. Tucker Elementary, the very school where the shooting took place less than a year before. The school principal there is part of my entourage, which is definitely star-studded.

The school principal brings to the table not only enthusiasm but female charisma that matches my son's rather well. Aware that beauty sells, I set her up with Francis at the front of the quartet of stars that I have concocted for this meeting.

I am the veteran in the group—and am fully aware that I am the least charming of the quartet. The fourth member is a story in himself.

We call him "Uncle Luke," though his real name is Luther Campbell and his stage name was once Luke Skywalker—as in the once famous rapper from the 2 Live Crew. Here I have to digress and tell a Luke story.

It was perhaps 1991 or 1992. I was mayor of Miami and reveling in the shadow of our eminently successful professional basketball franchise, the Miami Heat. These were the days before Pat Riley, Shaquille O'Neal, and LeBron James. These were the days when we struggled with a losing team and a forgettable coach named Kevin Loughery.

Loughery's team lacked the talent to be a contender. And Loughery lacked the glamour that Miami rightly deserved, as the world's newest and sexiest global city.

He was no Pat Riley.

On the day of this story, I was at a Miami Heat game and happened to have seats behind Luke's. He was right in the front row, where the fans literally sit courtside. And Luke was quite vocal as to the mediocrity of the team and its coach. Sitting close to the floor, with his bodyguard, he vented his frustrations on the poor coach. He yelled, time and again, "Get rid of Coach Loughery!"

The coach looked in our direction, and I could feel the blood flowing to my forehead in embarrassment, as I was in his direct line of vision. All of a sudden, Luke's bodyguard posed the logical question to Luke: "So, who are we going to hire as coach?"

Every fan in the vicinity was anxiously waiting for an answer from this brazen rapper king, who was known for his legal battles with prosecutors trying to ban his obscene music. The guy was a lightning rod, and he was right in front of me, ready to deliver his line.

Without skipping a beat, Luke turned to me and said, "The mayor should be the coach; he knows basketball more than Loughery!"

Omigod! There were at least five hundred eyes focused on me, and it was soon going to get worse. Not knowing anything about politics, the bodyguard yelled out, "Who's the mayor?" And Luke pointed to me.

That was the first time I had a conversation with Luke, assuming you could call that a conversation. Roll forward to 2012, roughly a year after my political renaissance. I read an editorial by Luke that criticized the Miami-Dade Children's Trust for not doing enough for the Black community. This agency manages about $100 million of taxpayers' money and is devoted to children of lesser means. In terms of mere economics, it should be focused on the impoverished areas of town, and that means at least a handful in predominantly Black areas.

So I invited Luke to my apartment and put the question to him. Soon I realized that we totally agreed on two things the school system should have been offering: universal after-school programs and vocational training for all—not just in the so-called magnet schools.

I pondered his arguments and waited for the opportunity to go global with the single-school prototype at Tucker Elementary.

And now, rolling further forward to the Wednesday school board meeting, here is the opportunity. Here are nine friendly school board members and a superintendent already invested in the initiative, with a name drawn from his own pronouncements (i.e., "envelopes of safety"). Here is a whole, large metropolis hungry for inspiration, hungry for solutions to the expanding youth violence, and saturated with negative national news.

Miamians think they're special. And they want something special from their leaders. On this day, they are about to see something very special.

We file in according to my instructions: the young, charismatic male-female couple at the front and the older, wizened, taller veterans behind them.

I knew we had the attention of the school board members. But I did not expect such a spectacular reaction; nor did I expect such a performance by the junior commissioner Suarez.

I still marvel at the video of the meeting, which my staff secured for me. I had gone to the meeting dressed in my best blues: a sky-blue suit, white shirt, and light blue tie. The school board is composed of three men and six women; two of the men are quite dapper, as is the superintendent, who clearly sets the tone for sartorial splendor. This is not a place to go underdressed, unless you are the local rapper king, in which case you can go in jeans and a loose-fitting shirt. Luther Campbell ("Uncle Luke") did not even wear jeans; he wore shorts and a rumpled shirt. But he was Luke.

Francis was not dressed as formally as I. But he sported a nice tan suit and an open white shirt. He looked good. And that was before he started talking.

There are people who look good just sitting there. (Think Justin Trudeau or Franklin Delano Roosevelt.) There are people who look good because they sound good. (Think Mario Cuomo or Jesse Jackson.) Then, there are people who look good just sitting there and doubly good when they start talking. (Think John F. Kennedy.)

Francis is in the John F. Kennedy realm. He looks the part and he plays the part. Extremely well. And on this day he brought his A game.

I have come to expect that, but this was a rather large stage. This was a school board that governed a huge county school system. This stage included the most flamboyant, most charismatic school superintendent in the nation.

Anyhow, suffice it to say that I did not expect such a scintillating performance by Francis. It was like listening to someone with the speech of Adlai Stevenson, the angelic face of Bobby Kennedy, and the stage presence of Ronald Reagan.

You had to be there to get the full impact; nevertheless, I will try to narrate it.

Francis begins his peroration. "We have done well to reduce crime overall in our community," he explains. "However, the exception has been youth violence, which has increased precipitously in the last couple of years."

Now, it must be admitted that throwing out words like "precipitously" is dangerous for any politician. For one thing, it is very difficult to pronounce. Besides that, it can make the speaker sound like, as former vice president Spiro Agnew once said, an "effete, impudent snob."

But Francis is a natural. He blends formality in speech with informality in body language. He exudes both confidence and humility.

Suffice it to say that by the time we finished the fifteen-minute presentation to the school board members, we had them in our back pockets. They fell over one another to sponsor the agenda item. And almost all made impassioned remarks about the merits of the idea, sprinkled with admiring comments about the father-son team and the rapper king Uncle Luke.

Soon after this star performance, it was time for me to decide whether to run for mayor of the county or to simply stand for reelection as a commissioner. The factors that go into that kind of decision are many, and they include the personal, political, and ideological. You want to do the right thing, the practical thing, and the thing most calculated to lead to domestic stability.

For all politicians, the decision to reach higher than their station is fraught with complicated, conflicting considerations. Most politicians decide simply to run for reelection, if they are not termed out, rather than risk a climb up the political ladder. In corporate law, it is called the quiet corporate life.

In politics, it is often a function of keeping your marriage stable.

37

To Run or Not in the Time of Zika

It's a glorious midsummer Sunday in Miami. The *Miami Herald* has a big banner on its editorial page endorsing the incumbent county mayor, Carlos Gimenez, for reelection.

I considered throwing my hat in the ring but decided for various reasons to stay put as one of thirteen county commissioners. The most compelling reason for not running for mayor was money: a candidate running countywide must be able to communicate his or her message to 1.4 million voters.

Imagine that. Just one simple mailer, if you can do it for the seventy-one cents per item (including postage) I was quoted, will cost you the better part of a million dollars. Gimenez's advantages of incumbency and a knack for fundraising had allowed him to raise close to $5 million.

At most, I could have raised a million. Being outspent five to one, no matter how good your platform and how bad your opponent's, is a prohibitive hurdle. I won a campaign for mayor of Miami when I was outspent three to one, but even that feat (in 1985) was due partly to the luck of having three well-known candidates and the fact that Miami is still a place where retail politics works.

The city of Miami, that is. In the city proper, which has about one-seventh the number of voters as the county, you can literally knock on doors and visit enough senior centers to touch and meet in person about ten thousand of the most likely voters.

That is close to half of what is needed to win, since only about 30 percent of the eligible voters bother to actually cast a ballot. More on that later, when I narrate the path taken by my son in his quest to become Miami's mayor, following my example of three decades ago.

Anyhow, back to the quickly approaching primary election, slated for August 30, when the county will elect its mayor and roughly half of the commission.

One opponent's name is on the ballot, which is quite a surprise. I assumed that I would not draw any opposition, as happened four years ago, when I was reelected for my first full term as county commissioner. But at the very last moment, on the very last day, I have drawn an opponent.

His name is not likely to warm the hearts of my district's large Cuban American constituency. He has the same last name as Fidel and Raúl—the twin architects of Cuba's brutal communist dictatorship.

So Michael Castro is not what concerns me today.

What concerns me today is a mosquito-borne virus that goes by the name of Zika. Just yesterday, the governor of this, the third-largest state in the most powerful nation in the world, announced that this little stretch of Miami Beach where I spend my summers is under a Zika virus outbreak alert. A handful of residents have reported being infected by the disease— which is generally harmless, except for pregnant women.

As was the case with the prior alert, involving a small area of Wynwood, located in the urban core, we should probably not panic over the situation. The total number of infected patients is still minimal, and the transmission of the virus does not seem to be driven by endemic conditions as much as by travelers who already bring the disease in their bodies.

We could probably end the alert by simply shutting out visitors from a couple of Caribbean islands. (That would be as politically incorrect as what Donald Trump would later do in regard to radical Islam: cut off entry to all immigrants from a handful of countries in the Middle East.)

Not only does that idea not cross our minds, but the correlation is not even mentioned. No one in the mainstream media or government mentions the possibility that the spread of the Zika virus is a function of the wrong people coming into Wynwood or Miami Beach, rather than the wrong bug.

So we spray insecticides and kill all the mosquitoes. We can do that in the U.S. We have resources not only to spray from airplanes but even to use traps. (I knew about mousetraps, but not mosquito traps...)

After a couple of days, we are told that the traps have gone from catching fifteen Zika-bearing mosquitoes to catching one. How we found out they were Zika-bearing mosquitoes, I will never know—let alone the more pertinent question, which is whether the mosquitoes are learning to refuse the bait inherent in any trap.

None of these questions can be asked in the various special meetings of the county commission. Nor can we delve into the rather scholarly argument made by our local mayor/savant, Phil Stoddard of South Miami, who is a neurological scientist at a local university.

Miami's good old "Dr. Phil" says that we are jeopardizing human embryos by spraying toxic insecticides, much more than the embryos are jeopardized by Zika-bearing bugs. In fact, he argues, there are no proven cases of microcephalic conditions in fetuses resulting from the Zika virus, but a lot of deformed fetuses from insecticides.

So now, we don't rightly know the cause and we don't rightly know the cure. But we are in charge of an $8 billion budget. You want to know how much that is? That is more than the budget of sixteen U.S. states. It is more than the gross national product of Cuba in 1959, when communism began gnawing away at the prosperous Cuban economy.

It is my fiduciary duty, as a county commissioner, to deal with the perception that a contagious disease is spreading in two of the hottest tourist attractions in this city-state that we call Miami-Dade. And I have to carry out that duty rationally, ethically, and selflessly. (I say "selflessly" because my compensation is nominal: $500 a month. Most weeks I work forty to fifty hours on county matters, so that puts me way below minimum wage.)

That's not a lot of compensation for someone who has two postgraduate Harvard degrees and who graduated number one in his engineering class at Villanova University. But who's thinking about that? Right now, in the time of Zika, I just want to succeed at governing Miami. And I have a strong ally: His name is Francis Xavier Suarez.

During my entire county commission tenure (2011 to 2020), I served in tandem with Francis. I am not sure what I would have done if he were not on the city commission, as well as on the county's transit board and presiding over the Miami-Dade League of Cities.

Let me put it this way: In the areas most in need of progressive initiatives, including mass transportation and affordable housing, the vigorous leadership exerted by Francis made the difference between slow but deliberate progress and total inaction. The same was true when I strayed beyond county government and tried to do something about our public schools. Had it not been for Francis, it would have been total failure.

Many times in those nine years I felt, in the immortal words of Simón Bolívar, that we had "ploughed in the sea." Still, as I write these lines, substantial progress has been made. Almost every bit of it has been due to the father-son team.

But for now, we still have to deal with the status quo.

The status quo, on this glorious Sunday, in the summer of 2016, in this glorious beach apartment, is firmly in place. The *Miami Herald* has endorsed the incumbent, Carlos Gimenez, for reelection as the county's mayor.

This is not the end of the world, by any means. Gimenez's opponent is the populist daughter of the city mayor; she targets for criticism Gimenez's inability to fund the People's Transportation Plan and his coziness with lobbyists.

She's right on both counts, but the voters don't care at this point. They are generally satisfied with the pedestrian incumbent, who has avoided major scandals and led the county through the "lean" years that started with the Great Recession of 2007 to 2009. Like Barack Obama, Gimenez benefits from having taken over the helm of a sinking ship, in a time of economic recovery that specially benefits municipal governments, which depend on real estate values for their operating revenues.

Miami-Dade, since 2009, has seen a hefty increase in its tax base. And its rate of unemployment has been cut in half, from about 12 percent at the height of the Great Recession to less than half of that now.

The incumbent is not a bad man. He is just a plodder. Lee Iacocca would have called him a "bean counter" as opposed to a "mover and shaker." God bless Iacocca for coining the terms.

Gimenez is the classic bean counter. I am the classic mover and shaker, and so is my son.

But Francis is more adaptable than I am. He doesn't have to be a mover and shaker. He can be a plodder, if he wants to. He can be both archetypes.

In the words of revered Miami developer Armando Codina, Francis "has a lot of bandwidth."

He has a lot of range. In terms of substance, I do too. But in terms of people skills, and sheer appreciation of the panoply of characters that it takes to make a major metropolis, Francis is supreme. Perhaps it is because he is less judgmental than I am.

He's also more patient than I am. I guess that is contrary to the conventional wisdom, which would make him the "young man in a hurry." Sometimes it seems that he is in less of a hurry than I am. Maybe he's just more tolerant, more accepting of the full human condition, more willing to suffer the fool.

Francis has an uncanny ability to roll with the tides. He has an affinity for change, which we share, combined with a deep respect for the establishment, which I don't share.

In the final analysis, he is humbler than his dad.

And we are both driven by the overpowering instinct to make our city work, and that means making our mass transit system work. We both troubled by the congestion in our roadways. And what concerns us both is how we have failed the average working stiff, the minimum-wage hotel employee who lives in Homestead and has managed to land a job in a downtown hotel, making eight bucks an hour.

Their plight was highlighted recently by Wendi Walsh, who represents the hotel workers' union. She showed up at county hall, without an appointment, to discuss the working conditions at various resorts and facilities, including Miami's airport. Her point was simple: If we don't pay more than minimum wage and don't provide affordable and efficient mass transit, the typical hotel worker will spend two hours commuting in each direction and an hour's pay in transit fares.

How could we let that happen? How could we ask a young man or woman to spend twelve hours a day to earn seven net hours' worth of pay, to miss spending time with his or her children while not missing a minute of work, being late for work, or looking for a better job? The latter causes the enormous turnover we see in the hotel industry.

Neither Francis nor I can live with this. We are determined to solve it.

We are also determined to solve the abysmal lack of affordable housing in our county. And the slow pace of government-funded development, whether it's for public spaces, tourist attractions, arts facilities, or classic infrastructure such as parks and public utilities.

We are both fiscal conservatives, meaning that we are convinced that increasing taxes is not the answer. We are also both progressives, meaning that we think government has a proper role in leveling the playing field, so that everyone has equal access to a good education, a decent job, a home, and affordable health care.

We are both followers of Teddy Roosevelt, Fiorello La Guardia, Franklin Delano Roosevelt, John F. Kennedy, and Ronald Reagan. As my reader can see, we don't care much for party labels.

We care about solutions. And we spend every waking hour formulating them and making them happen, mindful that we have been given the opportunity to serve our fellow human beings, each of whom is entitled to the same quality of life that we enjoy.

In the meantime, we both have to know—as the famous song says— "when to fold 'em." In politics, that translates to knowing when to abstain from a difficult race, even if it is an opportunity to climb another rung in the ladder to real, executive power.

My decision not to run for mayor of the county in 2016 was very similar to Francis's decision not to run in 2013 for mayor of the city.

Like most important campaign decisions, Francis's decision not to run for mayor of Miami in 2013 included personal considerations. Without stealing his thunder in describing personal details, the announcement of his withdrawal from that race followed important family news: His wife, Gloria, had just found out she was pregnant with their first child.

Francis and I both believe that the family is the fundamental cell of society. If the family is suffering or lacking in any way, it is difficult for the politician to serve the larger community. Francis and Gloria had been yearning for a child for half a decade; when she became pregnant, in the midst of a certain amount of campaign turbulence, it was a good time for him to reconsider running.

My wife was certainly not pregnant in 2016, but she was concerned about her health, and in particular the possibility that we might be left without health insurance. At the time, she was still four years short of eligibility for Medicare, yet anxious to retire from teaching and become a full-time grandmother.

The thought that I might lose my county insurance was worrisome to her. So was the memory of 1997–98, and the expected turmoil that a mayoral campaign brings.

But personal issues, in either case, did not provoke the final decision to abstain. As mentioned before, in my case the decision was based on cold, hard numbers: The incumbent's ability to raise millions of dollars was the biggest deterrent to me.

Francis, in 2013, did not have that particular problem. He was on his way to a million-dollar kitty, while the incumbent mayor (Regalado) was struggling to raise even a fraction of that.

What ailed Francis, in that race, was a succession of small mistakes, which portended a nasty struggle instead of the cool and collected blitzkrieg to victory that had been on every pundit's mind. The miscues included a municipal aide's putting on social media that she was tired of dealing with "brain-dead" constituents, and a campaign aide's using the internet to submit voters' requests for absentee ballots.

Stupid statements by an office receptionist are not a big deal—though they always create the quandary of whether to fire the aide immediately, as the media critics would prefer, or give the aide a second chance, as your heart tells you to do.

The use of the internet to submit requests for absentee ballots was a whole different story. The reason it got so much attention was not its intrinsic gravity; for it had none. The reason was the timing. And in politics, timing is everything.

The story of Francis's decision to pull out of the 2013 mayor's race may be one he will tell in his own book. Here I prefer to relate the story of our joint visit to the state capital of Tallahassee, where there is the power to spend each year the better part of a hundred billion dollars.

38

Father and Son at the State Capitol

The state of Florida has an annual budget in excess of $90 billion. About $10 billion of that is earmarked for transportation; most of it goes for highway construction and maintenance. Our county, which constitutes about one-eighth of the population of the state, gets about one-eighth of that amount, or slightly over a billion dollars.

Francis and I see our task as, on this trip to Tallahassee, diverting as much of that as possible to mass transit instead of more highways. That the joint voyage to the state's capital happened at all is itself a bit of a miracle, as I previously had avoided going to Tallahassee for the first five years I served on the county commission.

The reason for that begs explaining. To begin with, Tallahassee is more of a Deep South city than an overgrown North Florida town. Its cultural and geographic proximity to Georgia has earned it the nickname "Georgiahassee."

One time, when I was mayor of Miami, I went to what we Miamians call "Tally" to lobby for my beloved city. As I rode an elevator in the Capitol, a Capitol police officer got in; as always with police officers, I said hi and sort of introduced myself.

His response was unexpected and unintelligible. It wasn't so much that the officer was impolite—let alone rude. He was probably trying to be nice to us. But what he said was totally incomprehensible. It was a very, very short statement, dressed in a deep Southern drawl that made it sound like a cross between a cough and a grunt.

Anyhow, I couldn't follow up on that even if I had wanted to, as the logical follow-up would have been "What language do you speak, sir?" The guy was too big and too serious for anything like that.

But that is not the main reason to avoid the state capital. The main reason is that Miami-Dade politicians, surrounded by hordes of lobbyists, civic activists, chamber-of-commerce types, and even college administrators, flock to "Tally" for every legislative session in such large numbers, and in such an uncoordinated fashion, that the conflagrations tend to have, at best, no perceptible impact on legislation and, at worst, a dumbing effect on the entire process.

There have been laudable efforts to harness our vibrant county's clout, when added to the clout of our thirty-four municipalities plus the nation's fourth-largest school system and largest community school (Miami Dade College), the world's largest passenger seaport, and a public hospital network with more than ten thousand employees (with a $2 billion budget)—all possessed of at least one or two lobbyists. Those lobbying efforts culminate in a week visit (called Miami-Dade County Days) to the state capital, which is devoted to our county and includes what is by far the world's largest paella, concocted by Miami Hispanics for the culinary benefit of the legislators and their staff.

Paella, for readers who don't happen to know, is a dish that includes rice mixed with chicken and every kind of seafood known to our species. In Miami, it is garnished with generous amounts of wine, beer, and other alcoholic beverages. I am not sure if that is part of the Tally paella, but I suspect it is, even if no one acknowledges it.

Miami-Dade County Days in Tallahassee always makes for good fun, food, and socializing. But its legislative impact is doubtful, due to the sheer number of people and agenda items thrown into the mix. Expecting sensible legislation to come out of this occasion is like expecting a symphony to come out of the famous Woodstock festival.

Besides the above, there is a much bigger obstacle to lobbying successfully in the name of Miami-Dade County: The county commission is never able to agree on one legislative priority. *Hell, we can't even agree on ten priorities.*

Francis and I traveled to Tally for totally different reasons. He had been invited by the Greater Miami Chamber of Commerce—what we can call the bastion of Miami's establishment. I had been invited by no one but myself. Not being chairman of the county commission, or of any of its committees, and not being the mayor, I had no particular role to play.

I was essentially a freelancer.

But that is an exaggeration that borders on a misstatement. The simple fact is that showing up to Tally in the company of Francis means you are almost guaranteed to be taken seriously. And we were indeed taken seriously.

Part of the reason we were effective was that I adopted Francis's agenda. He was there for transportation; I was there for education. But his transportation agenda had been five years in the making. My education agenda, barely five months.

After seeing Francis in action over the past six years, I had learned to be a follower. It was a novel experience for me.

As it turns out, what made it doubly rewarding for me was that I was able to be more than just a supporting actor. By the luck of the draw, I was also able to be the chief enabler.

What I mean is that I ended up not only coordinating Francis's schedule but finagling the two most important appointments. As it happened, Francis *had not made any major appointments*. Using my contacts, I was able to secure meetings with the two most coveted people in the legislature: the speaker of the House and the president of the Senate.

The two meetings, which took place in sequence, were memorable for their sheer efficiency. And, of course, for the charisma of the presenter in chief—the junior Suarez.

As I said, Francis did not have a clear agenda for the Tallahassee trip. He had gone at the invitation of Florida International University's president, Mark Rosenberg, who also happened to be chairman of the chamber of commerce. I figured that was an important delegation and tagged on, fully assuming that Francis had a full agenda.

It didn't actually matter that he hadn't planned much; what mattered was that we were both in Tally for a lightning-quick trip. It began on a late Tuesday-evening flight; we arrived at the hotel at midnight and had an early breakfast with our lobbying team.

This is not to say that either of us takes our lobbyists too seriously. These folks are needed by private-sector companies to wade through the thicket of legislation and regulation that emanates from the state capital. To Francis and me, they are merely facilitators—useful for scheduling the meetings and guiding us from the Senate to the House and back to the Senate side of the Capitol, where both chambers of the legislature (as well as the governor and cabinet) have their offices.

Over breakfast, the leader of the county's lobbying team, Joe Rasco, did his best to brief Francis on the difficulty of having his pet piece of legislation approved. "Commissioner," he said, "that bill, even if it passes both House and Senate, will be vetoed by the governor." Having spent some time on the flight to Tally discussing this with Francis, I quickly chimed in: "Joe, the way we plan to present it is as merely removing a cap on what the state can contribute; it will not be a fixed amount of spending."

"It won't matter," said Joe. "The governor will still veto it."

Francis did not take too kindly to this double dose of negativity, saying, "I don't want to hear it, Joe. If you are going to predict failure, then I don't need your help." As if to make up for this faux pas, Joe immediately changed the subject to an event scheduled in just a few minutes by the chamber of commerce. It startled Francis, who realized that this was the reason he was in Tallahassee—to woo legislators in the company of the chamber bigwigs.

Meanwhile, I went my own way to meet with legislators regarding two education items that I was sponsoring: one related to after-school programs and one to apprenticeships. The complete story of how these initiatives slogged through the legislature will be told later. For now, suffice it to say that I subsumed my well-planned agenda under Francis's ad hoc one on this trip.

And it was a good thing I did, since he was going on instinct and charisma rather than planning. Thank God I had done some planning. And that got us to successive inner sanctums of the two top legislators in Florida, House speaker Richard Corcoran and Senate president Joe Negron.

Corcoran is a classic straight arrow. A devout Presbyterian with six kids. A man who is bothered by any kind of government spending that doesn't have a direct connection to the limited role he thinks state government should play in the lives of the citizens.

During the time we were there, he was particularly incensed that the state has sponsored a marketing campaign involving the flamboyant musician Pitbull. We're not talking a $50,000 or $100,000 fee. We're talking more like $3 million, for a musician who appears with ladies in very skimpy clothes and has sexually suggestive lyrics.

Clusters of other solicitors were milling around the inner reception area. They seemed a little surprised when we were ushered in within seconds of introducing ourselves to the receptionist. As we walked into the inner sanctum of the most powerful legislator in the third-largest U.S. state, I myself was surprised by the familiarity with which Corcoran treated Francis. (It turns out that Corcoran previously had endorsed Francis for a mayoral campaign that had been started and abandoned four years before.)

This should have put me at ease, but instead it made me more nervous. I had no political chips to offer this man, and now it appeared that he was the one who could cash in on chips previously earned. Besides, I was not a Republican, and I was there to advocate for a very progressive plan to fund apprenticeship programs.

I used a bold approach and told him the story of how in 1991 the U.S. Conference of Mayors had tried to lobby President Bush the elder to divert $11 billion in transportation funds towards early-childhood intervention. Bush refused to meet with us and thus missed an opportunity to show his compassionate side on a matter that was not really liberal, since it spoke of preferring kids to unneeded "turkeys," such as the famous "bridge to nowhere."

I am not sure whether the approach worked. All I know is that two weeks later, the chairman of appropriations in the state House was supporting $750,000 in appropriation for my apprenticeship program. And doing so *at the request of a freshman Democratic legislator no less*!

Needless to say, three quarters of a million dollars would not create career paths for many young Floridians. But it was a start.

In the meantime, I had barely finished my presentation when Francis immediately launched into his. The state cap that prescribed no more than a 12.5 percent state contribution to new mass transportation projects should be lifted, he argued. It really makes no sense to have an artificial cap for projects like ours, which could affect tourism and commerce in the largest county, which also contains the largest cruise port in the world and an international airport that sees close to fifty million passengers a year.

Anyhow, a cap is an artificial constraint, and removing it does not guarantee a single penny of funding. You still have the power to fix the amount, if any, that the state will contribute.

Speaker Corcoran seemed persuaded, and he admitted that the recommendation of our strong ally, Representative Carlos Trujillo, was a big factor. (Trujillo has since served as U.S. ambassador to the Organization of American States.)

It was pretty much the same reaction we received from the Senate president (Negron, which in Spanish means "very black," though this guy was anything but). In this case, the key ally we counted on was the president pro tempore of the Senate, who happened to be the daughter of a very good friend and former campaign aide.

In effect, both top legislators were already predisposed to support our agenda, whatever it may have been. Still, an observer might have noticed that we were a pretty brazen pair of advocates, using Republican allies to argue on behalf of progressive causes.

Francis and I would have responded, "Whatever works."

But I was still skeptical that we would accomplish much, and I was in a hurry to head home. Because I had planned my trip at the last moment, I could not get a flight out of Tally on Thursday, so I was determined to hitch a car ride to Miami.

I had to be in Miami for a commission meeting where I was the main opponent of the mayor's new executive order that would crack down on "sanctuary" cities and counties. (How that would play out is another story.)

Thankfully, I managed to hitch a ride with a member of the opposing party, a freshman legislator named Robert Asencio.

The good fellow was already on his way out of the capital when I begged him to turn around and pick me up so that I would not have to spend the evening on what had started as a very cold day in Tallahassee and promised to be an even colder evening.

Asencio and his aide kindly gave me a ride home. They drove a very modest compact; sitting in the back seat, I felt like we were riding in the most luxuriant comfort known to man.

People who have not traveled Florida's Turnpike on a crisp, clear February day have no idea of how idyllic automobile travel can be. Add to that setting the advances brought by the age of communication, and the company of an idealistic legislator and his equally noble, though much younger, aide, and you have the perfect car ride for a political junkie like me.

Before we got too far on the way home, I had to marvel at the warm bipartisan reception that Francis and I had experienced in Tally. "I truly did not expect that a bold agenda like we had put on the table to these legislative leaders would be so well received," I told Asencio.

Like the noble, forthright man that he is, Asencio spoke from the heart. "Commissioner, you should not be surprised at all. Perhaps you don't realize it, but you guys are royalty to these folks. They've never seen a father-and-son team like you two. Hell, most of them have never seen one politician like you two."

I pondered that for quite a while that day, and thereafter. What exactly was that quality—and what exactly would such a reputation entail for us, as we continued our half-decade rise to prominence that had thrust both of us into a privileged position in the world's newest global city?

We had gone to Tallahassee on the spur of the moment, with a wildly ambitious agenda, and had walked out with all kinds of well wishes. Would that translate into real success? Or would the very high degree of difficulty in our combined agendas result in disappointment?

Within three weeks, we found out.

Francis never expected to hear back so quickly from the transportation powers-that-be in Tallahassee. He was hoping that the bill changing the cap on the state's contribution from 12.5 percent to 25 percent would work its way through each chamber of the legislature, and that in mid-May, if the effort was successful, the battle to avoid a gubernatorial veto would begin.

Instead, we read in the paper that the Florida secretary of transportation had unilaterally decreed the lifting of the cap, in a letter directed to Francis as president of the Miami-Dade League of Cities. This was an amazing result, obtained in an incredibly short time and predicated on an unexpected use of administrative discretion.

It augured well for the continuing effort to fund the SMART plan, estimated to cost no less than $3.6 billion. To accomplish that would require a lot more than regal bearing and charisma. It would require constancy of purpose and consolidation of power, in the midst of a mayoral run for Francis.

Coincidentally, on the same day that Francis received the letter from the secretary of transportation, the *Miami Herald* reported that he had surpassed the $2 million mark in campaign fundraising. And that was without a serious opponent.

The qualifying deadline for the mayoral run was in September, which was also the month in which the county commission approved our budget. Getting the commission's approval was our best chance of obtaining at least half of the $200 million yearly revenue stream needed to start funding the SMART plan.

We were building up momentum at the two ends of the state. Only time would tell whether father and son would be successful in kick-starting a transportation project that had been stuck in the planning stages for more than two decades.

39

In Search of Affordable Housing

Besides a dysfunctional system of mass transportation, Miami has a major crisis in livability. It is due to the price of homes and the high taxes and fees new homeowners have to pay.

In this matter, Miami has no equal. There is no major metropolis in the world in which so many of the residents—the people who own or rent a domicile—are born somewhere else. In greater Miami, only about one in five residents was born here. That means 80 percent are technically foreigners or transplants from northern and western states.

Add in the consideration that a substantial percentage of residents live here only for a portion of the year, and you have a unique phenomenon: Residents who are eligible to vote comprise fewer than half of the permanent residents of our city. In Miami proper, which has about half a million residents, just about 40 percent are registered to vote.

Other than perhaps New York, Rome, or Paris, we have a higher percentage than anywhere else in the world of people who spend only a fraction of the year in town. That percentage can be gleaned from two numbers: the number of people who can claim a "homestead exemption" from real estate taxes (about six hundred thousand) versus the total number of residential units (about 1.6 million).

Miami, in sum, is not demographically stable. But if you think that is a weakness, don't tell the builders and developers. They thrive on that anomaly. For them, the number of snowbirds from the North plus the number of Southerners who want to escape with capital, or at least have a potential nest in case they need to escape, is a huge benefit. It fuels building booms in places like Brickell, Aventura, and Doral, where a mixture of Venezuelans, Colombians, Brazilians, Russians, Chinese, and assorted other immigrants (or part-time residents) all want to have a pied-à-terre.

For the builders, lawyers, and realtors, this high housing demand is a major bonus. For the middle- and working-class residents, it is a nightmare of high prices, constant fluctuations, and, ultimately, a crowded home, where three generations often struggle to not have domestic violence. When your kids cannot move out to a place of their own, and they begin having kids, the benefits of economies of scale clash with the reality of crowded living, crying babies, and a higher propensity for broken homes.

And, I should add, the lack of affordable housing combines with the lack of affordable mass transportation to create a society in which a staggering majority of the people (62 percent, to be precise) spend more than 50 percent of their income on housing and transportation. Among members of the working class, 70 percent of their income goes towards these two needs.

There is no way to overstate the unfairness of our real estate taxing system. In theory, owners of the smallest homes, who are the least affluent, would pay little or no real estate tax. They would be exempted, just as the working poor are exempted from paying income taxes.

Often it doesn't work that way. And there are two important reasons. One is the fact that the appraised value of a home is based as much on location as on size and quality of construction. In the seventies and eighties, you could buy a house in the "Roads" area of Miami for $60,000. It might have had three bedrooms and two bathrooms.

Today a house there could sell for ten times that amount. The reason? Because that area is five minutes from downtown, which is by far the largest single workplace in Miami-Dade County. Its nearness to downtown was not so important forty years ago, when driving and parking in the few office buildings there were fast and cheap. Now, due to our congested streets and pricey downtown parking rates, owning a house close to a place that employs close to 20 percent of our workers is a huge bonus.

So let's say you paid $60,000 for your house. Then the guy next door sells his house for a ton of money, and the property appraiser immediately applies that price tag to your own house. All of a sudden, your house is worth $600,000 and the property tax, which at 2 percent of the home's value started out at about $1,200 a year, or a hundred bucks a month, has become equivalent to a mortgage at a thousand dollars a month.

Policy makers realized that this was a problem for the working middle class and quickly found a remedy that works well for those who already own a home. They passed legislation that holds down yearly increases in property valuation to less than 3 percent. Later they coupled that measure with one that allows existing homeowners to "carry with them" the accumulated cap in valuation increases, so that they can exchange a home for a new one and not lose the benefit of the accumulated exemption.

It all works fairly well for those of my generation, who were able to buy homes a couple of decades ago. Not so for the new homebuyer; he or she can expect to pay about $200,000 for a modest home—and that assumes it is located a fair distance from downtown, in a place like Doral or Westchester to the west or Miami Gardens to the north.

By way of illustration, my son bought a modest home in 2007 for about $400,000. As soon as the tax appraiser picked up the sale in the public records, his property tax bill came in at a cool $7,000 a year. With one story, three bedrooms, and two baths, it was not an ostentatious home by any means. The shingle roof and small yard made it a classic suburban working-class home in any part of the country.

But the local government wanted $7,000 each year in taxes, for the simple right to have trash picked up and the neighborhood patrolled by some police. Oh, and Francis got some access to neighborhood parks.

Not fresh water or a pipe to send wastewater to the treatment plants. That was an additional cost, built into real estate taxes. (The county bureaucrats would crow about having the lowest water rates in the United States. What they didn't tell you is that Miami water comes courtesy of two aquifers that are easily tapped, extremely pure, and so large that it would take an avenging angel to muck up the works.)

Simply stated, we have the best natural plumbing system in the world. You would think that the government would offer us free water. Never mind building homes for us; just let us tap into the world's largest aquifer!

Besides lowering property taxes, the government can create incentives and eliminate disincentives for new affordable housing.

After his election in 2009, Francis moved very quickly on two related measures. One had to do with giving density bonuses to developers who included a minimum percentage of affordable housing. The other was to waive parking requirements for multi-family housing projects built close to mass transit. This measure, coupled with expanded, free trolley service to most Miami neighborhoods, effectively reduced the cost of housing in most of the urban core. By the beginning of his mayoralty, in 2017, Francis was able to announce full funding for as many as 12,000 units of affordable housing.

40

A Second Media Honeymoon

We are now in the fall of 2016. I have just been reelected to the county commission by an overwhelming margin and concocted a spectacular visual in connection with my swearing-in. Although I have never been much for photo ops, in this case I decided that the person who would swear me in as a newly reelected commissioner would be Francis.

Dealing with Francis is always a logistical nightmare. The guy's charisma is exceeded only by his insouciance about details such as timeliness. There is something unpredictable in my son; he seems to march to the beat of his own drummer.

Which is OK. I just wish the drummer (personified in this case by the officer who drives him to official functions) would give me some advance notice of expected lateness. So here I am, awaiting the single most important ceremonial moment of the county's two-year electoral calendar, and there is no sign of Francis. Ordinarily, it would not be a big deal, but as I said, he is supposed to swear me in for my next four-year term.

And, as it appears, he has gone to the wrong venue, driven by a different officer than the customary one, who is sick today.

The ceremony is scheduled for ten a.m. at a facility that is literally five minutes from Francis's house. He has an official driver. And, as it happens, this morning he and I happened to have met for a beautiful Thanksgiving mass in which my granddaughter (his niece) played the Pocahontas role at her parochial school celebration. What could possibly have gone wrong?

Eventually, Francis and his driver realize that they have gone to the wrong facility, and they reverse course in time to reach the right auditorium a bit late—but before the actual ceremony starts. After much nervousness and multiple exchanges of texts and phone calls, we are ready for the fireworks.

You can't beat the optics of this ceremony. The oath of office, accompanied by speeches, is taking place in an auditorium that fits a couple of thousand people. When a county mayor and seven commissioners are sworn in, the majority of the audience is what nowadays are called stakeholders. That means county staff, lobbyists, and media; public officials from the thirty-five municipal governments in the county, the school board, and the legislature; a few judges; and the state attorney.

Today, there are maybe a thousand people in the auditorium; I would guess about half are stakeholders and family of those being sworn in. I don't know who the other five hundred might be, but my guess is that most are close friends of the county officials. Perhaps one hundred are citizen activists. If they knew how much this whole affair is costing, in terms of manpower wasted and staging costs, they would probably wonder why we could not have done this ceremony as part of a regular county commission meeting.

But I am not in a position to change any of that. My only objectives today are to be light in my comments, entertain the stakeholders, please my colleagues, and perhaps score a point or two with the media.

Scoring points with either the mainstream media or social media requires good optics. The others accomplish that by bringing in hordes of relatives, including as many toddlers as possible. I can't (or, more correctly, won't) compete with them on the number of relatives surrounding me.

Frankly, my kids and grandkids have more important things to do. Even my wife has school to teach, and I am not about to ask her to take a day off to attend what is mostly a boring ceremony, trivialized all the more by the lack of gravitas of the participants.

But I have brought my ace in the hole. Whereas the other officials have somber judges swearing them in, I ask my son to do the honors. And that turns out to be a real coup.

Francis Xavier on this day is as funny and handsome as ever. Put simply, he brings his A game. He wins the crowd over with pure charisma. His self-effacing comments are well received by a crowd that is used to my too-sober, too-analytical, and too-serious comments.

Needless to say, I follow suit and keep my comments short and sweet.

The mainstream media go on to ignore both of us in their reports, concentrating instead on the mayor's comments, which were totally devoid of substance. (He spent about five minutes trying to convince us that driverless cars are a couple of years away, and that the bigwigs at Ford Motor Company informed him of that. Yikes!)

Thankfully, social media posts do feature visuals of Francis swearing me in. Different bloggers publish the picture of father and son doing our thing. One picture makes it to the weekly publication *Miami Today*, which has a particular interest in mass transportation. Its readers are mostly downtown professionals, most of whom see Francis as the leader of the future and many of whom ascribe to me the positive energy that Francis emits.

With that article in hand, it is easy to multiply its impact by posting it on Twitter and Facebook. Other politicians post selfies; I prefer to post pictures published by third parties, which gives an air of impartiality to the publication. (Political and marketing consultants refer to that as "third-party validation.")

As it happened, the father-and-son visuals didn't reach one hundred thousand *Herald* readers, but they did reach perhaps twenty thousand readers of *Miami Today* plus twenty-five thousand social media followers of Francis and myself combined.

It is a new age in media. And it helps to have a younger, more charismatic partner in crime.

41

City of Miami Election of 2017

As the qualifying deadline approached, it seemed clear that Francis would not draw a serious opponent for the mayoralty. But that was not nearly enough to satisfy us. Miami's mayor was still not a "strong" mayor. Other than appointing the city manager and presenting a yearly budget, the mayor of Miami (in stark contrast to the mayor of the county) did not have much executive power.

Miami's four thousand employees report to the manager—not the mayor. And the city commission approves the budget, passes all the ordinances, and makes all decisions on procurement, planning, and zoning. The commission also selects the city attorney and the city clerk. And even on the appointment and dismissal of a city manager, commissioners can override the mayor by a four-fifths vote.

Going into the elections of 2017, Francis had solid relationships with three of the five sitting commissioners. He had supported all three in prior elections and had generally gotten along with all.

But two seats on the commission would be open in November. And one, in particular, presented some worrisome scenarios. It was the one that involved the Carollo brothers, one of whom (Frank) would be termed out and one of whom (Joe) was seeking to replace him.

It should be noted that the runoff in the Little Havana district was not of the essence for Francis. He already had an ally in the person who replaced him as commissioner, to go with the other three incumbents and thus provide a supermajority of four allies. In the seat vacated by Francis, an old Miami warhorse (Manolo Reyes) was elected. His main opponent would have been quite acceptable, too, but in the end Reyes captured the support of most of my own and Francis's neighborhood "captains." It was not necessary to endorse him outright or to raise substantial funds for him.

Reyes's son was close to Francis, and Reyes's in-laws were close friends of mine. He was a reasonable man, a high school economics teacher, and a friend.

But the Little Havana district was not so easy to control. Miamians at large viewed this battle like people look at a fishbowl. It is a space where some dangerous fish live, but they are not a danger or a factor in the lives of those outside the fishbowl. Even if a little shark penetrates the fishbowl, it is still a little shark. It cannot harm the commonwealth.

That is really wishful thinking. Joe Carollo is toxic; everything he touches turns to dissension and distrust. The result is not just disruption; it is destruction of civility. He is a big shark in a small pond with the ability to jump out and wreak havoc in the bigger pond.

There was no way I could abstain from the battle to put him back into his little hiding place in the private sector, where (to quote Adlai Stevenson) he could retreat into the "estranged recesses of his deranged mind."

Carollo is particularly noxious in a diverse, polyglot community like Miami. He uses racial terms to criticize his enemies, a practice carried over from his days as a police recruit, when he placed KKK pamphlets in the locker of an African-American colleague.

He uses the police department to investigate his political enemies, as he did in 1998, when he had virtual control of the city administration, having placed the ethically challenged Donald Warshaw in the roles of both city manager and police chief. He files suits with reckless abandon, taunts the media, and erodes public confidence by hinting at scandals that don't exist.

He was the master of "fake news" before that term appeared in the national lexicon.

And he particularly relishes the technique of guilt by association, which he mixes with "red baiting" in the most obnoxious ways. When Carollo has the bully pulpit, if you say anything positive about a liberal politician, such as a Kennedy, he will pounce on it. And God help you if he ever finds you pictured with Bernie Sanders—even if the event involves many other people and you just happen to be standing next to Sanders in the cloakroom.

Having Carollo on your city commission is bad news. I had to endure it for two years, from 1985 to 1987. As described before, he stirred up controversy and ultimately sank a beautiful project in one of our spoil islands (Watson Island) with his unfounded accusations.

From 1998 to 2001, when he served as mayor, his tenure was characterized by turmoil.

By the fall of 2017, the mainstream media had seen through Carollo's veneer of muckraking, populist rhetoric and realized the underlying venom. They had been shocked when he had first convinced the mayor of the small city of Doral to appoint esteemed former county manager Merrett Stierheim as city manager, and then promptly condemned Stierheim as being anti-Hispanic.

When a disgusted Stierheim resigned from his post, Carollo cajoled the mayor of Doral into appointing him and then quickly turned on him also, accusing the mayor of being in the pocket of Venezuela's leftist dictator, Hugo Chávez.

Everyone who had been following his latest antics was finally convinced that the man was a sociopath. No self-respecting politician would even think of supporting him.

No one, that is, except for the most powerful politician of all: Miami-Dade County mayor Carlos Gimenez.

I am sure the pundits gave that as an additional reason for thinking that Carollo would be the odds-on favorite. By coincidence, Gimenez's pollster, Dario Moreno, was also a Carollo sycophant. And so the moment Carollo announced that he was running for his brother's seat on the commission, at least one poll had him as a prohibitive favorite.

I actually thought that Gimenez's support would turn out to be a hindrance to Carollo, given his recent misstep in trying to scuttle the rail expansion plan. But lo and behold, the same hurricane (Irma) that helped seal Francis's mayoralty put Gimenez front and center.

Mayor Gimenez thrived on emergency management. He was the ultimate firefighter dressed as a mayor for all emergencies, and particularly as a mayor for hurricanes.

In the span of a week, he gobbled up more airtime than Donald Trump.

He was on every channel, every few hours, for five or six straight days. It was as if Miami television were owned, produced, and directed by him.

By the time hurricane season ended, Gimenez's support was not a hindrance to Carollo. Instead, it was a substantial asset, as it meant financial support and some measure of credibility. Here was a former city mayor, supported by a current county mayor, running for a seat on the city commission. Here was a Cuban demagogue, possessed of every weapon available to those who have no ethical compunctions, ready to start a slow but devastating climb up the political ladder.

Here was Joe Carollo, Miami's Joe McCarthy, on the brink of a political renaissance. The only obstacle to his success was the conscience of the community, and the conscience was us.

"Us" in this context should have been all local people of goodwill. It should have meant the business community, the *Miami Herald*, the Cuban exile leaders, the civic activists, anyone with any interest in the environment, anyone with any shred of civic dignity, all good-government groups, and everyone's favorite aunts and uncles.

And it really did, theoretically, include all those people—except most were not willing to publicly oppose Carollo. In an ideal world, all people of goodwill would be mobilized to make sure that "Crazy Joe" would not make a comeback. And all of Carollo's first-round opponents, who had borne the brunt of his attacks and his divisive campaign, would unite behind the one who made it to the runoff.

But most of his first-round opponents avoided taking a stand. Most politicians, and many civic leaders, are afraid of a bully. It's the old story of failure to stand up to a dictator when someone's own personal interests are not affected.

Another logistical problem was the minuscule size of the district in question. Single-member districts, important as they are for minorities, also lead to parochialism. The commissioner from Little Havana doesn't have to pay much attention to the *Miami Herald* or the mainstream media. He doesn't have to pay much attention to social media. He only has to buy enough Spanish-language media coverage to convey his message to the elderly in north Little Havana and hope that the younger residents of the district simply don't turn out on Election Day.

Ultimately, our effort to keep bad-boy Carollo off the commission failed, in part because this rather cagey pol had moved into the Little Havana district, where his McCarthyite rants against those he called "Chavistas" (followers of leftist Venezuelan strongman Hugo Chávez) found at least a minor echo.

The runoff opponent, Alfie Leon, was like a hobbit with a lion's heart. By dint of a Herculean twelve-month house-to-house canvassing marathon, the previously unknown little lion had come in ahead of two dynastic candidates and barely ten points behind the former mayor.

In Miami, the runoff election is only two weeks after the initial one. Unfortunately for Leon, the race for second place was so tight (seventeen votes) that it took the supervisor of elections almost three working days to certify the second-place finisher. By the time Leon was certified, Carollo had raised substantial funds and begun his well-oiled hunt for absentee ballots; in those he had exceeded Leon by a two-to-one margin in the first election.

Ordinarily, a well-established candidate who obtains only 30 percent of the vote against newcomers is in trouble. The problem here was twofold: the advantage that Carollo had in the absentee ballot hunt, and the effectiveness of negative campaigning when it is done by a media-savvy veteran like Carollo.

This second factor has to be elaborated on, particularly in light of the peculiar penchant of the mainstream media to publicize negative allegations. This two-week runoff was testament to that unfortunate reality.

Interestingly, by 2017 the *Miami Herald* had wised up to the media manipulation tactics of Joe Carollo—but only at the editorial level. The editors, to their immense credit, consulted me as to the editorial support in the runoff. They had two evident concerns.

One concern was an allegation made by Carollo that Leon had issues of residency—that he had lived and voted outside the district even while claiming to be a longtime resident. It was at best trivial and at worst bogus, since there was no question that Leon had lived in the district a lot longer than the required one year and forty-five days.

The one who had residency issues was Carollo. But the discrepancies and ambiguities in his supposed leasing of property on the very eve of the qualifying deadline were not made public until two days before the election. And by that time, Carollo's barrage of attacks on Leon had influenced close to 75 percent of all the votes, which had been cast either by absentee ballot or early voting.

The other issue that concerned the editorial board—and one that was shared by pretty much all people of goodwill both in and outside the district—was whether Carollo, if elected, would constitute a destructive force that would derail the entire Francis Suarez mayoralty.

What troubled the *Herald* editors, in this regard, was the dichotomy in the involvement of my son and myself. Whereas I was clearly opposed to Carollo and helping his adversary, my son (who had just been installed as mayor and was enormously popular) was uncommitted. Moreover, Francis insisted that he could work harmoniously with either candidate.

Was that the height of naïveté? Or was it the calculated, mature decision of a young statesman on his way to being a "superb" one, as the *Herald*'s editorial board had wistfully suggested?

I cannot give my reader any kind of emphatic answer. A part of me felt let down by my son; it argued that his endorsement of Leon, as well as his full-fledged support of my own endorsement of Leon, surely would have led to a victory against the destructive demagogue.

Another part of me fully identified with his thinking, which was logical enough: The newly elected mayor's neutrality would be very effective insurance against a victorious and vindictive Carollo. A necessary component of that theory was the concept that Carollo was no longer a major force, either for good or ill. That he was old and fully exposed in his mischievous ways, to the point that he would no longer be influential with the community as a whole.

A man whose character already had been assassinated by his own misdeeds, the theory continued, could not engage in the kind of character assassination that had been his forte. Besides, went the theory, a city commission post representing Little Havana was hardly the pulpit from which to wield power.

Those were probably the fundamental ideas behind Francis's decision to stay neutral, and I accepted them. Francis did not want a continuation of a thirty-year blood feud between the Suarezes and the Carollos. No more Hatfields and McCoys in Miami politics.

But that assumes a sort of equality in the adversarial camps. And a willingness to engage in a fair fight—but there is no such thing with Joe Carollo.

Dealing with this man makes me reminisce about the historical quandary faced, at a much higher level, by Winston Churchill and FDR when they had to deal with Joseph Stalin. It is said that when they were discussing the unpleasantness of it, FDR turned to Churchill and said, "Winston, I would deal with the devil himself it if was necessary to achieve peace." To which Churchill retorted, "The devil yes, but the devil's mother?"

Even without Francis's involvement, there was a good chance Carollo would have lost if the *Herald* had not been schizophrenic. Having the support of the editorial board did not insulate Leon against Carollo's dirty tactics. The *Herald*'s beat reporter, David Smiley, still covered every allegation Carollo made and gave equal space to his and Leon's pronouncements. One glaring example is a fundraising reception given for Leon by a Coral Gables commissioner. It was an impressive event and should have been covered as such.

But Carollo quickly seized the venue to attack the event. The key mistake here was made by Smiley, who was covering the city commission race. Instead of just reporting on a very successful event, hosted by a very credible politician who happened to be a city commissioner from the neighboring city of Coral Gables (Vince Lago), Smiley immediately sought a comment from Carollo.

Predictably, Carollo made fun of the event, calling it elitist because it was held in a luxury hotel outside the district boundaries. This was class warfare at its best: Carollo was stigmatizing a very positive fundraiser by his opponent, who was clearly the grassroots candidate.

By airing Carollo's comments, the reporter disseminated the impression that Leon was a wealthy outsider—the establishment candidate. In one quote, Carollo managed to dispel the reality of his own affluence, as evinced by his living in a million-dollar home in a swanky section of Coconut Grove and his signing a lease on a luxury apartment in the district on the eve of the qualifying deadline.

Poor Leon had labored in the vineyards of the Lord, canvassing house to house for twelve months. He had a distinct advantage in the younger sections of the district, comprising about half of all its precincts.

Carollo had a distinct advantage in the absentee ballots and in a senior residential complex known as Robert King High Towers. This facility, which housed about three hundred mostly Cuban-American voters, was deeply rooted in the Carollo modus operandi—which recently had been utilized by Carollo's much younger brother, Frank.

How Frank Carollo had utilized it is worth recounting. This guy would habitually show up at the very doorsteps of the district's senior voters (particularly at Robert King High Towers) on their birthdays. And he would not show up empty-handed. He would show up with a birthday cake!

Combining that deeply ingrained modus operandi (limited to the senior residential complexes) with his demagogic anti-Communist rhetoric, Joe Carollo was able to maintain a solid base in north Little Havana, even as his antics and Leon's fresh grassroots approach ate away at the rest of the district.

Unfortunately for Leon, and for the people of Miami, the younger residents of the district don't take municipal elections, which happen in odd years, too seriously. They come out only in congressional and presidential elections, which happen in even years.

In the end, Carollo eked out a four-point victory over Leon. Would this be a harbinger of four years of turmoil and demagoguery or merely a transitory comeback, equipped with a mini bully pulpit for Miami's bad boy?

I was fairly sure it was the latter. More important, Francis's decision to abstain from the fray was his to make, not mine. He was our municipal leader, and had to make his own mistakes.

It was his first "learning moment" as mayor.

In the meantime, there was unfinished business at the county level. There also was an opportunity to begin cleaning house early. The occasion was the midterm resignation of a county commissioner.

42

An Early Opportunity to Reform the County

Miami-Dade County has about 1.5 million voters. Since there are thirteen districts, that means each district has about 115,000 voters. In any county commission election, a candidate who starts off as an unknown, and who has minimal fundraising ability, has no chance.

The situation is even worse if the election happens suddenly.

Such was the case in mid-2018, when Commissioner Bruno Barreiro suddenly resigned to run for Congress. The sudden resignation was evidently a stratagem to give an advantage to his own wife, Zoraida Barreiro, since it meant the election had to be set for just forty-five days from the vacancy. Name recognition would be the overriding advantage.

Filling this vacancy was important to all of us who wanted to have competent and ethical government in the county. The district in question connects Miami's downtown to South Beach, which is the nonpareil tourist attraction on which our metropolitan area relies.

Connecting those two regions by some form of rail, some kind of mass transit, has become our highest priority. So has protecting them both from the ravages of the sea, including the storm surges that invade both areas during hurricanes. Neither Barreiro nor his wife had much of an understanding of either issue, or of the related matter of how to finance the needed infrastructure without imposing new tax burdens on citizens already impacted by enormous real estate taxes, highway tolls, parking fees, and utility costs for things that used to be free, such as garbage pickup or parking at various public facilities.

Even so, conventional wisdom said that Zoraida was the front-runner. I met with her and her husband and talked about the above issues, as well as about the county government generally and the need for reform of the bureaucracy.

The discussion was far from satisfactory; later, I learned that the deal to have a sudden election had been engineered by another commissioner who had extracted a promise that Zoraida would cast her vote for the sitting commissioner who would be seeking the commission chairmanship.

That was not acceptable, by any means.

In the meantime, the *Miami Herald* did something quite unexpected: In its election editorial, it supported a fellow named Alex Díaz de la Portilla, described earlier.

Miami only has one English daily newspaper. The *Herald*'s endorsement has a disproportionate weight, even in a large metropolis like Miami. I was shocked enough to inquire about this; and so I called the editor of the *Herald*'s editorial board, a thoughtful, progressive, decent lady named Nancy Ancrum.

Ancrum was quite forthcoming and did not reject my inquiry. She admitted that Eileen Higgins was the most qualified candidate for the vacant seat. "But," she said, "Eileen does not have a broad base of support." (Which was a nice way of saying that a non-Hispanic who had little money and little support from the establishment did not have a chance.)

"What about Mrs. Barreiro?" I asked.

"She didn't know diddly-shit" was the quick and frank answer.

I had come to share that view, and ultimately decided to go public with my support of Higgins. I knew full well what I was getting into; this lady was the proverbial "Madam Librarian" from *The Music Man*. If she came in a distant third, supporting her would be considered another Don Quixote effort by me—tilting at a windmill.

In addition, there were scant resources to convey the endorsement. I had to rely on "robocalls" and on social media.

But there were three reasons why this kind of election might have unconventional results. Reason number one is that it was a special election, with a very low turnout. Although in theory there were over a hundred thousand voters, in practice there would probably be not more than ten to twelve thousand. Anyone who can mobilize a couple of thousand voters can surprise.

The second is that the district included a substantial number of "yuppies" (young, upwardly mobile voters). Those in this demographic live in constant connection to the internet. Their medium of communication is social media: Facebook, Twitter, emails, texts, and derivations thereof.

The third reason is a widespread dissatisfaction with the status quo. In *Democracy in America 2010*, I chronicle that voter alienation. In 2018, two years into the Trump presidency, the angry voter was in the majority. And that anger was particularly palpable among young Democrats, who loved Eileen Higgins's profile: progressive, Democrat, and female, with no ties to developers.

In the end, that profile and those other factors not only transcended the conventional wisdom but put Higgins on top.

The question now was whether she could survive a runoff against the established candidate. The runoff was scheduled only two weeks after the first vote. So there wasn't much time to ponder or strategize. Because it was a special election, there were just days between the first vote and the runoff. And I had to concentrate on my own fundraising event (for the county mayoralty), which was scheduled in that very short span of time.

By the time I focused on it, it was Thursday of the week before the absentee ballots would be mailed, so we had just one weekend to mobilize: barely seventy-two hours before the ballots were mailed and about ninety-six hours before they were received.

It didn't take long to figure out what was needed or how quickly it was needed. Clearly, the crucial segment of the electorate was the Hispanic absentee-ballot voters who had voted in the first round. These folks would be the most likely of any identifiable segment to vote in the runoff. The reason? Because they would automatically get a ballot mailed to them by the Elections Department.

By my estimate, at least half of all the voters in the runoff would be voting by mail—which is to say, by absentee ballot. If Higgins could pull even 35 percent of those, she could win—assuming that she also won the votes of 65 percent of those who would turn out at the polls on Election Day.

In other words, if the opposing candidate won 65 percent of the votes cast by mail, with those voters comprising half of the total number of voters, and Higgins won 65 percent of the votes of the half voting in person, she would have what the experts call a "path to victory."

That's all simple math. But how do you get on that path? And how much time was there to formulate a strategy?

As I said, there were about ninety-six hours, or four days, to carry out the operation. And twenty-four of those were wiped out by the upcoming Memorial Day holiday. So we had a Friday, plus a three-day weekend to pull off the operation.

As a practical matter, it's hard to mobilize a major operation during a holiday weekend. (Miamians take their holiday breaks very seriously...) And this one, as it happened, ended up being a super soggy Memorial Day weekend.

And I mean super soggy.

The most obvious strategy—the one conventional wisdom dictated— was to woo major endorsements from important figures who previously had supported the candidate who came in third. In this case, those figures were Alex Díaz de la Portilla (DLP) and Joe Carollo.

As stated before, DLP was a lovable rogue and the *Herald* had endorsed him in the first round. But he was a diehard Republican. Higgins would need to mobilize two factions: the elderly Hispanics and the young, activist Democrats who would ordinarily stay home.

The other possibility was to use Carollo himself as the point of the spear. But this was unthinkable. Could we invoke the maxim "The enemy of my enemy is my friend"? Could reasonable, decent people seek to rub elbows with the likes of Carollo in order to defeat a common enemy?

I soon realized this was not an option. The idea was ruled out by the one person whose endorsement in that district could make the difference: former mayor Maurice Ferré. He was, after all, the grey eminence of Miami politics.

Luckily, Ferré and I were on good terms once again. I had asked him to introduce me at my book-signing event the year before for *Democracy in America 2010*. The timing and the theme were perfect: The book is about philosophy, science, history, and theology—all topics that Ferré was conversant with and interested in. I had dedicated the book to him using the moniker "Miami's philosopher-king."

I sensed that I was on his good side.

No one thought Ferré would jump in. But I had to at least try to get him to neutralize what Carollo might do to mobilize the conservative, elder Cuban voters. So I called him and was elated to find out he would readily endorse Eileen Higgins.

I then set about drafting my own endorsement of candidate Higgins. I used the term *"la gringa,"* meaning a non-Hispanic woman, taken from her ads. Cubans are a noble people. They are grateful for the *gringos* who have helped us, supported us, accepted us into this great country, and even helped us to build up Cuba. Among the latter are the Augustinian priests who founded Villanueva, which was the lone Catholic university in Havana. I drafted my endorsement letter by referring to Villanueva's rector, Father John J. Kelly, as the *gringo* who had been arrested by the G-2 (Cuban secret police) with my father.

Fr. Kelly was the *gringo* who had been with us when things went bad.

As soon as I reached Ferré, he was in all the way. Yes, he would support Higgins. He began by complimenting me on my role in getting her to this point. He wanted to be part of it.

We set up a meeting for Friday morning at his home. Higgins would pick me up.

I kept thinking, how would this wily old patrician react to this totally unvarnished schoolteacher and "Madam Librarian" spinster? At his apex, Ferré had been the lion king of Miami politics. Together with Claude Pepper and an African-American activist named Charlie Hadley, he controlled Miami politics for twelve years, until I came along and took him down.

Ferré had wielded power like Mayor Richard Daley in Chicago (as per Mike Royko's book *Boss*) and Mayor James Curley in Boston (as depicted in the equally famous book *The Last Hurrah*, by Edwin O'Connor). His style was slick, hard-core, Democratic machine politics. And it all changed with the arrival of the Cubans, who tilted the scales towards the Republican side of the spectrum.

(New-generation Cuban Americans were politically much closer to the national norm, but the older Cubans were more prevalent in the district in question at the time of the runoff election with Higgins, and they were definitely inclined towards the Republican side of the spectrum.)

Bruno Barreiro, now represented by his wife, was the darling of the Republican *viejitos* ("old-timers") of Little Havana and South Beach. He had ridden that wave for twenty-plus years.

How could we change that without having to cater to Carollo, which was now clearly verboten? I figured only a well-crafted effort by Ferré and myself might do the trick (emphasis on "might").

But we owed it to this great city, and this great country, to try. (It wasn't the first time I had backed an underdog candidate, by the way. I had done it with Steve Clark running against Miriam Alonso as I left the city mayoralty in 1993. Many were surprised that I would back a spent old Anglo warhorse over the flaming populist Alonso. They were less surprised when Alonso, after losing the election, was indicted on public corruption charges.)

I don't know what motivated Ferré to join the Higgins bandwagon. But he sure did, and with gusto.

As we drove to his place, I prepared myself for the shock of his physical appearance. He had personally confirmed what I had heard in whispers: that he had a rare form of cancer. I had heard he had lost his mane of hair to chemotherapy. This would not be the iconic Maurice Ferré; this would be a worn-out warlord.

When we arrived, the maid, Celia, planted a kiss on my cheek. "I love your son, like I used to love you" were her first words. Thankfully, Francis had always courted Ferré and treated him as his mentor and éminence grise. Clearly, the adversarial relationship in the elections of 1983, 1985, 1996, and 2001 was not a factor anymore. Ferré was on his way out, and he felt included by Francis in the new regime. My own courtesies of having him introduce me at my book signing and calling him the philosopher-king had erased a lot of bad blood.

The thing about Ferré is that he *is*, deep down a philosopher-king. Before I even met him, I had been told that his political bible was the same as mine: *Man and the State*, by Jacques Maritain. Unfortunately, his pragmatic side would often supplant Maritain's philosophies with Machiavelli's. And his other flaw was that he was, at heart, an elitist. How could an old elitist patrician support a naïve populist like Eileen Higgins?

My guess is that idealism creeps in the older and sicker we get. Ferré has a good heart. He missed the opportunity of a lifetime when his golden son, Francisco, died in a plane crash. A lot of that affection was transferred to my own son, also named Francis, who treated him as a father even as he opposed every crazy idea that Ferré brought to the Metropolitan Planning Organization, where he stymied us for about three years as we crafted the SMART plan, while pushing for more highways, tolls, and buses.

Ferré followed all the wrong policies when he listened to the Cato Institute and its faulty market view that highways ought to be taxed to build new highways, when in reality the taxes previously imposed are a burden on the middle class, and those taxes are used to support a big, bloated government full of bureaucrats who don't seem to grasp what the working class is enduring.

Unsurprising to us who engage in the politics of the county, Zoraida Barreiro's candidacy, as I mentioned, was built on her commitment to vote for a particular commission chairman in an election that would take place at year's end.

Ferré shared my concern about that deal; and it strengthened his resolve. I suspect that he also wanted to line up behind a good Democrat—in particular one who was an ally of his grandson-in-law, Florida State Senator José Javier Rodríguez.

The Friday before the ballots would be mailed ended on a good note. We had the two letters and the pictures and the signatures—scanned in Ferré's case and taken from a proclamation in mine. We'd had a bump in the road—the money to do the mail-out had not come in—but that was solved by Friday evening.

By Saturday we had the money. Mike Eidson, my biggest donor and a rabid Democrat, had come through. We were in business.

I called Higgins and told her, "Whatever else you are doing on Memorial Day weekend, cancel and monitor the mail-out. Ferré is loved by 25 percent of the *viejitos*, and I am loved by another 25 percent. (Of that 25 percent, I would guess 20 percent is because of Francis and 5 percent is my own.)

Whatever. I told Higgins: "Just make sure that mail piece goes out the same day the absentee ballots go out. And make sure it's first-class mail. And that it is delivered to the post office on Tuesday morning, first thing."

The message to the candidate was basically: *Do not delegate. Repeat: Do not delegate. Be there until those damn letters are received at the central post office in Doral. Take them yourself. Or call me and I will take them.*

This is what politics is all about. It's about being at the right place, at the right time, with the right message. It has almost nothing to do with theory. But it's fueled, if it's right, by the best of intentions. And we had those.

The reward for our efforts came a couple of weeks later. On June 19, 2018, the voters of central Miami and South Miami Beach elected a reform candidate to the county commission. In the process, two Miami dynasties (Díaz de la Portilla and Barreiro) suffered a sudden and unexpected setback.

And yet we had only twenty-four hours to celebrate.

The day after the election, the entire county commission (sans the newly elected commissioner, who had not yet been sworn in) voted 9–2 to extend the county's highway network into the hallowed western fringes. Worse, the agency in charge of that highway extension was none other than the MDX, which had tormented commuters with toll after toll after toll.

It was a sad spectacle—the epitome of bad government. I decided that something had to be done about it. Democracy requires that its true leaders raise their voices at all important moments in the governance of the region in question.

This was an important moment. This was the moment in which nine county commissioners went against every principle of good government and stuck their collective finger in the eye of the electorate.

It was time to accelerate that reform clock—lest the inertial force of decades of inept government crush the spirit of the electorate, of the people governed.

43

From Confrontation to Conciliation

et's go back before Higgins's election to September 2017. Neither Miami nor Miami-Dade had any kind of a working government. The mayor of the city and the mayor of the county were continuing their blood feud. Each wanted to trip up the other.

I have often used this kind of rivalry to push public policy initiatives. In the case of the city of Miami, when two of my commissioners were vying for prominence, I called it "internal creative tension." It was an effort to make lemonade when you were sold a lemon.

Or two lemons, in this case.

Miami in 2017 was a lot like America as a whole: divided, disconnected, despondent, and determined to make the politicians pay.

In the county, the rail expansion initiative was faltering. Mayor Gimenez had all but abandoned it.

In the city, Mayor Regalado was making life miserable for Francis, calling special sessions without consulting his commissioners to see if they could attend. It was particularly inappropriate to call together his legislators without first knowing if they were ready, willing, and able to meet and support a lame-duck mayor's grandiose plans.

Two of those special meetings happened right before Labor Day, when government is typically somnolent, resting for the budget hearings to come in September. I could see the pressure building on Francis. And here I was adding to the pressure by fighting with the county mayor over a $3.6 billion rail expansion.

We met for lunch midweek. I sensed the pressure on him. I had already decided the night before to work with the cards dealt to me. That there was no need to tilt at windmills, no need to be Don Quixote.

More than that, I had decided to snatch victory from the jaws of defeat, as the saying goes. Sometimes in life, and often in politics, you have to proclaim even the smallest victory. It isn't out of personal vanity; to the contrary, you do it out of a collective need to celebrate.

For half a decade, I had been the proverbial Don Quixote. Most of the time I had challenged Mayor Gimenez quietly and behind the scenes. That had ended after his reelection in 2016, when I began to go public and excoriate his trying to abandon the rail expansion plan.

To that end, I had reached out to the commission chairman, a *simpatico* fellow named Esteban "Steve" Bovo, to determine if he had thrown in his lot with Gimenez. Again, because of the Sunshine Law, I had to do this by convening a sunshine meeting with him and the chairman of the county's transportation committee, Bruno Barreiro. A fourth commissioner, Daniella Levine Cava, had attended, as well as more than twenty assorted staffers and lawyers.

It had not been a happy event. Cava, who was arguably the most progressive member of the commission (and the most marginalized), had simply stated her modest objective. "I am here," she said, "because I am worried about the cuts in the existing Metrorail/Metrobus system. The recent cuts in service, to save $5 million, are not acceptable. That's my most important priority."

Her statement was tantamount to defeat. Barreiro went next, and he was even more despairing. "I have come to the conclusion," he pronounced, "that the only feasible approach is pay-as-you-go." He was ready to walk out of the meeting, and it was like a death sentence to any financing plan— particularly coming from the chairman of the transportation committee.

It was everything I could do not to gag. I stammered, "Commissioner, that reminds me of an article written by the brilliant Cuban-American writer Carlos Alberto Montaner, where he described the presidency of Balaguer in the Dominican Republic." Balaguer, I continued, would wake up in the morning and call his treasury secretary and ask him how much money was in the bank. When the treasury secretary would answer that the republic had a balance of $1 million, he would immediately authorize a capital project for that amount. It sounded crazy, explained Montaner, but in fact Balaguer had completed more capital projects than any of his predecessors.

Balaguer and the Dominican Republic aside, it was clear that two out of three commissioners in my sunshine meeting had clearly bought into the mayor's minimalist approach to governing. I was only waiting for Chairman Bovo to make his position known. But he, for reasons I could not discern, was uncommitted, ambiguous, and wordy. He spoke of how the north and south corridors should now be treated as part of the "spinal column" of the county's mass transit system.

It sounded flowery and nice, but there was no mention of either rail or how to fund it. For a week or so afterward, I seethed with anger— interpreting his ambiguity as being equivalent to his having made a deal with the mayor. As a test of his loyalties, I pressed him on the issue of whether the east–west connector (reaching from the airport to the western fringes of the county) would be done with buses or rail. Here again he was noncommittal.

I left the meeting feeling not only that my quixotic lance was broken but that the windmills had sliced me in half. I was completing six years as a commissioner, coinciding with Gimenez's six years as mayor, and all we had to show for that time was a promise of more big, lumbering buses— not to mention more tolls to pay for them.

I vehemently complained to Francis, asking why he had not come to the sunshine meeting. He apologized and explained that he'd had some personal matters to which he had to attend on that day. He simply could not make it. I told him I was not sure I could do three more years of this.

But the anger and frustration were like passing clouds; Francis immediately came to county hall and suffused me with his own sunshine. It helped that he had started working out again and had a marvelous suntan. He pledged that after his election, he would give the county mayor an ultimatum: in effect, "Either get back on the train or we will do it without you."

I was mollified. The cavalry was on its way. A leader was about to arrive, in full mayoral regalia.

And he was my son.

Soon after the sunshine meeting, I attended, for the umpteenth time, a meeting of the countywide transportation planning organization's subcommittee. It was called the Fiscal Priorities Committee—a name that meant absolutely nothing to me, since I refused to be forced to prioritize the various branches of the rail expansion plan.

It was unusual for the chair of that committee, Dennis Moss, to convene a meeting during the August recess. But I didn't mind. I figured I would go through the motions, that I would be a good soldier even if the war would be lost.

At the appointed hour, Moss and I were the only two committee members present. Eventually, enough commissioners showed up for quorum. And then the fun began.

The executive director of this transportation planning agency, a very pleasant lady named Aileen Bouclé (which we had figured out rhymed with Bublé) did her best to explain the new financing plan. It consisted of shifting federal surface transportation funds, previously used for highway construction, to mass transit.

The plan was not artfully drawn or coherently explained. It wasn't so much that it fell on deaf ears as that it fell on confused ears. The climactic oxymoron came when Ms. Bouclé explained that the reassigned federal funds would count as a "local contribution"—meaning they would count towards state funds.

In other words, *we would be using federal funds as a local match to leverage state funds*! Then as added leverage, we were hoping to use the 50/50 state-to-local matching funds that Francis had negotiated during the prior legislative session.

Never had someone concocted a more artificial, more unintelligible, more blatantly deceiving shell game.

It rankled my sense of transparency. How would one explain this to the electorate?

I went home that night thinking this was a nonstarter. And then I saw the light: This is the best we've got. This is the optimal solution that can be obtained with this cast of characters. If so, why reject it? Why not go with the flow and claim a partial victory?

Why, indeed.

Great leaders like Martin Luther King Jr. and Abraham Lincoln were at similar crossroads and managed to act victorious, even when defeat was at their doorstep. The key for a leader facing almost certain defeat is to encourage the more timid souls in his or her midst to do heroic things, hoping against all odds that victory can be had.

The scene reminds me of the movie *Kingdom of Heaven*, when the crusading king of Jerusalem places his sword on a young plebeian and makes him a knight. It was time to make everyone a knight.

And it was also time to ride the biggest wave available. In this I was reminded of a scene from the life of former New York mayor Ed Koch.

Koch had turned a scene of pandemonium, defeat, and near anarchy into a magnificent symbolic victory.

How he did it is told in the next chapter.

44

Taking a Victory Lap

Sometimes my impatience with the bureaucracy blinds me. In this case, I was dealing with the proverbial double whammy.

Part of my problem is that I can't stand to deal with committees—except maybe committees of the whole. In other words, I am impatient when sitting as a legislator on a board that can only act collectively, but hardly ever does. I am even more impatient as a member of a subcommittee of such boards.

To be frank, it had never dawned on me that the Fiscal Priorities Committee of the countywide Transportation Planning Organization could be useful. I accepted the appointment because rejecting it was verboten. You just didn't do it.

I also did not put much stock in the bureaucrats who ran the various agencies involved in transportation. There were three of those: Charles Scurr, who managed an entity that received the half-penny sales tax and squandered a quarter-billion dollars a year; Aileen Bouclé, who managed the countywide transportation planning organization, which dealt primarily with federal transportation funds; and Alice Bravo, who managed the county's transportation department, with its half-billion-dollar budget.

As Churchill said, put them all together in a room and what do you get? "The sum of all their fears."

Not that it was their fault. The main fault for issues like this lies with the elected officials and the appointed board members of those agencies. They are the ones who have the fiduciary duty to the people. Unfortunately, they don't get paid, or they get minimal pay.

And for the most part, they don't have the technical know-how to battle the bureaucrats. And that was particularly true in this case, as the bureaucrats were armed with paid outside consultants.

Average citizens sense that the bureaucrats are overpaid and over-reliant on consultants. They sense that municipal government managers purposely overstate the technical complexity of what are classic services, none of which has changed much for half a century.

Yet the mainstream media buys into the myth, and so does academia. I have already given reasons why the media side with the bureaucrats; as to academics, I suspect that they profit from the consultancies. They are not about to bite the hand that feeds them.

But that is a topic for another book. Here in Miami, I had to work with the cards dealt to me. And they were, surprisingly, stronger than I had realized.

From Monday through Thursday of that week, I had gone from skeptic to true believer. The first phase of that awakening was realizing that the Fiscal Priorities Committee had some real significance.

It had not dawned on me until the chairman called the emergency meeting, which was set for September 6—the day before the county commission was to meet to vote on the $8 billion budget, and eight days before the countywide transportation planning organization was to meet.

I had asked my executive assistant, "Why the emergency meeting?" She had no clue, and neither did my legislative aide. They were probably afraid to tell me the procedural reality of things: Without a subcommittee approval of the newfangled financing plan, the entire project could not move forward.

Eureka! I realized that to these folks, these procedural niceties were important. As mayor of Miami, I had convened my five-member commission whenever I wanted and put on the agenda whatever I wanted. It was a simpler form of government, and it worked well despite the weak nature of the members of my city commission.

Here in the county, we had a weak mayor (though with strong-mayor powers); a disjointed, divided commission; and an even more dysfunctional countywide planning agency. Add to that a highway authority that derived a quarter-billion dollars a year in tolls, and a transit authority that divvied up a quarter-billion dollars in sales tax surcharges, and you had the perfect recipe for municipal anarchy.

Only a magician could bring us together.

Or rather, a duo of magicians.

Pondering all these things, I thought of something that Mayor Koch had done in New York to snatch victory out of the jaws of defeat. Or perhaps I should say to join the parade, making it look festive. Or to turn a liability into an asset.

The circumstances were a transportation workers' strike in New York, and the most effective alternative to taking public transportation across the George Washington Bridge, which connects Manhattan with New Jersey, was to cross it on foot. From the window of city hall, Koch was watching the hordes of commuters crossing the bridge and thought, "What am I doing here? I need to be where the action is."

And so he went down to the place where the bridge reaches Manhattan and started waving with his arms, as if inviting the people to cross it on foot. It was reminiscent of Moses parting the Red Sea, and the media caught the moment as such.

I was saying as much to South Dade state representative Kionne McGhee, who had been our emotional leader in the battle for rail. He promptly agreed that we needed to embrace wholeheartedly even this halfway measure.

"Sometimes you have to take a victory lap," he said, "even if the victory is partial."

The more I thought about that, the more I realized that victory laps are rare in politics. And they are important for the masses, who are fed a steady barrage of communal failures by the media.

In this case, it was all the more important to have a bright flag of optimism to usher in the new city mayor. I thought about that, and about Adlai Stevenson's eloquence after John F. Kennedy's death, when he lamented that we would never know "how different the world might have been had fate permitted this blazing talent to live and labor longer at man's unfinished agenda for peace and progress for all…"

In Miami, in the fall of 2017, it looked like fate would indeed give us a blazing talent as our leader.

It was time to rejoice, and then to get to work on our unfinished agenda.

But first, there was this little, meteorological event – of the kind that can bring make or break a municipal leader.…

45

Hurricane Irma

t is late September 2017, and there are just eight days left to qualify for mayor of Miami. Only one person has done it so far: Francis Xavier Suarez. He is the only person likely to qualify, unless there is someone who is willing to fork up a thousand-plus dollars for the privilege of being mentioned as the proverbial also-ran.

It is hard to put a percentage probability on that scenario. There are many, many people who have resided for the required period (more than a year) in Miami and who have a thousand bucks to spare to pay the qualifying fee and be listed on the ballot.

So it's really a crapshoot.

What is not a possibility anymore is that a formidable opponent will officially file in the next week. I have already discussed, in prior chapters, how the two most formidable ones (Raquel Regalado, the mayor's daughter, and Frank Carollo, the termed-out city commissioner and brother of Joe Carollo) had their potential campaigns derailed by events.

There is always the possibility that an unknown but very wealthy entrepreneur type (à la Michael Bloomberg) could challenge Francis. Such a challenger often rises up when the mainstream candidates become identified by the voters with a failed system of government. It tends to happen when there is a natural catastrophe or when crime is rampant, and a city simply becomes unlivable and unmanageable using the traditional Democratic or Republican policies.

None of that is a factor in Miami in late September of 2017.

And yet the beguiling question keeps popping up: Would it help for

Francis to have at least token opposition? On this day, just eight days from the qualifying deadline, a sister poses the question to me via email.

Earlier this year the same question was posed by none other than a national figure: U.S. senator Marco Rubio. He reportedly answered it in the affirmative, arguing that having some token opposition would allow Francis to publicize his plans and his persona.

I was not privy to that conversation. Had I been, I would have argued emphatically against.

I have always welcomed opposition when running for reelection, and I think that, as a general rule, it is good for the democratic process. But every rule has an exception, and these are exceptional times.

Let me elaborate.

A very practical issue comes up the moment one considers having to campaign beyond September 23 (the qualifying deadline): The campaign monies stored in political action committees (PACs) stay intact if there is no substantial opponent. The funds amassed (in this case in excess of $2 million, over and above the million dollars in regular "hard money" raised for the campaign itself) are then available for future campaigns.

Francis, as the proclaimed mayor-elect, and still having more than $2 million in the bank to support other candidates, would be a bonanza with no known precedent in municipal politics—at least in these parts.

It means that Francis could delve into any one of the two commission races that will also be on the ballot in November, and which will determine how strong his legislative coalition will be. Miami has a very small legislative assembly, with five members, and Francis is supported by all three incumbents whose terms are not ending in November.

They are merely reciprocating the support he has given all three (Ken Russell, Keon Hardemon, and Willy Gort) over the years. If the two new ones are faithful allies, then Francis will have a very solid commission behind him as he takes office.

He could strengthen the coalition enormously by appointing the most reliable of the three incumbents, or maybe even one of the two new commissioners, as chairman. (That would be totally within his power.)

He also could choose the new city manager without excessively consulting the commission, which could reject the appointment only by a four-fifths vote. Last but not least, he could greatly influence the appointment of the new city attorney, which is done by the five-member commission.

I was not able to do any of that in 1985, when I became mayor. The city manager was appointed by the commission as a whole, and they chose a likable fellow who was ethically challenged and not particularly competent. For three terms, I had to live with him as manager, which meant that he was the true executive; he made all the appointments, including those of police chiefs and department heads.

Francis would have much more executive power, and that would be added to having no opponent and a huge, mostly unspent war chest.

Having ample funds to support or oppose municipal candidates in 2017, and state and federal candidates in 2018, would enormously strengthen the new mayor's hand.

But that is not the gist of the reason that winning by acclamation is important. The gist of the reason is symbolic.

And the symbolism is growing by the minute, aided by the appearance and strength of Hurricane Irma. Whereas politicians can be brought down by unexpected natural disasters (think Chicago's 1979 mayoral election in which a devastating snowstorm led to defeat for the incumbent), Irma is doing the opposite: It is showing Francis at his best.

It was as if Francis was single-handedly taming the worst hurricane in the past quarter century.

The morning when the hurricane hits, when winds are still at near-maximum speed, Francis commandeers a SWAT armored vehicle and goes out to inspect two construction cranes that are dangling dangerously in the downtown area. I happen to be sitting inside my car, charging my iPhone, when I hear radio station 560 AM (the only one that I can hear well) interview Miami city commissioner Francis Suarez about the dangling cranes.

The interview goes something like this:

"Commissioner, what can you tell us about the cranes?"

Francis answers firmly and evenly, without much pause, "There are two loose cranes—or rather unattached cranes, as neither has collapsed entirely. We have asked all residents of the areas in question, which were evacuation zones to begin with, to abide by those evacuation orders. We have done so directly, knocking on doors of homes and apartment buildings."

The interviewer then asks the logical question: "Why were these cranes, if unable to absorb one-hundred-mile-an-hour winds, not required to be removed, given that we had clear indications of a hurricane of that magnitude, or even higher?"

Again, without hesitation, Francis answers, "We tightened all laws and regulations after Hurricane Andrew in '92; some, such as the regulations on cranes, were contested by the builders. In fact, that particular regulation is still being contested in court; it is currently before the Eleventh Judicial Circuit. After the experience of Irma, we will seek to tighten any loopholes that exist, and should prevail in court."

Francis goes on answering questions as to the likelihood that a detached crane could collapse only vertically down and not go flying horizontally to the immediate neighborhood. He prefaces his comments by saying he is not a structural engineer, which only gives him more credibility for not sounding like an expert on everything. (Not doing this is a trap that I occasionally fall into.)

In the end, it sounds like Francis has tamed not only the cranes but the hurricane itself. It is a Churchillian moment, reminiscent of when Churchill went to the scene of a London fire and helped to quell the flames before the real firefighters arrived.

Other scenes during and after the hurricane show Francis at the city's Emergency Operations Center (EOC), speaking and acting with authority that he technically doesn't have. The reason he sounds and looks more authoritative than he has a right to is that the mayor has been out of town during most of the action.

And so has the police chief.

Miami has a very complicated system of government, and it gets even more complicated during an emergency. When I was mayor during the 1989 civil disturbances, I ascertained that I could take over police powers, *but only with the consent of my other four commission members.* Today's government grants the mayor more power than I had then, since the mayor can appoint or remove the city manager at any time, and the manager can appoint and remove the police chief at any time. So, if there is any doubt as to who's in charge, the mayor can pretty much exercise plenary powers without consulting the commissioners.

But there is no mayor at the scene this time, and no police chief. Plus, the city manager and acting chief do not look or sound like major-city officials, by any stretch of the imagination.

So, a huge vacuum has been created, and Francis has quickly filled it. He is articulate in two languages, he is close to being declared mayor by acclamation, and he is logistically prepared in every possible way.

The most important logistical advantage he has over all other city officials is that he has been at the key location the entire time. Francis, together with his wife and three-year-old son, are staying for three full days at the city's EOC. They are even sleeping there.

Now, it must be clarified that not everyone can pull this off with grace. Not everyone has a supportive, attractive wife (Gloria) and a reasonably rambunctious but also reasonably well-behaved child. From day one, Francis's son (Andrew) has been in love with first responders; he thrives on wearing the gear of firefighters at every opportunity, riding their trucks at parades, listening attentively to their sirens, and so on.

Perhaps that affinity for first responders, or else the sheer activity of fifty adults in uniforms moving around with a clear purpose, is keeping three-year-old Andrew at peace.

The decision to have Gloria stay in town with Andrew was fraught with the usual personal considerations, which will remain confidential. Suffice it to say that getting them safely out of Miami was certainly considered. In the end, Francis and Gloria made the decision to stay, and to ride out the storm in the one location that not only was safe but was sure to have 100 percent communications capacity.

Francis, as you by now know well, is a great communicator. As I've said, he has the sunny disposition of Ronald Reagan and the self-deprecating style of JFK. But he can be grave when the circumstances call for gravitas. His eloquence in Spanish was recently on display after the death of Fidel Castro, and it is again during this hurricane.

Hurricane Irma is the "perfect storm" logistically to show a steady hand at the wheel. And it helps that *Herald* reporter David Smiley is also on hand at the EOC. And that he decided to follow Francis just when I joined him on a pre-hurricane patrol of senior centers.

Covering emergencies like riots and hurricanes is taxing for reporters. They don't have the benefit of drivers or vehicles that are ideally suited to go from place to place during such emergencies. Many of them also don't have the physical strength to go on patrol, as first responders do.

Francis does, and he used those assets to visit a couple of senior housing facilities that were in dire straits in the last pre-hurricane hours. Moreover, he capped the opportunity by inviting reporter Smiley to join us on one such patrol.

(I had joined him, in a supporting capacity, at the city's EOC; the county's own EOC was at the opposite end of town, and it had more commissioners there than one would want. They constantly appeared behind the county mayor at press conferences, looking for all the world like mummies in some sort of exhibition of Egyptian pyramids…)

The main destination on this pre-hurricane patrol was the Robert King High Towers, in Little Havana, with eight hundred residents. They had lost power even before the arrival of the high winds. This was not a good start to a hurricane.

Francis went into action. He communicated with the tenant's association president, Maria Campos, who was on-site and in charge, whereas the housing administrators were probably securing their own homes and nowhere near the senior center.

Luckily, a Florida Power & Light truck arrived on the scene as we were walking up five flights of stairs. We could observe it from a distance working to fix the broken transformer next to the facility. Smiley took a picture of Francis in a telling pose as he stood on the fifth-floor balcony pointing at the FPL lineman in the distance, as if he had made it happen.

In these situations, it is important for the politician not to take credit—to be self-effacing. Francis has that quality—which he probably inherited from me, since my engineering mind does not allow me to claim cause-and-effect credit for things that are not scientifically certain.

So his remark was candid and humble: "I hope no one believes that I made this happen, because I clearly did not," he muttered loud enough for Smiley to hear.

More important perhaps is the trait that he inherited from his mom: his sheer love of people. On the fifth floor was an Afro-Cuban family of about eight people sharing one little apartment. One of them was visiting from Cuba and remarked that Cuban public officials "did not mingle with the people" like we did.

All of them wanted pictures with Francis; only one or two of them wanted pictures with me.

Which was OK with me, to be frank. I shied away from the pictures; instead I did my best to take pictures of the scene. There's a reason for that: I am not photogenic, and Francis is enormously so. Not to mention that in this case, I am not going to be on the ballot in two months...

Besides, Francis is the protagonist in this scenario. It has been a quarter century since I was mayor, and it's his turn to shine and to lead us.

The final scene of Hurricane Irma takes place in Francis's neighborhood, as he is cutting off branches from a fallen tree. I tell the officers and a couple of aides (who are cautiously watching him from afar) a story. That morning, as we reveled in the aftermath of getting power to one residence (mine) and having three families sleep there and take showers for the first time in three days, I saw Francis showing the grandkids a music video.

As he did, he became teary-eyed, and I asked him why he was emotional. (This is not a strange thing in our family; we are all big-time criers, particularly in church when we hear hymns like "On Angel's Wings" and "Pescador de Hombres.") But this was a happy moment, and it was strange to see him cry. He told me, as he walked away, that the song was called "Feed the World" and that he kept thinking of the people who had no food.

That has been a very proximate reality in our city during this hurricane. The senior centers have cafeterias, and they feed the elderly two or three times a day. In a hurricane like this, when power is lost and delivery trucks cannot bring supplies, they cannot be fed by government or private agencies and must rely on relatives, the Red Cross, and donations.

After watching the music video, Francis was prompted into action, and by the end of the day had managed to supply a handful of senior centers— in particular the ones still without power—with hundreds of meals and thousands of bags of ice.

After I told the above story to one of his security squad, a Black sergeant named Wayne Tillman, he said, "I want to tell you a story of Francis. You probably saw a picture of him carrying two twin boys; they were African-American kids, and he was playing with them and with an older sister, who walked around with him holding his hand. Well, their grandma came and immediately expected the kids to jump into her arms, as she said they always did. But they did not; they stayed with Francis."

"Commissioner," he blurted out with enthusiasm, "the grandma said those kids never, ever take to strangers."

And then he added, "Your son is a natural."

46

Wynwood Camelot

As you have no doubt figured out by now, Francis did become mayor. Now it is about a month later, and the occasion is the fortieth anniversary of the priesthood of Father José Luis Menéndez, who is the epitome of the domestic missionary.

Let me explain.

"Domestic missionary" is my term for a celibate priest, nun, or rabbi, or a lay doctor or nurse, who chooses to work in the inner city, serving the poorest of the poor in our country. In Los Angeles, there is a Father Greg Boyle, who has basically adopted hundreds of wayward teenagers and given them a sense of direction and tough love.

In Miami, it is Father José Luis Menéndez. People like him are the sociological antithesis of "white flight." He is a tall, Caucasian, Cuban-born hunk of a man who could easily have been a lawyer, doctor, or politician. Give him a little money and put him in the running for Congress, and you have a sure winner.

But he chooses to live in a poor, crime-ridden neighborhood, where the church to which he is assigned is falling apart as the once wealthy parishioners move to the suburbs. Far from becoming entrenched in his big but bedraggled church, Father Menéndez decided to expand by building a handful of new, small mission churches, so that people wouldn't have to walk or drive as far to worship their God, which is his God.

Today he is celebrating his fortieth anniversary of priesthood, and the archbishop plus a dozen priests and nuns are present to honor him. I have been asked to introduce him, but in reality the ceremonial role in this priestly anniversary luncheon belongs to the newly elected young mayor, my son.

I have always thought that I am the main attraction. Even in the worst moments of my exile from politics, I figured that sooner or later, I would become the "big dog," the leader, the main man.

I have worked hard to be back at the top. I have fought the media, struggled to convince the big-money boys that I am still viable, picked fights with powerful special interests and bureaucrats who make life difficult for the working class, alienated elitists of the left and the right, and worked my way back to a position of being perhaps the most popular commissioner in a county of close to three million people.

But it's one thing to be a popular county commissioner and a whole different thing to be the most charismatic young mayor in the nation. On this occasion, Francis is not just charismatic but beloved. At this gathering in Wynwood, which is essentially a religious get-together of salt-of-the-earth Central Americans, a Polish archbishop who speaks Spanish and Creole, and the Cuban-born honoree (Menéndez), the unquestioned star is the young mayor.

That is as expected. He is the heir to a tradition of inner-city involvement started by me; the parishioners attending this celebration have memories of battles we fought to preserve and improve their neighborhood.

They particularly remember two near disasters.

One disaster was market-driven. Wynwood had for many years been the site of a parking lot for cargo containers. Occupying an area of about forty acres, these huge steel containers worked their stealthy way at night from the Port of Miami into the mostly residential neighborhood.

Miami's port is no small thing. It is the launching pad for about one-third of all the high-tech cargo that goes to the entire world from the United States. Besides being the world's largest passenger cruise port, it is one of the primary ports for high-priced, low-weight cargo. In other words, for appliances and computers.

That high-value freight comes in by cargo containers, and when the containers are emptied, they need to be stored somewhere. Wynwood became the storage site, and the rusting containers ended up stacked two and three high in the heart of the mainly Hispanic working-class neighborhood.

Leave it to an elitist politician, of Puerto Rican descent no less, to conspire against what was the largest Puerto Rican community in Miami-Dade. I refer to the debonair former mayor of Miami—Maurice Ferré. Hard to believe as it is, this man tried his best to enlarge the cargo container cemetery in the last year of my mayoral term (1993). But I was still mayor and had my people in place.

One of my people—perhaps the most effective community leader in all of Miami—was Father Menéndez, and he had important and disturbing news. Ferré, now a county commissioner in charge of seaport issues, had approached him with a deal: If Menéndez supported the enlargement of the container site, Ferré would donate $150,000 to the parish church. Menéndez, of course, said no. And then came the classic, materialistic query: "Just what amount will make you change your position?"

Menéndez told me how he answered Ferré: "There is no amount of money that will make me change my position. Period."

I attended the town hall meeting that was held in Wynwood; Father Menéndez had done his homework, and the community had responded. The crowd echoed in unison to the cry to preserve the residential character of the neighborhood.

And I had barely stoked the flames of resistance. Menéndez had done the organizing. And, in the process, we had upheld the principle of subsidiarity, which prescribes that all decisions reflect the will of the people most affected.

Wynwood, now rid of all cargo containers, became the venue for a new, shining commercial district called Midtown, around which were built residential towers. Historic neighborhoods in the periphery of Midtown could continue thriving, and hopefully could maintain their demographic composition and historic character.

That was one battle. The other one was a little more violent. It involves the arrest and subsequent beating death of a Puerto Rican drug dealer named Leonardo Mercado.

Mercado was not a Wynwood citizen in good standing, and he probably deserved to be roughed up for resisting arrest when police came to charge him with drug dealing in 1988. But his death from internal injuries sustained during what appeared to be a severe beating by the arresting cops caused a strong reaction in the mostly Puerto Rican community of Wynwood.

The civil disturbance that ensued brought back memories of the Liberty City riots of 1980. Mobs of angry youths again combed the community and refused to obey curfews. This time, two commercial sites were burned pretty much to the ground.

One of the businesses burnt was a shoe repair shop. And Father Menéndez immediately set his sights on making that the venue for a neighborhood rally that would eventually lift the spirits of the entire community. His call to me went more or less as follows.

"Mayor, the only local business that was seriously damaged was a shoe repair shop. The owner is a parishioner and good friend, and doesn't understand why his store was targeted. We are meeting there in an hour and would love it if you can attend."

I did attend, and it was a moving scene; the store had been looted, and there were charred remains of shelves and single shoes that had been left behind. But the place had been mostly emptied out, and there was space for a meeting of perhaps forty to fifty community leaders, including some youth.

Father Menéndez led us in prayer. He seemed to evoke the Bible's story of Jesus's resurrection, saying that the store would be rebuilt in three days. Then he surprised us by telling us that it would not be a shoe store, but a chapel.

And so it happened. It was perhaps a year later that I was invited to attend the first Mass in a small, brick chapel that had replaced the shoe store. Interestingly, there was a domed roof, but the chapel was missing large portions of the upper walls, where Menéndez was hoping to install decorative glass bricks.

In the meantime, the newly built chapel was exposed to rainstorms. It seemed as if Menéndez wanted to impress us with the urgency of raising what he said was a couple of thousand dollars.

Around that time, my law office was borrowed by filmmakers producing a Sylvester Stallone movie called *The Specialist*. As they were shooting the film in my office, a stone sculpture that had been given to me as a gift was broken. The movie producers offered to compensate me with insurance proceeds.

Since the rock sculpture had been a gift, I assigned the insurance proceeds to Father Menéndez's new mission church. But first we had to determine the value of the sculpture. Enter my wife, who promptly identified a local store that sold such rock sculptures. When I asked what the name of the shop was, she exclaimed, "Why, it's Art by God."

And so the little mission chapel got its decorative glass bricks and became reasonably waterproof. And Wynwood slowly improved, to the point that two decades later, in 2017, there are now no signs of civil disturbance or rioting youth; instead, there are revitalized parks and streetscapes, and there is a thriving business district called Midtown just to the north.

Wynwood is still being led by the same, charismatic priest, who has built a handful of mission churches. And Miami is being led by a charismatic mayor, who is heir to a tradition of walking and playing and praying in the poorest neighborhoods of the city.

And on this Sunday, gathered in a parish cafeteria for a gala lunch to celebrate the pastor's fortieth anniversary, a couple of hundred parishioners are pouring their love on me and my son.

Politics doesn't always have a happy ending. But if there ever has been one, it is on this Sunday, among these humble folks and their minister. A priest and sociologist named Andrew Greeley once described the collective feeling of faith that happens when people gather to celebrate a common, inspiring theme that lifts their spirits in a special way.

He called it "esprit collectif," using the French term. It is felt on this Sunday, at this gathering of mostly Latino parishioners. Two civic leaders of two generations who speak their language and share their faith are here to feast and to thank their religious shepherd.

And those two civic leaders—a father and son holding office in county and city, respectively—are being treated as part of the texture of the community that they have served.

The only question that remains is whether this collective spirit can be transferred to every neighborhood in Miami. On this Sunday, it seems an easy task.

47

Launching a Herculean Enterprise

D uring the 2017 holidays that ended the "year of Francis," I made a decision to run for county mayor. Before I did so, there was some flirting with a congressional race.

It happened that our longest-standing congresswoman, Ileana Ros-Lehtinen, had announced her retirement, to take effect in November 2018. The district had two features I found very tempting: It was almost an extension of my commission district, and it was the nation's most volatile one, in the sense that the congresswoman was a Republican but the district had voted overwhelmingly (by a 20 percent margin) for Hillary Clinton in the presidential election of 2016.

It was made for an independent like me.

Besides those favorable demographic indicators, there were other, more personal factors that pressed me to consider running there. There was this little thing gnawing at me that said it was time to head in a different direction. Being a county commissioner for another three years, until my term was done in 2020, didn't seem exciting. I was sixty-eight years old, and the idea of continuing in my present role well into my seventieth year of life was not too inviting.

For the better part of the fall and winter of 2017, I pondered the idea of being the single independent congressman in a House equally divided between the two major parties. I could imagine being the decisive vote in a chamber consisting of 217 Democrats and 217 Republicans.

How cool would that be? A member of Congress is one-fourth of 1 percent of the greatest deliberative body in the world, yet I would have a national voice. If ever there was a way to bring unity to Congress, this would be the one that was doable. I would simply have to win against a single candidate from each party, during a two-month general election, in a district where I already was a known commodity.

On the Democratic side, nearly a dozen candidates were vying for what would probably amount to no more than ten thousand votes. On the Republican side, it didn't really matter. The district was leaning heavily towards the Democratic side, and those not registering as Dems were registering as independent (technically, "no party affiliation"), to the point that the independents were almost one-third of all the voters.

There was something especially agonizing about the decision I was about to make. Put simply, it could be the final political decision of my life—particularly if I were to lose. I could see myself in November 2018, approaching age seventy, with all my political capital spent and all my PAC funds depleted.

In other words, I could see myself falling right back to the bottom of the political barrel, just as I had after being ousted from office by a court decision two decades before.

And this time I would be a lot older.

The other problem with running for Congress was that I would be abandoning Francis. I thought about the two Castro brothers from Texas who had served simultaneously—one in Congress and one as mayor of San Antonio. With that power base, one of them had made it to the cabinet, as secretary of Housing and Urban Development. But that stint ended, and then he disappeared, reducing the duo to a single entity.

As much as I hated to admit it, the presence of Joe Carollo (clearly the ultimate gunslinger) on the city commission made me hesitate to leave Dodge City. It was at about this time that a trial court ruled in favor of Carollo, denying his rival's argument that Carollo had failed to establish legal residence in the district.

By staying on the county commission and building up a strong financial base for a future county mayoral race, I not only would be supporting Francis with my county position but also would be grabbing the pole position as the front-runner for the immensely powerful county mayoralty. The more I thought about it, the more it made sense.

In the end, my decision to stay in my seat and start the Herculean effort to win the county mayoralty seemed a no-brainer.

Afterward, I couldn't believe that I had seriously considered running for Congress as an independent. What had I been thinking? That the two national parties would let me waltz into Congress from an urban region that had never elected a nonpartisan candidate?

Not only that, but the battle would have left me ideologically bloodied. Each party would have featured ads that would have knocked me out of consideration. The Democrats might have focused on my pro-life views. The Republicans might have targeted my stalwart votes against urban sprawl, or my refusal to go along with symbolic "urgings" like the one that opposed having a Cuban consular office in the county.

That particular vote and a similar one in Miami Beach are worth discussing, as an illustration that Miami politics still had a strong component of foreign policy. One must begin the analysis by noticing the way the issue was approached by the two municipal governments. Whereas the county commission passed a resolution rejecting the placement of a Cuban consulate within the county borders, the mayor of Miami Beach, joined by a Cuban-American commissioner, actually wooed the Cuban government into locating a consular office within the borders of Miami Beach.

Ironically, both governments acted improperly. The county should not have tried to dictate foreign policy by impeding consular services within its borders for people legally wanting to travel to Cuba—particularly since many, if not most, travelers were visiting Cuba for humanitarian purposes.

As for the Miami Beach officials, it was unseemly beyond comprehension for municipal officials to prostrate themselves before a brutal totalitarian regime in an effort to bring a problematic consular facility to a city already chock-full of less controversial businesses and attractions. In both cases, the city and county elected officials were pandering to a particular voter base—conservative for the county and liberal for Miami Beach.

And in neither case was the actual business of governing advanced.

I was as well known and well liked as any of the potential candidates for the county mayoralty, and was the only one of all of them who was fiscally conservative, a social justice progressive, and a well-respected environmentalist. Heck, I was the only independent commissioner in a county with more than 600,000 registered Democrats, 400,000 Republicans, and 500,000 independents.

And I expected to have labor on my side.

How important is labor? Let me explain. Winning the county mayoralty involves two elections.

The first election takes place in late August and has the feel of a primary. Often it is not decisive—particularly when the incumbent cannot run again because of term limitations. When that happens, there are as many as ten candidates; four of those are usually viable.

That means a runoff, which happens when no one gets a majority of the votes. And the runoff is in November, coinciding exactly with the presidential election.

Here's what that means. In the August election, the turnout is in the 25 percent range, meaning about 350,000 votes. In the runoff, when the voters come out *en masse* to choose a president, the total can exceed a million. That's the amazing ratio: *Three times more voters come out in November than in August.*

Now let's get back to the August election. The people who vote can be divided into two classes. One class is the faithful "super voters"— the mostly elderly absentee-ballot voters, who automatically receive their ballots in the mail. The other class is the "stakeholders."

There are two subgroups of those. One group of stakeholders is composed of the public-sector unions (and their relatives). In Miami-Dade, there are close to one hundred thousand union members who work in government, with thirty-five thousand of those being county employees and another forty thousand being school board employees. (The rest work for cities, the public hospital, and various branches of state and federal government, and for the state attorney and public defender.)

If the unions are not with a candidate, and the elderly Hispanic absentee voters aren't either, there is little likelihood that the candidate will make it to the runoff.

Then everything changes. The August election is retail; the November one is wholesale. Furthermore, the first election is nonpartisan, whereas the second one is colored by partisan allegiances.

But first I had to reach the run-off. And thus, as the 2018 calendar year began, my task was fundraising.

48

The Politics of Fundraising

After I decided to pass on the congressional race, it was time to get started on the county mayoral effort. And that meant fundraising. Political fundraising depends on a handful of factors. In no particular order, they include the ability to tap existing relationships, the ability to create new ones, constancy of effort, and salesmanship.

Underlying the entire effort as a precondition is the perception of viability. In order to launch the ship of funds, the donors have to believe that you can win.

It should have been relatively easy for me to win. I had been the mayor of Miami. I was a reasonably well-liked and extremely well-known commissioner from a wealthy district. And my son currently was the mayor of Miami.

But I did have a problem of perception, and it was rooted in my past record of running penny-size campaigns. The most notable of those was in 1996, when I ran for county mayor and was out-financed and outpolled by no fewer than three candidates. And by a big margin.

That faux pas had been bred by stubbornness. In a county with almost one million voters, I had tried to run for mayor with a couple of hundred thousand dollars. Starting off tied for first in the polls with another former Miami mayor (Maurice Ferré), I faded out of contention when my three major opponents financially outperformed me by factors of 2–1, 3–1, and 5–1.

The candidate with the 5–1 advantage was a charismatic new major player in the county named Alex Penelas. Everything about Penelas, including his name, was smooth. He was a smooth talker, a smooth dresser, and possessed of smooth manners.

He was Marco Rubio before Marco Rubio: boyish face, quick wit, likable to the core.

And he overwhelmed us all with his fundraising, which had a narrow but powerful base, as it tapped deep into the industrial city of Hialeah, whose business magnates had long yearned to have one of their own as the golden boy of countywide politics. All of a sudden, it seemed like every wealthy entrepreneur in Hialeah had a stake in Penelas. The city didn't have too many multimillionaires, but it had enough millionaires to finance their favorite son.

I learned a valuable lesson in 1996: Countywide races require major fundraising. Now, two decades later, it was time to test my ability to tap existing relationships, create new ones, and display effort and salesmanship that were up to the task.

I have never lacked constancy of effort. And I assumed that by now, I had enough existing and potential relationships to tap into.

And I am a decent salesman, when given a forum for my ideas. The problem for me in political fundraising is that applying salesmanship to political connections is uncomfortable for me, to say the least.

For all but the most idealistic of donors, the sales pitch has two components: the likelihood that you will win, and what you will do for them if you're elected.

I do pretty well with the first of those, and I did particularly well with it in the immediate aftermath of my son's winning the city mayoralty with 86 percent of the vote. Doors opened to me quite easily, as I soon found out.

What was not so easy was marketing myself once I was inside the plush corporate offices or elegant restaurants where I would be giving my sales pitch. (As a general rule, the super-wealthy took appointments in their office, over coffee or catered lunch, whereas the more moderate millionaires enjoyed being invited to lunch at a place where they could be seen with the candidate, in a pose that showed who was wooing and who was being wooed.)

I could handle both settings with ease. I knew the world of business generally, and the business of doing business with government, which many of the donors were involved in.

The problem was closing the sale, which often required making promises. An ethical politician can make only one promise: to be accessible. But not all access is equal. The classic saying around these parts, which is cynical but true, goes like this: "Those who give you early money get front-row seats at city hall. Those who come with late money get second-row seats. Everyone else gets good government."

Donors who give early money, in sizable amounts, expect a special kind of access. The automobile mogul Norman Braman fits the mold of this type of donor.

Dealing with billionaires like Braman is worth a chapter.

49

How to Woo a Billionaire

Over the years, I have dealt with many wealthy people. Early on in my career, I dealt with Joe Robbie, who was the multimillionaire owner of the Miami Dolphins. In those early years, I also rubbed elbows with the up-and-coming class of ultrarich Cuban Americans, including two whose presence or legacies have lived on till the present.

Those two are Armando Codina and Jorge Mas Canosa. Both made their fortune in construction—the former in classic real estate development projects and the latter in utility infrastructure.

Dealing with the super-rich is always an exercise in two virtues: patience and humility. It is also an exercise in figuring out what makes them tick.

I consider there to be three main types of multimillionaires: the classic philanthropist, the classic entrepreneur, and the civic activist extraordinaire. A special type is the ultrarich civic activist who splits his energy between domestic and international affairs.

Such was the case with Norman Braman.

Braman and I go way back to 1983, when he decided that Miami's then mayor, Maurice Ferré, was too divisive to be the mayor of a polyglot city. Ferré had defeated Cuban-American firebrand Manolo Reboso two years before, in 1981, in an election characterized by racial accusations.

That year (1981) marked the high point of racial politics, as Reboso's Bay of Pigs buddies inflamed Spanish radio with talk of having a Cuban mayor, and Ferré countered on Black radio, using firebrand radio commentator

Les Brown to harangue the Black community with tirades about how Reagan would control Miami if Reboso were elected.

It was Cubans against Blacks, with the Anglos sandwiched between the two warring sides. To their credit, Norman Braman and Armando Codina both decried the racial politics and vowed to support an alternative to Ferré in 1985.

In 1983, when I met Braman, Codina had not yet broken ranks with Ferré—perhaps thinking that both sides had been equally responsible for the racial fireworks of 1981.

Braman had other reasons for wanting to oust Ferré, whom he considered a tax-and-spend liberal who had no clue as to how to run a city. (He was right on that point; in every major public project, Ferré's administration was characterized by inefficiency and cronyism.)

So Braman adopted me and proceeded to fund my campaign with maximum contributions from approximately fifty different corporations that he owned.

We were getting along famously until the Ferré campaign started a Black-audience radio war on Cuban Miami. Using the voice of popular radio host and community activist Les Brown, Ferré broadcast harangues that painted the prospect of my election as an outright takeover by the Reagan White House.

It was blatantly racist, pitting Republican Cubans against Democratic African Americans. And it was totally out of sync with reality, as I was a progressive independent, with no intention of implementing Reaganomics at the local level.

Braman was rightly incensed by the divisive tone of the ads, but he was also convinced that they were working. He was worried that they were not only fueling a higher turnout among Blacks but also influencing liberal white voters to support Ferré. His recommended strategy? To air the Les Brown ads on mainstream radio stations that catered to the average Anglo voter.

I didn't like the idea at all. I was embarrassed by the racial tone that the campaign was taking on and wanted to totally defuse the tense atmosphere. Plus, I thought airing those ads to Anglo audiences might just have a counterproductive effect. So I avoided the constant calls by Braman, figuring it was good to avoid a confrontation with my principal donor for a few more days, until the election was over.

But Braman tracked me down and suddenly confronted me with a very difficult dilemma—a threat, really. He said that if I did not air the ads, he would convene a press conference and ask for his money back. I knew there was no legal way he could force me to air the ads—and no legal way he could force me to return his contributions. Yet I also knew that he would use the opportunity to criticize my campaign and make me look like a total political amateur, as well as a hapless tool of a billionaire activist.

In the end, I caved. Braman said he would air the ads with his own money if I was unwilling to do it with my campaign funds. I sensed trouble all around me, and deep inside I made a decision that would affect the next two decades of my political life: to avoid the ultrarich donors and sink or swim with small donors.

I thought I could win at the game of modern politics by relying on grassroots support rather than lobbyists or millionaires. And it worked for a while, as I managed to win my next three elections. I became mayor of Miami in 1985 and was reelected twice fairly easily—in 1987 and then again in 1989, when the mayoral term was lengthened to four years.

It was my own personal "Era of Good Feelings," when politics seemed simple and pure. All you had to do to stay afloat was to keep your nose clean and pursue the public interest with verve and a little bit of luck.

After eight years at the helm, I retired from politics with a view to spending more time with my growing family.

By the time I surfaced again, in 2011, Miami politics had been changed pretty much along the same lines as national politics. The game had become much more dependent on money and media, and less dependent on the masses.

Thankfully, there appeared in my life a new billionaire, whose help propelled me to power in a sudden, unexpected special election.

His name is Armando Codina, and wooing him was easy.

Like Braman, Codina did not need government to make him rich. Or at least he didn't need it anymore.

Codina comes from upper-crust Cuban stock, but he made his money here in America by sheer entrepreneurial skill. I don't think he has a college degree.

He started off managing medical practices and later became involved in classic Miami real estate development, where he is the epitome of his own definition of a developer. He likes to say that a developer is a *"come mierda* [lightweight] with credit."

On his way to the top of the real estate heap, Codina hired Jeb Bush as his deal-meister; the relationship with Jeb and his father undoubtedly brought Codina to new business heights. He soon found himself on the board of major companies like American Airlines and Winn-Dixie.

During my "wilderness" years (1998 to 2011), I made it a point to stay in touch with Codina. I would schedule a meeting from time to time and would bring a sketch of one project or another—typically with a view to connecting Miami's downtown with its northern suburbs by activating the railway line owned by the Florida East Coast Railway, of which he had become a major stockholder and joint-venture partner.

On one visit, he said to me, "You know, Xavier, I have to tell you that you look so well settled, so *tranquilo* [calm], that maybe you ought to continue practicing law and stay out of politics." I was pleased that he didn't contrast the quiet life of a Miami lawyer with my somewhat turbulent political history. But he went on, and it got better.

"Having said that, if you ever aspire to political office, I will help you."

I carried that promise with me until an opportunity arose when the mayor of the county was recalled and the commissioner from my district resigned to run for that office in a sudden-death special election. It was 2011, and it was the largest municipal recall in the history of America.

My friend Norman Braman had funded the recall of the mayor and one commissioner. And the race to fill those positions was scheduled to take place in a mere forty-five days.

Whenever there is a sudden, unexpected election, you need two things: name recognition and a campaign war chest.

Knowing that a big war chest would be necessary, and having such little time to raise it, I called on Codina. It took a while to persuade him to do a fundraiser at his house, which is the classic residence run by a housewife—only ten times bigger.

Pressed by me to allow a fundraiser at his house, Codina ultimately acceded, though he had some clear conditions: Only thirty people could attend. Each should be committed to bringing $5,000.

To emphasize the magnitude of this concession, Codina added, "Look, Xavier, the only political events ever held at my house were for people whose last name was Bush. You will be the lone exception."

I was happy with the conditions, figuring to raise the tidy sum of $150,000 in one evening. But I never expected the thirty-person rule to be implemented as strictly as it was. Codina's secretary would call me on an almost hourly basis to name the people invited. Couples counted as two people, not one. The sitting mayor of Miami, Tomás Regalado, asked to be invited, but he was dating someone and that would mean two slots of the thirty. I had to tell him no.

Codina's lawyer, John Shubin, called him and said he had heard of the reception and wanted to come and support me. Codina's answer was clear and succinct: "You are welcome to come if you bring a five-thousand-dollar check!"

I think the only guest who did not bring any money was Anthony Kennedy Shriver, and I suspect that being of Kennedy "royal" blood was enough to be allowed in without the donation. But a lot of people were surprised, and not a little miffed, to find out that they were not allowed to bring partners or associates—let alone spouses—without a large check.

So it goes with the super-rich. They have their quirks, and you'd better get used to them. It's a bit humiliating to deal with them, but not nearly as painful as dealing with the professional donors. These are the lobbyists and clients who do business with the county.

Relying on the contributions of professional donors is almost a necessity, unless you are rich or so deeply established, so well known, so immune to negative attacks that you can bypass them and thus avoid what is called "pay to play."

50

Pay to Play

Miami is now a big city and Miami-Dade an even bigger metropolis. Combined, their budgets exceed $10 billion, and they control a major downtown, a large port, and an airport. Their daily population is close to three million people.

We are big-time, and to be mayor of the city or county, you'd better be prepared to woo those who do business with the local government. It is obviously not the way things should be, and no self-respecting politician would contend that it is.

The practice is called "pay to play." In short, it means that the companies who seek county contracts or rezoning of their properties feel compelled to make sizable contributions to politicians who will be voting on their projects or contracts.

It is about as clear a conflict of interest as you can get.

The influence of those with money at the national level has been a factor since the middle of the twentieth century, when John F. Kennedy was bankrolled by his father, the former U.S. ambassador to England and Wall Street financier Joe Kennedy. It was a far cry from what had taken place a century before, when Abraham Lincoln rose from log cabin to the White House by sloshing through Illinois debating a senatorial opponent named Stephen Douglas.

American democracy was not always so earthy. In my book *Democracy in America 2010*, I quote prominent historians for the proposition that the founders of America, in their eagerness to protect the people from a monarchy, did not bother to protect them from the rule of moneyed aristocrats. And, of course, the framers of the U.S. Constitution were mainly wealthy landowners.

In Miami-Dade, the money factor came into full view with the election of Alex Penelas, who was the first golden boy of county politics, succeeding the affable, hard-drinking Stephen P. Clark. In the 1996 race for county mayor, Penelas outstripped three other well-known figures (Arthur Teele, Maurice Ferré, and yours truly), with a barrage fueled by close to $2 million.

By 2016, that figure had been dwarfed by Carlos Gimenez, who spent close to $6 million to win his election for a second full term. Like it or not, if I was to become a serious player in the 2020 race for county mayor, I would have to raise a couple of million at the very least. The reason for that figure is that I have always reckoned that a well-prepared candidate who has a proven track record and no skeletons in the closet can outperform a less able candidate even if outspent two or three to one.

A heavyweight boxer with small gloves should win the fight over a lightweight with big gloves.

Even so, I had to bite the bullet and do some serious fundraising. And the best place to start (really the only place to start) was by tackling those who did business with the county.

Right off the bat I realized that I had one big problem: I had voted against the biggest players. Let me list those cases, more or less in chronological order.

My first negative vote was in relation to moving the Urban Development Boundary (UDB). This was a legal constraint that prohibited any kind of commercial development beyond the borders of what is mostly dry land into what is mostly wetlands, on the western boundary of the county.

By holding the line on the UDB, I alienated the biggest developers in the county, including the huge homebuilder Lennar plus individuals like Sergio Pino, Jackie Soffer, and Bob Easton.

Similar land-use votes on which I sided with the neighbors against the developers put me at odds with rum mogul Facundo Bacardi and the wealthy owners of a charter-school network, Fernando and Ignacio Zulueta.

As if having the biggest developers against me wasn't enough, I also had the misfortune of ending on the wrong side of two major sports franchises: the Miami Dolphins (football) and the Miami Heat (basketball).

Those two are worth a separate chapter—particularly when discussing two other billionaire entrepreneurs who sought to do business with the county.

51

The Mega-players and the Local Politician

D ealing with sports franchises and other supersize entrepreneurs is perhaps the best test of a local politician's mettle. Presidential candidates have to deal with gun and abortion advocates, religious zealots, the ACLU, and what Dwight Eisenhower called the military-industrial complex. Local pols deal with billionaire land developers and owners of football, basketball, and baseball franchises—as well as their rivals, the environmental activists.

The enviros use social media to convey their priorities. The mega-entrepreneurs use campaign contributions, but also something even more powerful. They use the threat of a major attraction moving to another city.

The Miami Heat is an established NBA franchise that finagled its way into a bayside sports palace that is the envy of any professional basketball team, ensconced as it is between the spectacular Biscayne Bay and the most desirable tropical urban downtown in the world.

When the Heat first manipulated us into building them a new arena, almost two decades ago, downtown was an embryonic residential area with maybe twenty-five thousand residents. Now it is a bustling mini-city with about a hundred thousand residents, most of whom have enormous purchasing power and spare time. The Heat owner (cruise ship magnate Micky Arison) negotiated a very favorable lease of the new $200 million sports palace by the bay over a decade ago. It was so favorable that after fourteen years of occupancy, the county had not received one penny from the profit-sharing formula.

But that wasn't enough for the Heat. These guys wanted another sixteen years of favorable lease terms. So they pressured us to renegotiate the lease midway through its term. The reason? Well, there really was no reason whatsoever, but they had to make up one, so they used the implicit threat of taking the team to another city.

Who on earth would buy that story? Well, a majority of the thirteen county commissioners did. How ridiculous was the story?

Think about it. Here's a franchise that has won three world titles in twenty-five years, that has the legacy of Shaquille O'Neal, Alonzo Mourning, LeBron James, and Dwayne Wade, and that still has the sport's most famous and glamorous coach (Pat Riley) as president.

Here's a franchise that has an established brand, a great track record, and a perfect venue. Why would they even consider leaving the city that is the international crossroads of the Americas and thus the perfect platform for the sport that is competing with soccer for the world's attention?

Why, indeed.

I made these points to the Heat's lobbyist. His answer will astound you. When asked why the Miami Heat basketball team would want to renegotiate such a favorable lease just halfway through its term, he said—in what has to be one of the most condescending, elitist statements of all time—that the owner (Arison) wanted "to secure the legacy to his son."

Imagine that! In one short sentence, he encapsulated the economic inequality in modern American society. On one side you have a billionaire owner and, on the team, his twelve multimillionaire, ergonomically gifted employees, most of whom never finished college. On the other side you have the masses, the working men and women who cannot afford to attend a single game and who are wondering how to pay for cable TV that used to be free and for tolls on highways that used to be nonexistent.

My reader might rightly ask, "This inequality is just a sliver of the problem of economic disparity in America; since it favors African-Americans, who make up the bulk of the athletes, why make a big deal of it?"

Yes, my reader, except that professional sports franchises are monopolies protected by government from the application of antitrust laws. They also are subsidized in two key ways: by public financing of their facilities and by free use of each city's brand.

In other words, the Miami Heat not only gets public waterfront property on which to build an arena; they also get to use, exclusively, the name Miami for their product. That means an automatic brand identification with the residents of a metropolis that numbers close to three million folks.

The leverage enjoyed by the owners of the basketball and football franchises in Miami is also bolstered by the popularity of their superstars. When the vote on the Miami Heat's lease extension came up, the owners were not present; they were represented by basketball icon Alonzo Mourning. When the vote on the Miami Dolphins' use of public funds for their stadium's new roof came up, the owners were nowhere in sight; they were represented by Hall of Famers Jason Taylor and Dan Marino.

Mourning, Taylor, and Marino are so popular that if they ever decide to run for mayor of the county, it would be hard to defeat any of them.

And so my colleagues voted for both the new lease (for the Heat) and the new roof (for the Dolphins). I voted against both—thereby pretty much waiving any possibility of financial support from those two powerful local businesses, as well as from their billionaire owners.

Not only that, but I basically distanced myself from what is in many ways our biggest source of community pride. Whereas the mayor of New York or Philadelphia can be seen prominently at the basketball and baseball games, basking in the glory of what has become America's number-one mode of entertainment (sports), the mayor of Miami is lucky if he or she gets to participate in the festivities accompanying a world championship in any of the three leading sports.

That doesn't keep my colleagues from trying their hardest to grab some of that glory. Their antics are worth at least one vignette.

52

How It Took Twenty Dignitaries to Honor an NBA Champ

n 2013, the Miami Heat won the NBA championship. They were crowned world champions in a sport watched almost as much as *fútbol* (soccer). Kids throughout the world know and admire basketball icon LeBron James. Only a fraction of those kids know who Joe Biden is.

I had been elected county commissioner two years before the Heat won the NBA championship. It is an American tradition to have a big parade in the downtown area of the city whose team wins a major sports championship. And so we had one in Miami, with a crowd big enough to populate a medium-size city.

The parade culminated at the sports arena, which was filled with perhaps eighteen thousand fans. The highlight of the parade was gifting the keys to the city to the team president and players.

In most major cities, the gifting is done by one person: the mayor of the city. In Miami, which has thirty-four cities and a county government, the number of dignitaries who wanted to share the limelight was embarrassing. I counted twenty: twelve county commissioners, one county mayor, five city commissioners, one city mayor, and one city manager.

If I had attended that ceremony, it would have been a cool twenty-one. When they named the county commissioners, they read out my name. But

I was just watching on television at home—anticipating some faux pas or another. Hell, the whole thing was a faux pas!

Inside the arena, there were other fun distractions. One involved a city commissioner (Frank Carollo) who insisted on carrying his newborn onto the stage for the key-giving ceremony. (I was told later that the kid had to be given back to the mother.)

In the meantime, another county commissioner was just champing at the bit. This rotund fellow was the chairman of our sports committee; naturally, he was convinced that he was a big-time sports impresario.

I knew better. I was sure that none of the Heat players, none of the Heat executives, and perhaps not even the owner had any idea who this guy was. But the poor man was convinced otherwise, and he made sure he was the last of the twelve commissioners present to greet and hug Pat Riley.

The optics were not good for him. Riley is about a foot taller than this guy and has an athletic build, whereas the commissioner is shaped more like a billiard ball. So when the last of the twelve shorter commissioners finally reached Riley, it must have seemed like a never-ending repetition of nonentities paying homage to the king.

The worst part is that the poor commissioner was sure that Riley would recognize him and hug him. But that was not to be, as Riley simply gave him the stiff arm and held him at bay.

It reminded me of Jason Robards in the movie *A Thousand Clowns*. Except that the clowns in this comedy numbered twenty.

This was not an isolated instance of ceremonial matters being at the top of the county's priorities. From the first day I stepped inside county hall, I realized that for these folks, activities such as giving a proclamation or honoring a thirty-year employee or a state high school sports champion were the most important functions of a commissioner.

Those ceremonial events often took up the first two hours of a commission or committee meeting. It was truly unnerving for me, since they pushed back the business of running a county with twenty-seven employees and – as of 2020 – almost $9 billion in combined operating and capital budgets. With scores of citizens, business owners, lobbyists, media, and county administrators in the chambers, we would award little plaques to a handful of long-term employees, and each presentation was preceded by speeches by at least one or two supervisors plus one or two family members, and finally by the employee.

This happened with each of my three committees, and those met each and every month. It would also happen, on a bigger scale, whenever a high-level administrator was retiring; in this case it would be at a full commission meeting, a meeting of the transportation planning organization, or a meeting of any of the other boards of which I was a member.

In those cases, the mayor would sing the praises of the retiring bureaucrat; that bit of ceremony would be followed by each commissioner's sharing stories of the retiree with the adoring masses. Then, at the next commission or board meeting, a whole new ceremony would take place, with a whole new set of commendations and speeches for the replacement.

And those were just the inside ceremonies. Outside ones involved foreign dignitaries, sports figures, musical icons, and business moguls. For a while after I was elected, there was an internecine battle between the commission chairman and the mayor over every ceremonial matter.

In Miami, we get a lot of distinguished visitors, and each one who asks for one gets either a key or a proclamation. Getting a key is tricky only if the dignitary has a spotty past (such as baseball player Jose Canseco) or a problematic ideology, such as leftist leanings or a cozy relationship with Communist Cuba.

Getting a proclamation signed is also logistically complicated.

Here's why.

Instead of having a proclamation signed by the mayor or the commission chairman, each one is signed by the mayor, the chairman, and all twelve members. The county comprises a total of 2,400 square miles, and the thirteen commissioners live in every corner of it. Signing proclamations—particularly during a recess month like August—is therefore expensive.

One time I was staying in Miami Beach during August and received a call from one of the three sergeants-at-arms. These fellows provided security for us during meetings and were used by many commissioners as chauffeurs. Besides those two tasks, they were in charge of getting the proclamations signed.

It was a bit unnerving to get a call from a police sergeant over a holiday weekend only to be told that I was being located to affix my signature to a proclamation that could easily have been signed by a signature machine.

The ceremonial grandstanding, coupled with the lengthy and convoluted speeches by commissioners during the business part of each meeting, wore me out as I approached my seventh year on the board. What surprised me is that no one else seemed to mind.

It's a lot like Congress. Each member of Congress is beloved in his or her district due, in great part, to doing ceremonial ribbon cuttings, attending Fourth of July picnics, and receiving constituents in the exalted halls of Congress; yet as a group they are detested.

I suspect, though I never saw an actual poll, that the county commission as a group was not supported by much more than 10 or 15 percent of the residents. That would be in line with the approval ratings for Congress, which hover in the range of 10 to 15 percent. But commissioners are beloved in their districts, just like members of Congress are, even though collectively they are detested by the general public.

As the summer of 2018 approached, I was wondering how I could stomach another two years of service in what had become a totally feckless institution. Moreover, it was an institution run by an uninspired bureaucrat who had full executive control of more than four thousand managers and the full acquiescence of a dozen commissioners, whose idea of a good day at work was honoring a high school team or a thirty-year employee in the well of a chamber that would have pleased Louis XIV.

Then I realized that, like it or not, the commission was on the verge of being completely replaced, as term limits would kick in for half of the board in 2020, and the rest in 2022.

If I could win the mayoralty in 2020, I would have not only the full executive power of this huge, local government but also a whole new commission within two years.

All I had to do was put together a slate.

53

Slate Politics

In 2020, Miami-Dade had an opportunity for renewal that few cities or counties will ever have. In that year, not only would the county have a new mayor, but roughly half of its legislative assembly would be replaced by new blood.

In other words, the people of this huge, prosperous, blessed-by-nature metropolis would experience a total changeover. This historical coincidence naturally would excite any purist; but Miami-Dade had few purists at the time.

Instead it had a new commission chairwoman, Audrey Edmonson, who began her tenure by lamenting the fact that her colleagues had been "termed out" and that a whole bunch of institutional knowledge would depart with them. Imagine that!

Term limits were imposed by the electorate precisely because they are fed up with the municipal legislative assembly. It is an extreme reform measure – typically applied only to executive officials.

In general, it is a maxim of political science that executives (presidents, governors, mayors) should serve no more than eight years, while legislators (like members of Congress) can serve indefinitely, since their power is dispersed, diminished, and discrete. Legislators generally are many and are Lilliputian in terms of power but are long-lasting. Executives are few, powerful, and short-lived.

Miami-Dade residents have chosen to change that conventional distinction. Henceforth, county commissioners have a short tenure. Eight years is enough, said the voters! Some of the commissioners had been in office for sixteen or even twenty years. Now all county commissioners are limited to two terms.

The charter change took effect in 2020, coinciding with the end of Mayor Gimenez's term.

This was unprecedented and fortuitous for me. It simply meant that henceforth, all we had to do was pick the winners in the various commission races and win the mayoralty. Presto! A whole new face for the county's government.

I tend to be impulsive, and my first impulse was to endorse candidates in all the open seats. I did that before even announcing my own candidacy for mayor.

Of course, the first impulse is not always perfect, as we shall see.

I have a pretty good eye for politically viable candidates. Or at least I thought I did. Knowing that five commission seats would be open due to the term limits, right off the bat I identified five candidates to support.

Some advisors heavily criticized my idea of a slate. They worried when I first announced my proposed endorsements of five candidates for the open seats.

They screamed bloody murder when I confided that I was ready to announce an additional three endorsements: two for candidates for seats being vacated midterm by mayoral candidates (Daniella Levine Cava and Jean Monestime) and one for an incumbent seeking reelection.

My advisors cringed at the idea that I would endorse not five but eight commission candidates—including one who would replace an incumbent whom I had previously endorsed!

They saw the X-Man going wild. And I suppose I was that, but there was method to my madness.

Even a quantitative method.

Here's the way the numbers would work, according to my advisor. He argued: "If you support candidates in eight seats, that means somewhere in the vicinity of twenty-five candidates, of which you will turn off seventeen whom you don't support. Those will do everything in their power to oppose you."

"Good point," I admitted. "But see this: In at least five of the districts in question, I am supporting a prohibitive favorite. In the other three, it's more of a free-for-all. Let's analyze those."

One was the above-mentioned predominantly Black district, where the early favorite (Gilbert) was no longer a prohibitive favorite, or even a favorite at all. His opponent was quoted in *Time* magazine, for God's sake! She is the mother of Trayvon Martin and supposedly would have Whoopi Goldberg on her side. Her opponent is *pesado* (Cuban slang for "obnoxious").

The other district had an incumbent whom I had supported in a special election less than two years earlier. She was a disaster. And the former commissioner in that district wanted to come back. He was a moderate Republican, a nice man who could be counted on to support the SMART plan and, in particular, Baylink.

Around this time, in the summer of 2019, Mayor Gimenez screwed up royally and gave us one of those political "gifts that keep on giving." It had to do with the mentioned rail connector between downtown Miami and South Miami Beach.

The screwed-up proposal by Gimenez was delicious in its combination of bad elements. It contained something for every demographic to hate, as we shall see.

It was hated by the good government folks for its lack of transparency, by the free-market folks for the advantage it gave to a Chinese-government-owned transit monopoly, by the anti-gambling forces because it favored a big casino company, and by anyone with common sense for its disjointed, unharmonious components.

The local entity that drove the bad deal proposed by Mayor Gimenez (Genting) was purportedly a Malaysian company, but its stocks were traded in Hong Kong and its joint venture partner in this bid was a company controlled by the Chinese government.

Moreover, Gimenez had negotiated an unsolicited bid in secret, and it failed every test of logic, including the simple matter of national security: At a time when China was threatening America with aggressive military and predatory trade policies, why would we allow one of its government-owned companies to take over an important rail linkage that would lie right next to the world's largest passenger port?

Indeed. The deal stunk, in every respect.

Almost as illogical was another deal put together by the county administration at about the same time. It concerned funding for a new civil courthouse.

54

The Courthouse Deal

By late 2019, as my term was coming to an end and the mayoral race was heating up, the county administration cooked up a strange deal to build a much-needed courthouse.

The need to replace or repair the existing downtown courthouse, which was home to more than forty judges, was evident. The stately courthouse, built almost a century before, was in need of serious repair, particularly its interior. Electrical and plumbing systems were falling apart, and rusty, exposed rebar gave a clear impression of danger to the more than five hundred courthouse personnel and the more than a million litigants, lawyers, witnesses, and jurors who traipsed through this august facility every year.

The courthouse had not been designed to maximize space. Its upper floors, resembling Mediterranean edifices, thinned out as they rose into a quaint tower, to the point that the upper floors were quite small and not suited for courtroom use.

As is typical of bureaucratic executives, Mayor Gimenez's first proposal was for a super expensive facility that would cost the better part of a half billion dollars. Working with the administration, the commission chairman, and the other lawyer on the commission (Sally Heyman), we tweaked the mayor's numbers down to about a quarter-billion dollars.

The proposal of borrowing for the project via a general obligation bond, or GOB, was then put to the voters. These borrowings are constitutionally required to be approved by the voters, since the debt so financed is paid by a tax that supplements the regular tax for operations, which cannot exceed 1 percent of the value of one's property.

In effect, the Florida Constitution wisely limits the power of local governments to exceed the 1 percent tax on real property, which is actually close to 3 percent because the local school board and the cities also have a 1 percent maximum each.

Add the county's 1 percent to the city's 1 percent and the school board's 1 percent, and you get the maximum taxable amount for operations. GOBs, approved by the voters in a referendum, add to that.

Unfortunately, the voters rejected the GOB by a substantial margin. And so the county did what all frugal governments with common sense should do in that situation, which is to see what existing facilities could be used or modified for use as courtrooms, right?

Wrong. The administration did no such thing. It simply resorted to yet another bureaucratic sham, which needs to be explained, due to its esoteric character. While the bureaucrats concocted their sophistry, I did my best to propose a sensible alternative.

Let's discuss that.

As an alternative to more debt, I proposed relocating to the existing courthouse the mayor's office, the county attorneys, and most of the other bureaucrats from the majestic twenty-nine-story structure which had been built to house them, in Class A space (called the Stephen P. Clark building). This was not a particularly novel idea, since the courthouse had been the original office space used by the mayor and other high-level administrators.

Then I proposed selling the entire Stephen P. Clark building to the private sector, leasing back only such space as was absolutely needed for other county functions. In pursuit of that plan, I had an informal appraisal done of the Clark building and found out it could sell for about $200 million.

Under my plan, the county would use the proceeds to fund the new courthouse—or rather courthouses, since the idea of having not only the circuit courts (with jurisdiction over cases involving more than $15,000) but also the county courts (with jurisdiction over cases involving less than $15,000) all located downtown made no sense whatsoever.

No one listened to my plan. Instead, the powers that be ignored the rather clear voice of the electorate, which refused to be obligated by a quarter-billion dollars' worth of new bonds.

So what did the powers that be do? You won't believe it. It is so devious, couched in such blatant sophistry, and blessed by such unprincipled lawyering that it must be explained in some detail.

The term of art is a "covenant to budget and appropriate."

55

The Artful Dodger and His Bureaucrats

I t's kind of unfair to call Mayor Gimenez the Dickensian "Artful Dodger" for the devious way in which he avoided abiding by the will of the people. The man is not Machiavellian enough to concoct this kind of legal scam; he's simply not equipped, by intellect or creative instinct, to challenge the bureaucrats and their supporting cast of county lawyers – the group to which many commissioners constantly refer to as the "best law firm in the world." (In my view they are solid enough attorneys, but they are themselves classic bureaucrats – with guaranteed incomes and the kind of job security that precludes any kind of bold or creative thinking.)

As mayor, Gimenez was faced with a clear need for a new courthouse, a host of exalted judges (including the chief judge), a well-known and respected clerk of the courts and a legislative assembly of thirteen county commissioners, none of whom wanted to alienate the judiciary.

That combination of eminent public servants is hard to resist— particularly when they are clamoring to solve a real need. Gimenez was between a rock and a hard place. His electorate did not want to tax itself to build a new courthouse, and his exalted, downtown constituency wanted (and deserved) one.

So he became the proverbial Artful Dodger.

The artfulness was provided by the bureaucrats and their very compliant lawyers. The legal dodging came in the form of the previously mentioned "covenant to budget and appropriate."

What the words mean is clear: an agreement to take on long-term debt that will be paid from successive budgets. In other words, what the law calls a "general obligation," which ordinarily must be approved via public referendum, somehow morphed into a long-term obligation to budget using future tax revenues.

Any way you look at it, it is a sham.

And Gimenez forced it down the throats of the entire board of county commissioners. It was hard for me to swallow, so before the final vote came, I did two things to clear my conscience. One was to engage in private discussions with the county attorneys and make sure they were relying on valid judicial precedents as to the constitutional validity of covenants to budget and appropriate.

The other thing I did was to refrain from grandstanding. I simply did not speak during the proceedings. It was an example of what we pray when we use the famous words attributed to St. Francis of Assisi: "God, grant me the serenity to accept the things I cannot change, the courage to change the things I can, and the wisdom to know the difference."

Trying to explain to the public why our vote was a subterfuge, an avoidance of the legal obligation to get voter approval for a general obligation, was simply not practical. Angering the entire legal establishment by voting against the much-needed courthouse was not advisable. And so I kept quiet and longed for the day when a more logical, more clearly legal, fairer solution could be fashioned to meet needs of this magnitude.

In the meantime, while the county's mayor shepherded his meek commission, the city's commissioners were not so meek.

56

Mutiny on the City Commission

Francis had weathered the 2018 storm rather well. He had become a national figure, featured prominently in print media (*AARP the Magazine*, *Men's Health*, and even *Time*, the latter of which selected him as one of the next generation's top one hundred personalities) as well as on television and radio and in social media galore.

Being featured favorably in the media and enjoying a remarkable economic upswing, the city's mayor presumably could ride the wave nicely for the next couple of years. Unfortunately, his commissioners mutinied.

And what a mutiny it was. As expected, it began with the bad boy of Miami politics: Joe Carollo. The man has no shame. Even though he himself had recently been cited for breaking the law a total of five times in doing home improvements without permits, he now accused the city manager of doing the same thing.

It is hard to believe that a man who has been a high-ranking military officer, a National Security Council staffer, the head of the entire Immigration and Naturalization Service, and the director of Miami International Airport, and who was now the city's manager, would cut any corners to get a simple backyard deck repaired.

But that was the accusation, and it was followed by a supporting chorus of other disgruntled commissioners, who felt that Francis was ignoring them. Facing a mutiny by three of his five commissioners, Francis decided it was time to name a new city manager.

But he took a little too long, and for about a month or so the city commission was back to the days when it had gained a reputation as being like a banana republic, with confrontations and sudden adjournments of commission meetings, bickering that bordered on fistfights, and every kind of accusation hurled between the chairman (a Francis ally) and Carollo.

For a while, there was more rancor and less civility at city hall than in the U.S. Congress—despite the impeachment trial going on at the latter.

The Carollo saga is now in its fifth decade. Bad guys usually don't last that long, unless they have absolute power, like a Castro or a Kim Jung-Un.

Imagine a Joe McCarthy clone being active in municipal politics for more than four decades. It couldn't happen, in part because the media, which emphasize the negatives regarding their elected officials, would publish and rehash every transgression, every hypocrisy, and every vulgarity by the official.

But the *Miami Herald* has, for some unknown reason, occasionally fallen for Carollo's witchcraft. It did so in 1997, when it endorsed him for mayor of Miami, convincing a court to overturn my election and almost destroying all semblance of the good government I had brought to Miami during the prior decade.

The *Herald* also danced around Carollo's follies again for a brief time in 2014, when Carollo became city manager of suburban Doral. He almost destroyed that city, until the mayor and commissioner ousted him.

And the *Herald* tried to mollify him when he used every kind of slur and demagoguery to get elected to a city commission seat in Miami in 2017. It really begs the question: Why does a respected newspaper, with a substantial investigative staff and smart, experienced, and presumably fair-minded editors, keep feeding the monster?

I have no answer. It's for others to ponder.

57

Francis Quells the Mutiny

It didn't really take much to quell the mutiny. All Francis had to do was jettison the embattled city manager and find one who was acceptable to three members of the city commission.

He did much better than that.

On a "Super Monday" in February, Francis, as mayor of the city, announced his pick for city manager. Here, the process was as important as the result; the optics were as important as the substance of the decision. In a master stroke of strategy and timing, Mayor Francis won the media war and, in the process, gave the impression of strength where others argued he was weak and cornered.

Under the city charter, the mayor has two weeks to present his choice of city manager to the commission for ratification. Francis set it up for a one-two punch: He announced the appointment at the break of day and immediately sent his appointee to face the city commission, duly assembled to vote on his appointment, in the chambers below his office.

He knew, of course, that no commissioner could afford to vote against the man whom he had chosen, because they knew that the votes were there for ratification. More importantly, he carefully choreographed the optics. Having announced his choice, he refused to answer questions from the media until the vote had been taken.

Never has something so transcendent been decided so quickly, ratified so quickly, and discussed with the media so quickly. It was a true fait accompli.

In one fell swoop, the commissioners went from being a disorganized, bickering, and mutinous bunch to looking like five meek acolytes waiting for the mayor and/or his new city manager to hand them some goodies.

Francis followed that bit of legerdemain by inviting the new, roguish commissioner, Alex Díaz de la Portilla, to Paris.

I have different names for Alex, as my reader knows by now. I have called him the Rasputin of Miami politics. But I have also called him a lovable rogue. Whereas Carollo is a hateful rogue, DLP is a fun guy to be around. He doesn't always put the common good ahead of his own prerogatives, but he doesn't forget the common good entirely.

Deep down inside, DLP senses that if he sinks the commonwealth, he will go down with it. He is a totally different animal than Carollo, who is happy going down with the ship, as long as the story of the sinking ship leads off with his name.

As it happened, Carollo's ship was sinking on its own. The recall movement against him was gaining strength, just as the lawsuits against him were piling up. (Altogether, he had three lawsuits pending; each alleged misfeasance, abuse of power, and illegal conduct.)

Carollo has historically played the judicial system in his favor. In 1998, as I've previously explained, he convinced an appellate panel to undo an electoral defeat (which I had won convincingly in a run-off); more recently, he convinced a trial judge to rule that he had complied with residency requirements even though his utility bills showed no use of electricity in the claimed residence. But it's tough to defend yourself against three sets of lawyers who have evidence of wrongdoing, as well as against a recall movement that alleges the same basic wrongdoings as the lawsuits.

At the end of the second decade of the century, Carollo's reign of terror was coming to an end, just as the ascendency of Francis Xavier Suarez was gaining momentum. There are no guarantees in politics. Carollo's being in retreat and the Suarez dynasty's ascending, as the first quarter of 2020 came to an end, augured well for the Miami dynasty.

But before we finish our story, we must discuss the global pandemic. How Francis and I navigated it and how we somehow avoided a major battle with the alarmist media and the do-nothing county mayor is worth a chapter.

58

Coronavirus Episodes

The pandemic arrived at the beginning of Francis's third year of a four-year term. It had the traits of a true, novel epidemic—unexpected, unknown, uncharted. For reasons I might never fully understand, the reaction of the nation was pure hysteria.

It was called coronavirus, or COVID-19. The number at the end does not designate the virus's place in a sequence of similar viruses, but rather the year in which it was detected.

Everyone agrees as to its source: a region of China called Wuhan. Within a month of its appearance, the virus began spreading to the rest of the world. By the beginning of March 2020, it was spreading fiercely into Europe and more hesitantly into the United States.

March in Miami is a month of festivals. The big two before the pandemic were a musical festival called Ultra and the Miami equivalent of Mardi Gras, called Calle Ocho. Between the two of them, they would attract an estimated four hundred thousand people from as many as a hundred countries.

Mayor Francis moved quickly. He canceled both events, which were held within the city's boundaries. County mayor Gimenez initially took a contrarian view; he criticized Francis's decision as being premature.

Soon Gimenez was backtracking. In less than a week, he went from criticizing Francis to canceling county events, then to imposing a curfew on clubs and bars, and then to closing all hotels, restaurants, and other businesses except for "essential" services such as government and medical, plus grocery stores and drugstores. In a county whose largest nongovernmental work sector depended on visitors, the closing of hotels and restaurants was tantamount to putting over a hundred thousand people out of work.

Neither Francis nor I was consulted as Gimenez went from shutdown skeptic to shutdown champion. Then something happened that changed Francis's outlook: He tested positive for the virus.

It is hard not to take seriously an epidemic that hits that close to home. Within twenty-four hours, all public officials and security personnel who had come in contact with Francis had been tested for the virus and had tested negative.

It made one wonder how the virus could be so contagious.

Soon after Francis announced that he had been infected, it was clear that he would barely suffer any real discomfort beyond the kind of congestion one might experience from a mild cold. As the only politician with a confirmed case of the virus, he quickly became a national television figure. Only the president and his entourage, plus a couple of governors (Gavin Newsom of California and Andrew Cuomo of New York), appeared as often.

But only Francis did appearances in two languages.

In the meantime, Mayor Gimenez kept putting out executive orders.

Here in paradise, we love to say that we foster neighborhoods that are the best places to live, work, and play. Sometimes, when I speak or debate before a religious crowd, I say "live, work, play, and pray."

By the time Gimenez was finished signing executive orders, many in Miami could not work, could not play, and could pray using only electronic means. Jesus had preached that he would be present where two or more were gathered in his name. Pretty soon, under the county mayor's mandate, gathering—along with work and play—would be limited to the home.

The top governmental leader in the county became obsessed with the idea that he could control what became known as "social distancing." Police, who ordinarily enforced laws prohibiting violence or theft, now were dedicated to keeping people from doing business or having fun.

I myself was supposed to "self-quarantine." Typically, in any kind of crisis or widespread calamity, I take to the streets. Living in a high-income neighborhood (Brickell), where I luckily could buy a cheap unit in the oldest building around, I otherwise would not notice firsthand what the working class was enduring.

But even in my Brickell condominium, a waitress (who was a unit owner) told me that she had been laid off. She had no immediate prospect of reemployment and was just surviving on meager savings, hoping for the restaurant to reopen.

And I knew, of course, that the number of unemployed in our county would soon reach into the tens of thousands. What to do in a situation like this? I didn't have that many options.

As a county commissioner, I had been ignored by my own county mayor; as the father of the city mayor, who had the virus, it was hard to take lightly what other government officials, and almost every medical professional, were predicting—which was doomsday.

I was sure that the doomsday scenario was a horrendous exaggeration that would have horrific consequences for our leisure industry. But it was tough to argue against the combined persuasive power of the mainstream media and the political class. It felt like any politician who minimized the crisis, who delayed imposing the most draconian measures, might end his or her career.

The executive orders being signed by the county mayor technically had a short duration—seven days. I could insist that the county mayor put them to a vote each week before renewing each shutdown order. But there were legal and logistical problems. Legally, I could not consult my fellow commissioners privately; I had to do it in public. Logistically, I could not meet in any location with more than ten people. And there were thirteen commissioners, plus a county clerk, a county attorney, and at least one member of the executive branch.

Mayor Gimenez, as the famous saying by former Chicago mayor Rahm Emanuel goes, could not "let a good crisis go to waste." And, of course, he had no feel for the suffering of the working class.

So the chief executive was exerting plenary powers, while the legislators were quarantined or unable to convene, and the local economy was tanking.

And what about the church? Well, the good archbishop of Miami, with a flock of over a million Catholics, had closed the churches to the faithful and waived the Sunday-mass obligation. We had suddenly become a city where you could not work or pray, unless you had a ready computer and the ability to work or pray from home.

But what about playing? What about recreation? What about enjoying the wholesome benefits of Miami's excellent beaches and parks?

Oh no, Mayor Gimenez said, the parks and beaches are closed. Only the boats and the marinas were open.

That exception lasted just long enough for the television stations to show footage of wealthy boaters frolicking in Miami's gorgeous bay, connecting boats to one another for further interconnection and fun. A quick executive order plus some marine patrol boats ended that merriment for the upper classes.

Even so, inequality in Miami, which was already quite pronounced, became that much more pronounced. Members of the upper-middle class enjoyed their pools, the condominium complexes enjoyed their gyms and tennis courts, and the lack of commuters on the street meant that the cyclists enjoyed the sunny, breezy, and well-landscaped roadways that graced tony urban neighborhoods as well as suburban enclaves.

And no one worried much about the hotel, restaurant, and shop workers who lived from paycheck to now nonexistent paycheck.

Besides the temporary measure of providing funding support to displaced workers, the looming battle was over when to end the shutdown of the economy.

The battle lines to some extent depended on political philosophy. Liberals, for reasons I have never fully understood, seemed to be pessimistic about the health-care crisis at hand. Conservatives tended to be more optimistic.

And as the saying goes, there is the truth, there are lies, and there are statistics. A month or so into the health crisis, we could only hope that the draconian measures taken would not end up costing more misery than an epidemic that seemed (so far) to strike only a small percentage of Americans and cause the death of only a tiny percentage of those infected.

I watched and analyzed statistical trends on an hourly basis. I posted as much good news as possible without hiding the reality of the growing number of people who had the illness. Statistically, our local reality began to diverge from the reality of New York, which undoubtedly is the news and financial center of the world.

Unfortunately, the media focused only on New York and Italy. Both appeared statistically as exceptional cases, in the sense of numbers of people with the virus. But that was a distortion, for New York had very few deaths in relation to people infected (less than 1 percent), whereas Italy had over 8 percent.

All of those numbers were too much for the media—let alone the politicians. When New York City hospitals seemed overwhelmed with critical cases of the virus, one of my fellow commissioners (Daniella Levine Cava) sent the mayor a memo expressing her concern that Miami would soon be in the same circumstances. Apparently, she had not paid attention to my tweet in which I had given the total number of hospital beds in the county with virus patients as thirty.

That figure was infinitesimal in a county where the total number of hospital beds (public and private) was close to ten thousand.

But the specter of New York, or Italy or wherever, was all that made the news. The media downplayed the fact that warm-weather countries, including almost all in South America and Africa, had practically no fatalities, or that industrialized countries in Europe and Asia were quickly treating successfully almost all infected by the virus.

Miami needed a young mayor to come out swinging from his own contagion. He was looking good in quarantine; he needed to look good at city hall and put a positive light on Miami's recovery.

Our economy was a time bomb. God willing, we would soon see the leveling of fatalities. It was already happening at the local level, helped by the sun and the salty sea.

It fell upon me to remind my son of something he had once said to me: "Dad, try to get some sun every day; it's good for you." His mother, who took her self-quarantine much more seriously than I, had started taking long walks, with resulting improvements in her health.

I wanted to say to Francis, "Son, I can't get any sun if you sign an order telling me I must stay at home." Correction: "I can, because we have an open deck in my condominium, but many people don't have decks or any space in which to grab the loving rays of the sun."

And I wanted to add, "God gave us a paradise so that we can show the nation how to balance a health crisis with an economic crisis. Lead us without fear, or exaggeration, but always with an eye to those most vulnerable in society."

Roll forward to the middle of summer of 2020 and the heart of the pandemic.

59

An Election-Year Pandemic

t was July Fourth, 2020, and the novel coronavirus seemed determined to keep its grip on our city and our country. The rivalry between Mayor Gimenez of the county and Mayor Suarez of the city continued unabated.

Francis was getting the best of Gimenez—and it wasn't close. The young Miami mayor, in fact, had taken the nation's airwaves by storm. He was a regular on *Good Morning America*, CNN's *Cuomo Prime Time* and *The Situation Room with Wolf Blitzer*, and other Fox and MSNBC programs.

He also did National Public Radio, which transmits to every little radio station in every corner of the nation. He had become America's mayor, thanks to a combination of his heroics in dealing with the coronavirus and his effective handling of the protests after the George Floyd incident.

That incident deserves a more expansive narrative. It came smack in the middle of a summer of discontent in America, almost as if the gods wanted to punish us all one more time over historic inequities in the treatment of people of African descent.

The killing of George Floyd by a white police officer, who put a knee to his neck while the man was handcuffed, was broadcast repeatedly to a horrified nation. I probably saw the cruel act no less than twenty times, watching in awe as three other officers did nothing to save Floyd's life.

The nation erupted into demonstrations of protest, under a triple theme: (1) police brutality towards Blacks, (2) inequality of economic conditions between Blacks and whites, and (3) defiance of authority. Across the nation's big cities, the protests were more organic than those of

1968, when the civil rights movement and opposition to the Vietnam War blended under a cadre of leaders and organizations.

This time, the protests were spontaneous and mostly peaceful, yet they were often marred by radicals and an occasional looter or band of looters who showed cruelty towards the business owners who resisted.

For Francis, it turned out to be another opportunity to display both his leadership and his empathy. By the second day of demonstrations, he had mastered the delicate balance between tolerance for the right of free expression and the need to protect people and property from the freewheeling, own-the-streets tendencies of the Miami protesters.

The first day was not so felicitous. Demonstrations that day centered on the police department itself, and the police were not ready for the randomness of the protests or the tendency to take to the streets—and even to the elevated highways that converged in downtown Miami, as if the protestors were part of a huge hand whose fingers touched down in about five different places.

Due to faulty logistical planning, and maybe an underestimation of the size and aggressiveness of the protests, a couple of police cars were set on fire, which brought back memories of Miami's worst riots, going back to the 1980s.

By the second day, Francis had regrouped and guided his troops in what I later called the Muhammad Ali "rope-a-dope" tactic, which lets the adversary appear to have free rein to hit you (or in most cases insult you), while you back up and rest against the rope that holds you up. Then, when the opponent is hitting a constantly disappearing target, the very rope that stops you acts as the spring that jolts you forward for a counterpunch.

That Sunday of the first week of the protests, Francis passed the test of leadership. He showed up right at the front lines of the protests, engaged some of the leaders in dialogue, and offered his personal cell phone number. This offer was carried live on Facebook and effectively showed Francis as a leader with empathy galore.

Later that same day, when the protesters tried to storm the police lines and do some physical damage to those in authority, he led his troops in a much more unyielding approach that included some armored trucks, equipped with deafening sound devices and blinding lights (a sort of new-age, nonlethal field artillery) and accompanied by a phalanx of officers on bicycles, who charged the most threatening protesters and then quickly formed a horizontal phalanx that regained control of the front line.

It was finely executed, devoid of brutality, and effective. That neat execution was followed by a curfew; in the end, the protesters went home, and there were few arrests and no injuries to people or property.

By the end of June 2020, Francis had earned his stripes in both racial confrontations and an epidemic that had decreasing mortality rates but was increasing in infectious transmissibility.

In Miami-Dade, it seemed like everybody had a young relative with the virus. But few except the very old or infirm were dying, and those were hidden in long-term-care centers—where no one could visit them—or at home in a secluded part of the house or their own quarters.

The intra-county rivalry of mayors subsided, as county mayor Carlos Gimenez seemed to accept a secondary role as communicator and city mayor Francis Suarez accepted a secondary role on the minutiae of how people should act in public places.

In the meantime, I was just a few days from what was either the last 120 days of my career or a new beginning in which I could—for the first time—have direct control of a county with a $9 billion budget, twenty-nine thousand employees, and a bully pulpit that could be easily shared with my more charismatic son.

60

The County Election 2020

As I write these lines in the summer of 2020, I have a good but also uncertain feeling. There are only ten days between now and the day the first voters will be receiving their absentee ballots. For all practical purposes, the election is about to begin, even though the official date is forty days away.

As a general rule, Miami-Dade has a high dependency on vote-by-mail ballots, also known as absentee ballots or, more typically, ABs. That's been the norm now for about three or four terms of Congress and reached a crescendo in the last midterm primaries (2018).

This year, the trend of AB-intensive voting is surely going to reach another peak, at least in the first round of balloting, held in August. That round will contain very little that is exciting, since the world is awaiting the November election that will pit Donald Trump against Joe Biden.

But that's conventional wisdom; this year, there is a new variable that should increase the AB dependency. That is the fear of infection from the second round of coronavirus that is plaguing Miami. Voters are requesting absentee ballots in droves. And the county has reinforced the trend by sending no less than seven-hundred thousand applications for ABs in a recent mail-out; the ABs require no return postage and very little effort in terms of providing identification and filling out forms.

And so in ten days, we will begin voting. The expectation is a 20 percent turnout of the 1.5 million voters; of those, as many as 60 percent—and maybe even 75 or 80 percent—will vote via first-class mail.

Using sophisticated data banks and coordinated phone and computer tracking, we are doing our best to "chase" the likely absentee-ballot voters all the way from the Election Department to their homes and back. As we do this, we are getting some sense of how this key demographic, consisting of about 180,000 people, sees the race.

We have had what feels like a zillion Zoom and in-person debates. But nothing unusual happened at first. The pundits would say that the needle had not moved much.

Then came the big one, hosted by Channel 23, which is the nation's largest Spanish-language network. And it was a doozy!

To begin with, the network went crazy with buildup and staging. The stage used was the one for what is perhaps the most-watched Spanish television show nationally, *Sábado Gigante.*

We were asked to show up two hours early, presumably to put on make-up, do mic checks, and work out the logistics of what was billed as a live mayoral debate for a full ninety minutes on prime-time TV.

Providentially, the logistics favored me. I drew the number three from a hat—which would place me roughly in the middle of the stage, given that we had six candidates. And it got even better when one of the less-known candidates withdrew, leaving five of us—and me right smack in the middle of the stage.

I started off weak, with an opening that wasn't exactly a barn-burner. My main opponent, Alex Penelas, is well rehearsed in using talking points that are timed for exactly one minute, and one minute is what we got for our opening.

About halfway through the debate, things got interesting. The moderator asked me to comment on the use of the "half-cent" transit tax, consisting of a 0.5 percent tax on all sales. As I described earlier, the half-cent tax was supposed to fund a whole new rail system, and the critique was that it had been misspent on operations instead of capital improvements.

I answered the critique by bouncing it back to Penelas, who had "invented" the tax, and then pivoting to my two colleagues on the commission, who I said had misspent it. Both comments were fair; neither was inflammatory. *But inflame they did.*

Penelas, using his thirty-second right of rebuttal (since he had been mentioned) agreed with me as to the misspending; furthermore, he quantified it, saying that Daniella Levine Cava had misspent $500 million and Esteban Bovo had misspent a billion dollars of the revenues.

That set off Bovo, who pivoted in a totally different direction, accusing Penelas of being corrupt and making his friends rich with airport concessions that were not competitively bid on. For a second there, Bovo seemed to have the upper hand.

But Penelas counterpunched viciously, saying that Bovo was the corrupt one, who had benefited from contributions tainted by a scandalous $15 million lobbying contract given by Venezuelan leftist strongman Maduro to Bovo's friend and ally, former congressman David Rivera.

By the time he was finished blasting Bovo, Penelas had managed to associate him with a socialist dictator, an indicted former congressman, and a $15 million lobbying scheme that stunk to high heaven!

The fisticuffs between Penelas and Bovo would go on unabated past that debate, well into the last weeks of the campaign. It was hard to figure out why they were concentrating on each other. It was equally hard to figure out why most of the negative attacks ("hit pieces" in the lexicon of politics) were leveled at the three other principal candidates (Levine Cava, Penelas, and Bovo), but not particularly at me.

As I look back on it now, the entire campaign was hard, if not impossible, to understand. The main reason is that it involved circumstances that were unique throughout the entire history of our county—and arguably of the nation.

Let me explain.

As the military saying goes, the generals are always fighting the last war, and this saying applies particularly well to the 2020 county mayoral election. Every war and every election are unique, and this one was no exception.

In the case of the county mayoralty, the uniqueness was "many-splendored." Multifaceted. The election had many variables, which made it difficult to fathom, let alone predict.

Let me try to elaborate without boring my reader.

Miami-Dade County is unusual in a couple of important respects. It is probably the largest county in the nation whose mayor is elected in a bipartisan way. The mayoral election is held every four years and coincides with the presidential election.

But not entirely. The election of county mayor takes place during the state legislative and congressional primaries—typically in late August. If no one obtains fifty percent of the vote, then the runoff election for mayor accompanies the November presidential election.

I don't know of any county in the nation that has this peculiar timing. Add to that the fact that Miami-Dade is one of the largest counties in the nation, and that fully one-third of its voters (amounting to five hundred thousand) are independent, and you have a recipe for uniqueness.

Now let's add another element. Miami-Dade is the largest county in the largest "swing" state in the nation. It has a million and a half voters. Of those, about six hundred thousand are Democrats, four hundred thousand are Republicans, and five hundred thousand are independent (technically "NPA," meaning they have no party affiliation).

So the independents are the big factor in the general election. Unfortunately for me, they don't turn out all that much in August, for the simple reason that they cannot vote in primaries. The reason I say that it's unfortunate for me is that independents like me a lot—probably because I am the only independent county commissioner and the only well-known independent political figure in the entire county. For that matter, in the entire state.

The pundits should realize that being independent puts me in a particularly good position where it's down to a mano-a-mano contest, also called a runoff. In this case, there is a high likelihood that my opponent in the runoff will be a Democrat. Since I do well with both Democrats and Republicans, and exceedingly well with independents, the outcome in November should have been very favorable to me.

If only the pundits had understood that.

They did sense (or at least one *Miami Herald* reporter did) that the runoff election, timed to coincide with the presidential election, put an independent like me in a the proverbial "pickle." Whom would I endorse for president?

The question came up much earlier than I expected. Doug Hanks, reporting for the *Miami Herald*, put the question to me during a lunch that followed the profile interview that he did in June 2020.

The exchange went something like this:

Hanks: "Who will you be supporting for president?"

Me: "No one at this point."

Hanks: "For whom did you vote in the 2016 election, Hillary or Trump?"

Me: "I didn't vote for either."

Hanks: "So you didn't vote?"

Me: "Yes, I did; I voted for a write-in candidate."

At that point, there was a pause. Hanks hesitated to ask me whose name I had written in; I hesitated to offer it. But after a pregnant pause, he forced the issue, asking, "Are you willing to tell me the name you wrote in?"

"Yes," I said, but I hesitated once again, letting him speculate a little. Then I hit him with it: "I voted for John McCain."

He was definitely surprised. Then he leaned back and smiled, as if to say: "You got me there."

One good thing about always telling the truth is that you don't have to worry that someone will disprove it. But I have learned that often it behooves me not to answer a particular question. That applies to a vote I have taken in the constitutionally assured privacy of the ballot box.

In this case, I went ahead and answered. Obviously, it was a good choice, as McCain, while still alive and serving as U.S. senator, was very popular among Democrats, and although not as popular with Republicans, was a war hero and the nominee of his party in 2008.

The whole issue of the presidency was bound to come up during the ten-week runoff period. But I didn't make the run-off.

61

Postelection and Still during the Pandemic

never made it to the county mayoralty. With three opponents spending well over $10 million combined, my million-dollar kitty was not nearly sufficient.

I had speculated that since the three well-funded opponents were mostly attacking one another, I could silently stay in contention.

It didn't work out that way, and I have a theory as to why. It is a function of today's highly partisan atmosphere that a centrist candidate—even one with great name recognition and voter favorability.

Here's the reason. It's all about voter turnout. Since the county mayor's election takes place at the same time as party primaries for Congress and the legislature, the voters who turn out are highly partisan. Premised on that, the left-leaning candidate for county mayor (Daniella Levine Cava) did her best to characterize the others as being to the right of her politically. In the meantime, the right-leaning candidate (Esteban Bovo) did his best to characterize the others as being to the left of him.

In effect, I ended up losing my place in the middle lanes, for the simple reason that *there were no middle lanes in that particular election*. It was either Bovo on the right, or Levine Cava or Alex Penelas on the left. In the end, the two extremes prevailed.

I came in a distant fourth.

The only question that remained for me was whether to endorse one of the two runoff candidates. Ordinarily, that would have entailed an analysis of their positions on the most important issues facing our county. And that would have meant a more or less even split between Levine Cava (who prevailed on environment and social justice issues) and Bovo (who prevailed on fiscal conservatism and law-and-order issues).

But the equation was complicated due to the fact that we had not yet emerged from the coronavirus crisis. Or at least, by the media's reckoning, we had not emerged.

In reality, it was past the time that all businesses should have reopened. That was particularly true of the restaurants and clubs that catered to the tourists and constituted our most important industry, employing close to a quarter-million people.

Moreover, it was time for the schools to open at least partially so that the children of the working class (mostly hospitality workers) could be placed inside a schoolroom while their parents went to work on-site as waitresses, nurses, security personnel, chefs, valets, dishwashers, busboys, construction employees, and so on.

But Miami's establishment did not want to reopen either restaurants or schools. Convinced by the media that it was dangerous to reopen, and blissfully unaware of how "the other half" lives, the influencers argued vehemently to keep schools and restaurants closed.

The county's death toll from COVID-19 was minimal: about two thousand total in a community of almost three million. By mid-August 2020, the hospitals were discharging patients to the point that there was ample bed availability, in case of another surge.

Yet the media kept up a chant that argued for more testing, more masks worn outside, more social distancing, and more caution in reopening.

How could anyone break the stalemate? That was the $64,000 question for me.

In a county with two-hundred thousand more Democrats than Republicans, how could a mayoral candidate buck the national mood that dictated caution in reopening, as Bovo was trying to do? In order to even have a chance at winning, Bovo would have to go moderate.

And if he pushed the issue, he would be seen as a radical.

In the meantime, the mayors of Miami and Miami-Dade were, as always, at odds. County mayor Gimenez first had opened the restaurants and then immediately closed them, when people started being hospitalized in droves. Unfortunately for him (and for us all) he did it at the precise time when the state had ramped up its testing to one hundred thousand people per day, which meant a lot of confirmed cases.

Gimenez had been criticized by Francis and a host of other city mayors, but he would not budge, perhaps concerned that it could doom his ongoing campaign for Congress. And Francis was hemmed in by legal opinions that placed emergency powers on the mayor of the county, rather than the mayor of the principal city.

In the end, I decided to weigh in with whatever persuasive power I had. In two months, my commission term would end, a new mayor would take over, and Francis might be left as the sole voice of reason in local government. Or rather the sole voice of reason with a bully pulpit.

I no longer could join him in office. The dynasty, for now, was interrupted.

I'm sure that most observers see the interruption as being on par with the one stemming from the bizarre court decision that had annulled all the absentee ballots in 1998 and given the mayoralty to "Crazy Joe" Carollo.

Yet I came back from that and governed effectively for nine-plus years as a commissioner, from 2011 to 2020, serving in tandem with my son.

I say they were glorious years for Miami. But that is for my reader to judge.

62

Legacy

t is not necessarily the sunset of my life, although I am well past my seventh decade of existence. I don't sense my mental faculties failing. As for my physical faculties, I am in many ways more fit today than I was ten years ago. Let me explain.

In a few weeks, I will turn 72. Because I served for nine years as a county commissioner, I had ample health insurance and I didn't have to pay for it. So I had all kinds of what are called "elective" procedures done. That includes correcting a couple of hernias and removing a lump on the back of my upper leg.

In the prior decade, I had also done some corrective surgery on my right knee, which needed minor "scoping" so that the meniscus would stop making noise when I bent my leg. I had also done physical therapy on both of my shoulders, with the result that I could now throw a football or tennis ball or beach ball to my grandkids.

And I have passed a couple of kidney stones, which luckily were small. In summary, and thanks to the incredible American medical industry, as well as excellent insurance coverage, I am in better health today than fifteen years ago.

And yet my age is an automatic signal to all who know it that says: "This person is in his third age; he is over the hill; he should be retired, sitting at home and resting on his laurels, supporting his 11 grandchildren – at most writing his memoirs."

The reality is that I am able to support (with advice, babysitting and occasionally legal consultations) my children and grandchildren, plus teach a law school course, plus handle more clients than I have ever had, plus write three books.

Why is that?

Well, because I am more efficient than ever. My legal matters take me a couple of hours a day. My law school class a couple of hours a week. My grandkids have parents who care for them, plus nannies and teachers and coaches. I supplement that on weekends, when I don't work much on my legal matters.

And the research for my books is done mostly on internet search engines, which navigate through enormous amounts of data in microseconds, giving me citations and quotes in much less time than it took academics even twenty years ago. Modern technology, coupled with a lot of healthy habits, make me as productive as a fifty-year-old in another era.

Let me expand on that. In the process, l want to reflect on the societal legacy that I have passed on to my son and my other children, as well as my grandchildren. It is all intertwined with my son's amazing success.

The Incredible Ascendency of Francis

In the past few days, I have gone into my son's Instagram Page and found myself amazed at the quality and quantity of videos posted by the young mayor. The highlight, one could argue, is one with the famous basketball player, Magic Johnson.

That was a spectacular video, in which the tête-a-tête between a normal-sized public official and a humongous athlete is supremely delectable for its content and its pzazz. Francis has grown quite wide with muscle in the last six months – more or less coinciding with the exponential growth in popularity that he has brought onto himself by a mere four words that he sprung on the social media world.

It happened when a group of disgruntled tech millionaires and billionaires were having a collective meltdown over life in the west coast; or, more precisely, in what is called "Silicon Valley" because it has been the center of computer technology for about the last three decades. They were publicly bemoaning the restrictive COVID-19 environment, coupled with high taxes and inefficient governments, which allowed not only gang activities and attendant crime, but also ubiquitous tent cities where homeless men and women displayed the open sores of modern American society.

Francis was up late, and – inspired by fate – burst into their conversation with four words: "How Can I Help?" Those four words elicited what nowadays is called a "viral" response.

It was December 4, 2020. The initial reaction, consisting of close to two million responses, soon multiplied exponentially to the point that Francis became a national figure. Elon Musk, who was just then the richest man in the world, connected with him via Tweet. Tom Brady tweeted him. "Mr. Wonderful" from the television series "Shark Tank" took him out to dinner with the president of CNBC. The president of *Time* Magazine sent him a political contribution.

By the time of this writing, Francis has concocted a mayoral podcast where he interviews the best and brightest of the entertainment, sports and tech worlds. Someone invented the idea of calling these interviews "Cafecito Talks." In the last few weeks, he has interviewed Magic Johnson, David Beckham, Ben Shapiro and Marc Anthony.

Less known than such sports and entertainment superstars, but also much wealthier, are tech billionaires that have flocked to his side. One of them offered to help for a potential presidential campaign. When told that Francis had just started fundraising, and had $250,000 in his campaign coffers, the tech billionaire (named Chamath Palihapitiya) immediately matched it with his own wire transfer of a quarter-million dollars!

The combination of talents and well-honed communication skills that Francis embodies is something worth discussing. We tend to focus on the pathology of world leaders who go astray – the Fidel Castros and Adolf Hitlers. On the opposite side, we focus on the handful who achieved remarkable notoriety due to a combination of inborn and developed traits, plus the circumstantial aligning of stars that offer them a "platform" in which their skills can be appreciated by the masses.

In the days of John Kennedy or Pierre Trudeau, it was up to the journalists to cover and disseminate their charisma. In the modern, social-media age, it is often the public figure and his staff who create the platform.

None does it better than my son.

A Mayor's Amazing Social Media Platform

Francis began his first year as mayor with a series of miscues. For some unknown reason, he immediately announced a referendum that would change the city charter to one where the mayor has all the executive powers and earns a full salary, commensurate with the task of running a billion-dollar enterprise.

His enemies lined up in opposition to the measure and, in the process, painted him as a rich *arriviste* who lived in a million-dollar mansion and was determined to enlarge his power and his compensation. In what was a messy ending to his first full year in office, the voters rejected the increase in power by a hefty margin.

The second year in office was much better, but still plagued with bumps and bruises for the young mayor. The biggest hurdle – which he ultimately overcame rather adroitly – was having to replace the city manager, when it became evident that a majority of his city commission wanted the guy out.

By the third year, Francis had catapulted to the level of national prominence that had never been seen in any municipal leader south of New York. Francis combined the people skills of LaGuardia with the energy of Ed Koch, the good looks of John Lindsay and the ability of Rudy Giuliani to seize the moment and milk it.

I will leave details of his ascendency to his own autobiography and to other, more skilled biographers. Here I want to offer a recent vignette while it's still clear in my mind and heart.

63

Francis as Leader of the Cuban Diaspora

t was the summer of 2021; Francis had been in office now for most of his first four-year term. The last few days had been a whirlwind of activity for him, as he acted like a combination of mayor, police chief and exile leader.

I had never been fully able to do that. I had very little control over police operations, given a weak-mayor form of government in which the city manager (who was appointed by all five commissioners) was the only person who could hire and fire the police chief.

And he guarded that prerogative jealously.

I also shied away from dabbling much in exile politics. By inheritance, I was in the middle of the political spectrum; my dad had not been a supporter of the Batista regime, but had not supported Fidel Castro, even in the first heyday of what some, less thoughtful Cubans thought would be Cuba's renaissance to democracy.

As the classic academician, my father had been an observer of the Castro-communist ascendency; that was followed by intellectual opposition to the regime. At no point did the father of fourteen see himself as an underground, anti-Castro conspirator or even an open dissenter.

Despite his passive opposition, like most Catholic professionals, he was viewed as enough of a threat to be imprisoned in the preemptive round-up that preceded the Bay of Pigs Invasion. So he served for a short time in a communist jail. His brothers were formally tried and sentenced (thirty years) for more aggressive subversive activities; one died in jail and the other was bailed out by his sons for money and spare parts.

My solid background of anti-Castro family history and a personal inclination towards hard-line defense policies did not compel me to make foreign policy pronouncements or dabble in exile politics. I mostly waited, during my tenure as mayor, to be asked by the exile leaders for help in their constant, unyielding efforts to bring about regime change in Cuba.

Francis was not nearly so stand-off-ish. When, in the summer of 2021, forty Cuban cities and towns erupted into demonstrations against the regime, Francis did not hesitate. He took to the streets.

The initial street demonstration, as usual, was right smack in the middle of our city. The venue was in front of the iconic Versailles restaurant. Someone brought a truck with a very high superstructure and there soon appeared Francis, who had waded through a crowd of well over a thousand chanting demonstrators.

The ability to appear before a crowd and make an impression is something inborn. Francis has it; I don't. For almost an entire week, he appeared at every gathering, every press conference and every national news channel.

Simply put, Francis became the face of the exile mobilization in support of the Cuban demonstrators. We watched in wonder from afar; and then, suddenly, his sergeant called to tell me that he was outside our condo building and wanted to come up.

But the actual visit was delayed. When I went downstairs to meet him and open the elevator door, I realized that he was in the midst of a phone conference, inside his official car. The officer opened the window so that I could listen.

The young mayor was in total control of the planning of the next demonstration, which was on the coming Saturday. He had exile leaders on the phone and was basically dictating the terms of the gathering. They wanted a four-hour permit to close the streets. He said that was way too much; two hours would suffice.

Then he told the organizers that they needed to agree on a master of ceremonies: the consensus was the daughter of the most recent Cuban martyr of Castro-communism: Rosa Maria Paya. Everyone seemed to agree.

Last but not least came some emphatic instructions on the role of politicians. Francis was emphatic: "The master of ceremonies needs to say very simply that we thank the mayor and commissioners of the city of Miami for their support in this demonstration." And then he added: "And we thank the City of Miami Police Department for their presence and protection. But no politician should speak."

Once again Francis was acting as mayor, police chief and exile leader. The last of those was the toughest role. Not everyone can play it right, as we were able to perceive from the next vignette.

Francis and the Pichy Boys and a Not-so-Peachy Gal

The scene at city hall that afternoon had been somewhat chaotic. A group led by the social media comics called "The Pichy Boys" had shown up at city hall, ready for war. Outside, on the rotunda, they were complaining in harsh terms that the mayor had excluded them from a prior street-concert. They tried to question his patriotism.

It was drizzling outside and someone offered the mayor an umbrella. He refused it, knowing that sometimes a little water is good to cool down the tempers. When the discussion became chaotic, he suggested that they choose five members of their delegation and that they go inside city hall.

That always works. People like to be on the inside of the castle. They like to be treated as leaders, even if they are only self-appointed wannabes. And so they agreed to the more exclusive forum with the mayor.

What took place inside was classic. The five-member delegation included the two Pichy Boys and a rather histrionic, loud and plain pushy lady, who kept complaining that the government was keeping her from going to Cuba and defending the protesters.

This was Francis's finest moment. He pounded his fist on the table and said: "Look, ma'am, my family stood up to the Castro regime; my grandfather was imprisoned and his two brothers were sentenced to thirty years; one of them died in jail. We are as patriotic as anyone."

And he continued: "As to your desire to invade Cuba, there is no one stopping you. That Dolce and Gabbana purse you are holding can be sold for enough money to buy you a rifle and rent a boat. In Miami that is exactly 500 bucks. And no one will stop you."

The Pichy Boys and the hysterical would-be-invader walked away mollified. Yet another round had been won by the young mayor.

What remained was a national public policy debate as to what to do in regards to the most oppressive, long-lasting and troublesome regime ever to plague the American continent.

Mayor Francis took the lead on that too.

The Just War Theory

Francis is wont to act instinctively at times. I am more methodical.

In mid-July, 2021, the suffering people of Cuba took to the streets; it was the most massive and widespread anti-government demonstrations in the history of communist Cuba. As many as forty cities and towns were said to be involved.

Over a period of six-plus decades, the Cuba conundrum had plagued both sides of the Florida Straits. The first effort to dislodge Castro-communism had failed miserably; it was called the "Bay of Pigs" and it was the first and only time, since Korea, that the United States had been technically defeated in an attempt at liberating a country from communism.

The Bay of Pigs fiasco was mostly papered over by what the American media considered the successful handling by President John F. Kennedy of the "Cuban missile crisis." The reason I say "papered over" is because it is a matter of interpretation by historians; one could argue that the final outcome of the missile crisis was an abject failure, rather than a success.

Here's why. In exchange for removing middle-range missiles from Cuba, the Soviet Union (undoubtedly egged on by Fidel Castro) extracted a commitment from the United States to prevent any armed intervention in Cuba, by anyone leaving U.S. shores. In effect, the U.S. government agreed to protect the status quo in Cuba.

And so for the next half century, there was no military pressure on Cuba – whether by the U.S. or by the exile community. The consensus was that Cuba would either be liberated by internal processes or simply rot away under the pressure of its own economic failure.

The outside world would not lift a finger.

That consensus was shattered in mid-2021. Demonstrations in Cuba and the vicious repression thereof, coupled with massive and vocal demonstrations in Miami, quickly eroded the non-intervention doctrine.

Leading the clarion call for action was Mayor Francis. Initially, as I said, he acted on instinct. Later, he researched, reflected and practiced his lines to sound reasonable in what was the most reasonable of all demands: that the free world *do something!*

But what was that something? Therein lies the rub.

Right from the start, Francis threw what in football is called a "Hail Mary Pass." He voiced the verboten words: *military intervention.*

Many in the mainstream media recoiled at such a thought. How can we even think of going to war against a neighboring country? Why not try economic sanctions, United Nations condemnation, gentle persuasion?

Anything but war – particularly at a time when the United States was finally ending the occupations that followed military intervention in Iraq and Afghanistan....

In many ways, this was the worst possible moment to raise the hopes of the Cuban people that anyone outside their national border would even consider intervening with force. Besides the aforementioned final winding down of the intervention in Afghanistan, there were two other very important political realities.

One was that Americans were happy with their lot – incredibly happy. The polls, reflecting to a great extent the victory over the COVID-19 pandemic and the resurgence of the economy, showed the highest level of optimism ever recorded. The last thing most Americans wanted was to rock the boat.

The other factor was named Biden.

The Biden Doctrine: Whatever You Do, Don't Fail or Fall

Foreign policy in the U.S. is set, in the main, by the president. With majorities in both houses of Congress, peace abroad and a recovering economy, President Biden was not about to make any risky moves, or even pronouncements.

Few nations in the history of civilization have come to the aid of other nations or their people, unless the internal conflicts spill over and imperil the security of one's own nation. In both world wars of the twentieth century, England and the United States distinguished themselves in coming to the aid of fairly distant peoples, in the case of Britain, and enormously distant peoples, in the case of the U.S.

It is testament to the benevolence of those two countries, and to the wisdom and courage of the statesmen that led them – people like Winston Churchill and Franklin Roosevelt.

Suffice it to say that Biden is no Churchill. He is no FDR, who proclaimed the Four Freedoms after WWII and thus set the tone for what today we refer to as "social justice" – a concept that connects the welfare of each person to the others in society.

And he would never emulate Churchill by getting way ahead of events or do or say anything that would cause the media (and academia) to bestow the label of warmonger on him. The most that Biden would do is make pronouncements that criticized the violence perpetrated on Cuban demonstrators by the communist regime's police.

Francis found such pronouncements akin to appeasement of the Neville Chamberlain kind. He chose to emulate Churchill instead. For a memorable week in the summer of 2021, Mayor Francis Xavier Suarez emphatically made the case for some form or military intervention in Cuba.

At first it was just in FOX News, which expectedly hoped to put Biden in the proverbial bind of looking weak in the face of communist barbarism. But Francis had the good sense, and the courage, to do the same in the liberal channels, such as CNN and MSNBC.

In what was perhaps his finest day and hour ever, Francis confronted CNN's Chris Cuomo with verve and eloquence. He began by playing to Cuomo's vanity: "I want to commend you for your prefatory remarks, which show that you are willing to expose the horrendous cruelty of the Cuban police state..." (I suspect that Cuomo was impressed that a young, Hispanic mayor would even know what "prefatory" means.)

Then the clincher: "The 'Just War Theory' prescribes that nations have a right to intervene to defend a people from atrocities such as are happening in Cuba now."

Hearing the Miami Mayor citing principles of political philosophy that are taught in the same Catholic schools he attended – and that his father, Mario Cuomo, had quoted in many speeches before – it was more than persuasive to Chris. He melted and nodded in what seemed like acquiescence in the principle cited, if not the particular application.

In another interview the same day, Francis was asked by an MSNBC commentator whether he was advocating "regime change." "Heck yes," he answered, "we have all been advocating 'regime change' for sixty years…" It totally deflated the journalist (Craig Melvin), who must have known that the Bay of Pigs was an operation coordinated by the CIA and paid for by American tax dollars with the express purpose of achieving "regime change."

Francis must have known that Biden would do no such thing. Besides ideology, which suggested that Democrats were inclined to fine-tune democracy, but not fight for it elsewhere, there was the inherent weakness of the president.

A man that can barely walk up a staircase to an airplane, with railings to support both arms, is not going to risk much in either physical or intellectual exertion. In other books, I have described Biden as the ever-jovial, ever-present, everyman. Whether he could withstand the rigors of the presidency for one full term of four years or not, it would be way out of his league for this fragile character to rock the boat, when he could barely row or stand up in the boat during a calm sea.

But events could ultimately give credence to the pronouncements of the young, charismatic, and physically powerful mayor of Miami. A genocidal wave of repression, followed by a massive emigration in small vessels from Cuba to Miami; an incident involving an American citizen or a journalist; a direct confrontation with Church leaders who finally stood up to Castro-communism; any of these could ultimately turn the tide and make military intervention a practical necessity.

Only time would tell.

64

A Star is Born

This chapter could well be titled "My Legacy." But I'm not ready to speak of legacies, as much as to speak of alliances. I'm only 72, healthy and politically relevant – in part because a local managed-care company has decided to use me in radio and television commercials that reach a goodly number of the nearly three million people who reside in this metropolis.

The health-care ads have visually connected me to the nation's rising political star, who happens to be my son. Because my political life and his are intertwined in time and family identification, and because he is at the top, while I sit on the bench waiting for a chance to show my skills – his reality is my reality.

His game, right now, is my game. And what a "freak" he is. Let me explain.

In professional sports, the word "freak" is used to describe an athlete who excels to the point of seeming to be at a totally different altitude from the rest of the league. Currently, in basketball, it is used to describe Giannis Antetokounmpo, the player who just led Milwaukee to the world championship.

Giannis, the basketball "freak," can do things no one has ever done. He is stronger, faster, and more coordinated than any big man has ever been. The famous Wilt Chamberlain, who was the most freakish athlete of his time, would probably look immobile if he had to guard Giannis, whose lateral speed is that of a much shorter man and whose jumping ability is probably 50% greater than Chamberlain in his prime. (That's not a wild guess; it's an educated one. Chamberlain lifted his body about 30 inches off the ground; Giannis does about 45 inches....)

But let's go back to the *wunderkind* who is currently the nation's most popular mayor of the nation's most popular city.

He shares a first name with the Pope and a last name with me.

Francis Suarez: America's Mayor

It's hard to know where to start in describing the *wunderkind*. His ascent has been rapid, exponential, unbroken and shockingly unprecedented, in a metropolis that chews up its politicians. No Miami mayor has ever been elected governor or United States senator – let alone president or vice-president.

The iconic Maurice Ferre tried in vain to reach the Senate. He also tried, as I did, to get a cabinet appointment, when he unsuccessfully backed Scoop Jackson for president.

The mildly charismatic Manny Diaz managed to get elected president of the U.S. Conference of Mayors, was termed out and failed miserably in a run for the U.S. Senate. He also failed to win a cabinet appointment from the Obama administration, as it was blocked by local Democrats whom he had alienated. More recently, he backed Michael Bloomberg for president, and saw that effort result in the most dollars ever spent for the least electoral votes, as Bloomberg won one primary: the tiny island of Samoa!

Like Manny Diaz, Francis is slated to become the president of the U.S. Conference of Mayors. Unlike Manny Diaz, Francis begins his second term (2021-5) with a favorable rating of close to five-to-one (75% to 16%).

I had close to that kind of popularity once, in early 1989, after I walked into a civil disturbance and managed to avoid rocks and bottles to calm down my city, unassisted and unaccompanied by police. That four-to-one popularity (76% to 19%) lasted but a few weeks, as soon the *Miami Herald* was blasting me for not giving what they thought was a proper welcome to Nelson Mandela, who had not even set foot in Miami proper, and was well received in Miami Beach.

That messy issue of international protocol, coupled with my choice of a black (Athalie Range) over a Cuban (Luis Morse) for city commissioner, caused me to slide back to more mundane poll numbers, as was evidenced by my reelection in November of 1989 by a margin of 62%-38%. Not quite two-to-one but still a "landslide" as experts characterize it.

Francis Suarez has survived an awful first year as mayor, a difficult second year and has been riding a wave that is now 23 months of victory after victory, plaudit after plaudit, and national coverage that began when he was the first public official to get COVID-19, the first to do a podcast from his home during the quarantine, and the first to donate plasma thereafter.

By the end of 2020, Mayor Francis had turned the attention of both tech industry moguls and venture capital magnates towards Miami, using a now-famous tweet: "How Can I Help," directed at the harried tech/venture capital entrepreneurs of Silicon Valley and New York.

They took the message as an invitation, and flocked to Miami with their billions and a goodly number of employees in tow.

The success in attracting new industry, coupled with good looks and a startling ability to do podcasts (called "Cafecito Talks") from city hall, with the ease of a Chris Cuomo or a Bill O'Reilly, catapulted Francis into the ranks of *Time Magazine*'s "Next Generation 100" and *Fortune Magazine*'s top 20 leader in the entire planet.

Articles in every major magazine and appearances in every major national cable station completed the image of a young, fiscally conservative, ecologically attuned, socially progressive mayor whose city had battled not only COVID-19 more successfully than any other major urban area but also reduced crime and taxes, while other large cities were beset by spiraling crime and budget deficits.

All of which is startling, but not freakish, in the sense of national attention.

What came next was freakish. It was the generalized talk, in major media outlets, of a viable candidacy for the nation's highest office.

Two events gave substance to what might otherwise be mere hype.

Francis at the White House

Barely three months into his presidency, Joe Biden invited Miami's mayor to meet with him and Vice-President Kamala Harris. The topic was yet another COVID-relief package that would provide over a trillion dollars in federal aid.

Due to faulty allocation rules that cut off cities with less than 500,000 residents, Miami had missed out on a major aid package that had come down from the Trump administration in 2020. Mayor Francis had broken ranks with Florida Governor DeSantis on various issues related to the pandemic; consequently, Francis was seen as a prize target by the Biden folks.

Whatever the reasons for their embrace, the fact was that the Biden administration passed up the newly elected, Democrat mayor of Miami-Dade County (Daniella Levine Cava) and invited the Miami mayor to a very elite meeting in the Oval Office.

It was so elite that only four governors and four mayors were invited. Moreover, only one Republican mayor (Francis) was invited. And then, the coup de grace: the White House press briefing afterwards included no governors and only two mayors, a Democrat from Detroit (Mike Duggan) and the Miami Republican.

Francis could not have asked for a better line-up. There he was, at the podium with the presidential seal, being introduced by the ubiquitous Jen Psaki. There he was, flanked by only one other political leader: the hapless mayor of the most hapless city in America.

The poor people of Detroit had barely recovered from a bankruptcy less than a decade before when they were hit by a pandemic that – like most Northern cities – was totally mismanaged. I had not followed Detroit's struggles since the intervention of the formidable Kevyn Orr – a Stanford lawyer who came in as trustee in bankruptcy and efficiently restored fiscal order.

I followed that episode in part because Orr had been slated to start a Miami office for Jones Day when he was called away to do his civic duty in Detroit. What I didn't know is how much Detroit was suffering from COVID-19.

But I'm getting ahead of the story, since Francis went first and Detroit's mayor second.

Pictures in the media had already alerted us that Francis was tired. The one from the Oval office had him looking down as if he were checking his watch, when actually he was nodding off to sleep-land. As happens to people who are extroverts, the lack of sleep makes them even more relaxed.

Mayor Francis Xavier Suarez of Miami was one nimble, relaxed dude as he stepped up the mike at the White House press room. He smiled for the cameras as Jen Psaki introduced him as the mayor of Miami who is also vice-president of the U.S. Conference of Mayors.

Just as he was ready to speak, Psaki added: "Oh, and he also served eight years as a city commissioner...." Francis then performed what may be his best John F Kennedy moment. He smiled and quipped: "Those were eight 'dog' years!"

Because he was tired, and perhaps because of the momentous occasion, Francis was not at his best on the podium. But even when he's on his "B" game, Francis is better than most. Two things helped him enormously: He's bilingual and he's good-looking.

As he finished his remarks in English, Francis asked if he could say something briefly in Spanish; Psaki concurred. His Spanish, like his English that day, was not perfect. But it was better than that of any other major political figure in the entire country.

Overall, he gave the impression of being a young, up-and-coming, charismatic and simpatico politician, in a country that isn't quite full of that archetype. And then the coup de grace, as he was followed by the portly, balding and short Detroit mayor.

Sometimes what counts is how bad is the fellow that comes after you.

To make matters worse, the metrics given by Detroit's mayor Duggan were abysmal. I winced when I heard his initial comments, which went more or less as follows. "Detroit," he lamented, "had awful unemployment when we went through our bankruptcy, ten years ago. We had accomplished a great comeback, going from 20% unemployment to 7%; and then COVID hit. Now we are back to 20% unemployment."

Omigod, what bleakness, and what a bleak, aging figure to convey the bleakness of Detroit! In one minute, the leader of that city conveyed what droves of people in the nation were thinking right about then: "Get out of the northern, Democrat-run cities and head South to where a progressive, new-age Republican is going to greet you, with a rum-and-coke in one hand and a bottle of suntan lotion in the other…"

The vignette at the White House, complete with presidential seal and a nice suit and tie combination, was what consultants call a magnificent "photo-op." It was picked up by a series of articles in the national media that touted both the City of Miami and its mayor as the ultimate combination of mecca and its civic ayatollah.

From that precious moment, in the Spring, Francis continued to ride wave after wave of positive public exposure. Even a local tragedy could not derail his momentum.

The Collapse of Surfside

To most of the world, the term "Miami" means the entire metropolitan area. It is synonymous with "Miami Beach." It encompasses an urban venue of almost three million people, with a Hispanic majority whose entrepreneurial character and political views are quite different from the rest of the nation's Hispanics.

Put simply, Miami's Hispanics don't act like immigrants. A fair number represent the upper classes of Argentina, Venezuela, Nicaragua and Colombia. The Cubans are now beginning the third generation, graduating from private and charter schools and enrolling in Georgetown and Vanderbilt and the University of Florida, from where the best students end up at Harvard Law.

Hispanics in Miami are so successful that they constitute the majority of new Hispanic-owned businesses in the entire nation. The media occasionally distinguishes the working-class resident of Hialeah or the elderly of Little Havana – particularly when they want to emphasize political extremism or poverty; but for the most part, Miami means glamour, prosperity, Julio Iglesias and Jennifer Lopez.

Thankfully for Miami, the recent tragedy of a collapsed building in a suburban municipality named Surfside did not get identified with Miami or its glamorous mayor. As it happened, it was seen in the eyes of the nation as a county issue, involving the county mayor, named Daniella Levine Cava.

In fairness to Mayor Levine Cava, she visited the rubble and shared the pain of the victims on a daily basis, without exaggerating or trying to rationalize the negligence that brought a building to suddenly collapse, taking 100 lives in the process.

Mayor Francis was supportive and occasionally present at the site of the disaster. But he had practically no role to play. He was not the face of the disaster even one-tenth as much as Levine Cava.

In fact, for about a month, Francis was in a secondary role vis-à-vis the national media. And then, all hell broke loose in Cuba. That's when Francis grabbed the limelight and showed a special ability in a novel area of civic leadership – foreign policy.

Francis Meets the Secretary of Homeland Security

As mentioned before, the July 11, 2021 demonstrations in Cuba were snuffed out in 2 days. It took a while for the Biden administration to react. Ultimately, the best Biden could do was to send Homeland Secretary Alejandro Mayorkas to meet with Miami civic leaders.

As told to me by Francis himself, when asked to speak he began by giving a back-handed compliment. "Thank you for inviting me, knowing that I am not coming to praise the administration's response to the Cuban people's uprising." That was a funny (and arguably gracious) way of saying: "You had to invite at least one critic of the administration and it might as well be a Republican who has been critical of both his own party's president and governor in the past...."

But it got better. Francis proceeded in the same vein. "Perhaps you hoped that I would be here to emulate St. Francis of Assisi when he said, 'Lord, make me an instrument of your peace...Instead I will emulate Winston Churchill when he said: 'I was not born the lion, but it fell to me to give the lion's roar.'"

Other politicians who were there, including the county mayor (Daniella Levine Cava), Democratic Congresswoman Debbie Wasserman Schultz and Florida Democratic Party Chairman Manny Diaz must have been stunned by the literary audacity of this young politician. To paraphrase Sir Winston himself, "never have so few words said so much to overshadow so many words by others."

It was vintage Francis, but not in the customary way. His attire was formal; his words solemn, rather than festive; his message almost as much a warning as a simple strategic recommendation.

And the photo op also favored him: It captured him giving Mayorkas a fist-bump and towering over the receding figure of an aging Archbishop Wenski and of the diminutive county mayor, Daniella Levine Cava.

Rhetorically and literally, Francis towered over the other public figures there, including Secretary Mayorkas, whose benign smile at receiving a fist-bump in the era of COVID evidently pleased him to no end.

65

A Star Is Shaken

As the final days of Francis's first term came to an end, he suffered the winds of criticism in a most unexpected – and unfair – fashion. It had to do with the dismissal of a police chief who had come in, Christ-like, to the acclaim of the multitudes, who placed palm fronds in front of him and embraced him as a Savior.

The head cheerleader, unfortunately, had been the young mayor of Miami. Although the mayor did not directly choose the police chief, he was quite involved in the decision to hire this particular individual, named Art Acevedo and hailing from Houston, which had one of the largest police departments in the nation.

The process by which Acevedo had been chosen included a citizens' selection committee, which had chosen three finalists after interviewing candidates in an open forum. Why anybody would choose to use this strange way of naming a police chief is beyond me. When I was mayor, the city manager and I would simply caucus and pick a one of the assistant chiefs to take over for the outgoing chief.

Such internal succession is what the civil service system envisions. Invented by the British, the civil service approach to hiring and promotions envisions enormous objectivity and job security at the bottom, coupled with total subjectivity and lack of job security at the top.

Put simply, the rank-and-file are tested, hired and protected from arbitrary termination, while the upper ranks are expected to be replaced from time to time at the discretion of the elected officials (who act as a sort of board of directors) and their chosen chief executive, who is technically "city manager."

The mayor acts as the chairman of the board in the process; his choice of a chief is exercised through the manager, who serves at his pleasure. Due to a quirky provision in the Miami City Charter, the five city commissioners can approve the selection of a chief or, in the case of a dismissal or termination, disapprove of such a decision.

So it's a bit of a mess, frankly.

Good old Acevedo had a big mouth. That was a given. But with a very discreet and subdued city manager, and a mayor who enjoyed and thrived under the limelight, it was thought that the chief would tone down his rhetoric and stick to policing.

Think again.

In barely six months, Chief Acevedo caused a major furor by characterizing the top ranks in the city's police department as the "Cuban mafia," criticizing both judges and prosecutors for being too lenient on criminals and alleging that three of the five city commissioners (all of whom were Cuban-born) were interfering unlawfully with pending investigations.

The ultimate dismissal of the chief took place in three acts, of which the first two were open commission hearings. It is not an exaggeration to say that these were a combination of "kangaroo court" and opera bouffe.

Two Friday Hearings (Circuses) Under One Tent

This may be the first time in history in which a public official accused the majority of his government's legislative assembly of illegalities and immediately afterwards dared them to fire him.

Why he did that is another issue. Perhaps he didn't calculate the sinister, persuasive power of the main object of his accusations, named Joe Carollo. Or perhaps he was simply fed up with being police chief and was hoping to set his commission critics up for a "whistleblower suit."

He certainly did not win the public-image battle. It was, at best, a tie between two abysmal losers: himself and Commissioner Carollo.

As soon as Chief Acevedo sent out his ill-conceived, accusatory memorandum to mayor and manager, Carollo moved in for the kill. He knew that all the cards were stacked against the chief, in great part because as soon as the manager fired him, the only recourse was to ask for a hearing before the city commission. And the chief could not possibly win that.

Besides the sheer number, Carollo had done his research and knew that the chief had a lot of embarrassing – if not downright dirty – linen hidden in his closet. And that there are no hidden spaces in the new age of social media. All your peccadillos are available and retrievable in living color as if there were happening before your very eyes.

And so Carollo, with the help of his two commission colleagues, convened a commission meeting in which he showed multiple news articles and a couple of videos of Chief Acevedo at his worst. As happens in a litigious society, Carollo found a couple of lawsuits that accused the chief of sexual harassment, in rather lurid detail. He also found videos of the chief "dancing with [a female] star" in skimpy attire; not just dancing with her but even seeming to spank her with a traffic ticket in the roundest part of her anatomy.

You really didn't need two hearings. But Carollo found more material, including a very damning memorandum from a city department showing that the chief had been in a car accident with his city vehicle and had not reported it.

Of course, Carollo cannot just win a public relations battle. He has to gloat. He just has to overdo it.

In this case, he spread rumors that the chief intended to arrest him, or even shoot him, and insisted that the city manager give public assurances that no arrest of commissioners would take place.

It was bizarre. Beyond belief bizarre. It was a new low for Carollo.

But it was not good for the chief either.

The *Miami Herald* editors seemed bent on rescuing Chief Acevedo. In their blissful ignorance of political reality and of what makes a city great, they pressured Mayor Francis to come to the rescue of the chief.

This the mayor could not do, because the chief had dug his own grave.

It all lasted about three painful weeks. In the end, Acevedo's lawyers committed some sort of historic-level malpractice. They invoked the city charter provision that allowed a terminated police chief to get a hearing before the city commission and then failed to put on a defense.

To paraphrase Churchill: Never have so many high-paid lawyers done so little for their client and so much for so many public officials who want to get rid of their client....

66

Election Day, 2021

Today is election day, November 2, 2021. Miami Mayor Francis Xavier Suarez is expected to win big against a handful of non-entities and otherwise flawed opponents.

How useless is the opposition? Consider this: Of the five opponents, one was just arrested and charged with impersonating a police officer. Another one of the five had her candidacy disqualified by a court. That left three opponents and they had last names like Dutrow and Exantes.

Say what? I had never heard of or met anyone with those last names. I didn't even know that such names existed – which made it perfect for them to be the first two names on the ballot. The third name on the ballot belonged to a candidate named Maxwell Manuel Martinez, which sounds somewhat normal in a city where the electorate is over 50% Hispanic.

But it turned out the guy, who was otherwise pretty well educated and physically attractive, would stand at the corner of Francis's house and wear a sign that said: "I am not the mayor's son…" It was his way of criticizing the mayor's security detail as excessive; however, that was a tough issue for him, since Francis was not just the mayor of Miami, but the incoming president of the entire U.S. Conference of Mayors, which made him a national figure.

Compared to New York, whose mayor has a security detail numbering over 40, Francis's three officers, following him over the course of 18 hour days, seven days a week, was not all that excessive.

The final stroke of good luck came when the one opponent who had some "juice" was disqualified. Her name was Mayra Joli; she was

Dominican born, attractive and a lawyer. Just being a Hispanic woman, who happened to be a "Trumpista" (Trump supporter) would have enabled her to garner a few percentage points.

When a judge disqualified her candidacy in midstream, there was no way to eliminate her name from the actual ballot – which assured that all her votes would go uncounted. This added to the percentage that Francis would get, since it siphoned off the protest vote and nullified it.

The scenario was ideal and the national media seemed to sense it. It came to a head with an Associated Press article.

The AP Article Culminates National Media Exposure

The Associated Press article lifted our spirits at just the moment when we needed it. For reasons that would take a whole book to explain, the *Miami Herald* continued its litany of negativity towards Francis. One day it was the firing of the police chief, another it was that Francis wasn't doing enough for the homeless in Miami.

(The criticism of his homeless efforts was particularly galling, as Miami was on the verge of what Francis called "functional zero" homelessness. We had gone from about 6,000 homeless in our county of three million people to about 600 and were finally using our well-funded homeless trust to support volunteer outreach programs that leveraged government dollars quite nicely.)

The AP story culminated a spate of favorable national articles, from every major magazine and blog that recently included *New York Magazine, Florida Politics, Vanity Fair, Bloomberg News, National Review,* and *The New York Times.* From both the right and left of the ideological spectrum, the complimentary themes were identical: Francis had managed the COVID-19 pandemic exceedingly well, setting his own tone of caution without shut-downs, had reduced crime while adding police presence, and had reduced taxes while increasing city services.

Miami's poverty rate had plunged from 40% to 20%. It had attracted more tech companies than any other city. Its unemployment rate had plunged to close to 5%. Its real estate industry was bursting at the seams.

Miami was, in sum, the most attractive (and happiest) city in the nation, if not the world. And the AP story simply echoed those facts, while hinting that Francis's profile had attracted national attention; his name was being mentioned as a VP running mate for Nikki Haley – or perhaps as a candidate for the White House.

And why not? If you succeed in leading a city as diverse as Miami and also succeed in leading the entire national conference of city mayors, by being elected its president; if you were the only U.S. official to serve in the U.N. Global Commission on Climate Adaptability; if you were the only public official to be constantly featured in both CNN and FOX, why not think that you could run for President?

That was the stage as we prepared for election night on Tuesday, November 2, 2021.

And then what I witnessed was very telling.

The Aftermath of Victory

Over the course of 36 hours, what I witnessed is worth describing. Francis celebrated with the best of them, then did weights with the best of them, and then flew to Glasgow and rubbed elbows with British royalty.

Other than Pierre Trudeau, I doubt that any high-level politician has ever done such a triple-play in 36 hours.

Let me restate what he did. On election night, November 2nd, he drank Japanese whiskey and smoked Havana cigars well into the night. That was Tuesday. By Wednesday afternoon – precisely at 3 P.M., when most of us were recovering from the reveling of the night before, he was setting a new personal best of 275 pounds in what is called the "front squat."

Let me elaborate on what can appear as a trait of minor importance but is actually quite significant. Francis weighs about 180 pounds now; but when he was first elected mayor, four years ago, he weighed about 160. He looks good at either weight, because he is five-foot-ten with shoes on. At either weight, he is a fitness nut – kind of a Pierre Trudeau in his forties, with not a pound of fat.

But when he eats well and works out, gaining 20 pounds of muscle, Francis has an entirely different profile. Let me elaborate with a vivid, recent example of the problem faced by politicians who are slight of build and of medium height.

We last saw the problem when Donald Trump took on the very charismatic Marco Rubio. By all accounts, Senator Rubio is an accomplished debater; his ability to speak in complete, logical paragraphs is unsurpassed in current American politics. He is well read and well versed, particularly in matters involving foreign policy. He is also very, very confident in his own persuasive abilities.

Trump stands about five inches taller than Marco; he weighs about 75 more pounds. In effect, he is close to one-third bigger in size, if one thinks of "size" as "bulk." (In physics, it is called "mass.")

When Trump made fun of Senator Rubio as "little Marco," it had a devastating effect. From that moment forward, Rubio's voice seemed to become more like that of a child. His gestures seemed to be those of a little kid, compared to the bully standing next to him.

By contrast, Francis can "throw his weight around" in the sense that he has a commanding physical presence. As was the case of Trudeau or John F. Kennedy, he manages to convey an image of strength-from-fitness. Like Trudeau and JFK, he appears in sporting events in just the right attire to illustrate what nowadays is called his "sixpack," which is a metaphor used to describe the man who has a muscled abdomen.

Physical traits were not as important in the age of Fiorello LaGuardia or even Adlai Stevenson. But this is the television age, the "selfie" age, the age of Instagram, where Francis posts pictures and videos on a daily basis, always showing him in action, always properly attired for the occasion, always in command of the stage.

When you can party late into the night on Tuesday, lift 270 pounds on Wednesday afternoon and jet to Scotland that same night, to be photographed with Prince Charles on Thursday at noon, and do it all with grace, you are a media marvel. When your wife has movie star looks and your oldest son salutes – without prompting – during a ceremony commemorating the tragedy of the Twin Towers on 9/11, you have the complete visual package.

67

How Miami Became the Sports Center of the World

One of my most important legacies, in my 1985-93 tenure as mayor, was obtaining two new professional sports franchises: Major League Baseball (MLB) and NBA basketball. (I could add NHL hockey, which in its early days played at the Miami Arena; but ice hockey is a secondary sport in terms of worldwide audience; as I write these lines, the NHL franchise has moved north to Broward so I will not include it in the discussion.)

By the time Francis became mayor, Miami was already one of a handful of cities that enjoyed three of the five most watched professional sports. But we did not have the other two sports that rank among the five most popular sports worldwide: professional *futbol* (soccer) and Formula One racing.

To Francis obtaining these two became a challenge; in particular, Francis was dead-set on bringing MLS futbol to Miami proper, rather than some suburban venue. By pure luck, the opportunity presented itself when world renowned soccer player David Beckham acquired a franchise under the Miami flag. It had cost him a mere $25 million, in part because he had negotiated an option to buy way before he needed to exercise it.

The battle to locate the soccer stadium became a *cause celebre*. Initially, Beckham chose a site in the inner-city neighborhood called Overtown. This much-neglected neighborhood had been the venue for our first basketball arena, coming at a time (mid-1980's) when the people in that area were desperate for any kind of economic development that would bring jobs and a measure of glamor to Overtown.

By the second decade of the twenty-first century, Overtown was coming out of its poverty- and crime-plagued syndrome and seeing great residential and commercial improvement. The residents no longer welcomed any and all sports stadiums that one may want to place in their midst. And so they rose up in opposition to the Overtown site.

Major league soccer, by all rights, should be staged in the urban core, where residents could walk to the games. Downtown by the bay would be an interesting location, but the prime piece of real estate there had been snatched by the very successful Miami Heat Basketball franchise. Adding another stadium in that area would be prohibitively costly and a difficult sell to residents already saturated with basketball, concerts and running events.

And thus it came to be that the Beckham group, now possessed of local Cuban infrastructure builders, Jorge and Jose Mas Santos, proposed to redevelop a decrepit golf course sitting right smack in the middle of the city.

It is named Mel Reese, after a former city manager. It occupies a bit over 100 acres and is bordered by a river on the north, a superhighway on the south and two major arteries on the east and west. In effect, the Mel Reese Golf Course is isolated from the only residential neighborhood around, which is called Grapeland Heights.

My only involvement in the effort to attract the Major League Soccer (MLS) franchise was to do what I have always done in this situation: to propose as many viable sites as possible.

There are two reasons for that approach. One is to keep speculators from raising the price of land acquisition, when they sense that government is interested in their land.

The other reason is to forestall a phenomenon that goes by the acronym of "NIMBY," which means "not in my backyard." What this means is that stable, so-called "bedroom communities" are wont to object to a major new facility in their neighborhood – particularly one that entails enormous numbers of cars and very noisy crowds of fans flocking for events that often take place at night and on week-ends.

A "bedroom community," as its name indicates, is a residential neighborhood where people expect to go to sleep early and enjoy the peace and quiet that most middle-class Americans yearn for, when they are home from work and school. In today's urban condition, those neighborhoods resist any kind of change and, in particular, any new commercial facility that is likely to bring cars and noise.

The Beckham Group's proposal for Mel Reese Golf Course was certainly calculated to bring cars and noise. Besides the actual soccer stadium, it included a billion dollars' worth of commercial, mixed-use development – i.e., hotels and office buildings.

At this point it is worth discussing whether and why the commercial development became an integral component of what should have been simply a soccer stadium. Most media commentators missed the point regarding this issue. For them, it was a case of over-reaching by a soccer franchise that had been obtained on the premise that it would be located in Miami, which is what gave it value. Everyone assumed that the MLS executives who sold the franchise to Mr. Beckham for a mere $25 million were betting that Miami would become the epicenter of professional soccer in the American hemisphere.

The problem was that major league soccer requires a major league stadium, tailored specifically to major league soccer. That carries a price tag of $250 million, or ten times the acquisition price of the franchise. The typical way to fund the stadium is for government to either build it or subsidize it.

Most governments are happy to build or subsidize a new facility for a major sports franchise. In Miami, however, the recent history included three scandalous subsidies of existing franchises in baseball, basketball and football. One of those, involving the major league baseball Marlins franchise, had cost $600 million in taxpayer subsidies and brought down the county's mayor (a fellow named Carlos Alvarez) in what was the nation's largest ever recall of a municipal official.

Subsidizing any kind of sports franchise, except on terms that were acceptable to the taxpayers, would be a death-wish for any politician. And so Mayor Francis engaged in a four-year journey that included, as a prerequisite to further negotiations, a referendum vote of the people. The vote approving the stadium plan was held in a general election in Francis's first year as mayor. It passed by a substantial majority of over 60%, despite a concerted effort by media and many bloggers to discredit the proposal as environmentally unsound.

The environmental argument against the plan was mostly misdirected. The stadium proposal included, as a condition to development of the golf course, the eradication of toxic pollutants in the subsoil; these were the result of a prior use of the venue as a waste disposal site. Included in the stadium plan was remediation of the subsoil toxicity entailing expenditures, by the franchise, of some fifty million dollars.

The other environmental argument against the stadium was premised on the proposed reduction of green space, from about 120 acres to about 60 acres. That had some quantitative merit; yet it failed to take into account that the 120 acres presently devoted to golf, while looking quite green from the air, were not accessible to the general public, which didn't play golf, and even for those it was not free to use.

Moreover, golf courses are not exactly environmental preserves. They don't have much tree coverage; and the lawns must be constantly irrigated, trimmed by fuel-powered machines and fertilized by chemicals that feed the desired grass surface while destroying the undesired weeds.

If it had been up to me, I would have tried to negotiate with the Mas/ Beckham group a middle position that would have preserved the 18-hole golf course, allowed a 10-acre stadium and perhaps a small hotel and/or the small shops that usually accompany any sports stadium. I was not involved in those negotiations, but I suspect that the franchise owners made that idea non-negotiable. In their view, I suspect, if the city wanted a totally privately financed MLS franchise, plus a cleaned-up 60-acre commons usable by all, it would have to accept substantial commercial development.

In any case, that was the package presented to the public and approved by popular referendum, in a general election.

What remained were the details of the deal, which had to be approved by four-fifths of the city commission. In a commission of five, that meant only one "no" vote; and one commissioner was dead-set against the deal from day one. Therefore, all four remaining commissioners had to be enticed into approving the deal.

That "the devil is in the details" is a general proposition. That the devil lurked in the minds and hearts of certain commissioners was also a generally accepted proposition, given that one of them was the infamous

Joe Carollo, who had confounded and polluted Miami politics in four decades of truant and treacherous behavior.

Another was the Rasputin-like Alex Diaz de la Portilla, who had been less noxious, but not much less inclined to committing illegalities than Carollo in his three decades of public service.

The others included the mercurial Ken Russell, who always seemed to be running for some other, much-higher, position.

In this instance, Russell had embarked on a totally Quixotic race to dethrone Florida's Cuban-American golden boy senator, named Marco Rubio. Like him or not, Marco Rubio was a social media powerhouse, with about three million followers, which compared rather well with Russell's ten thousand followers.

For Russell, the final vote on the soccer stadium would be a career-defining moment. The liberal wing of the Democratic Party would never forgive him if he voted for it. His colleagues on the commission and the young mayor, plus most of the business community, would never forgive him if he did a *volte-face* on something that had been carefully tuned to provide a win-win for the average Miamian, who wanted the city to continue prospering.

How carefully was the deal tuned? Well, you can start with the formula for what everyone now calls "ROI," for return-on-investment.

This had been set initially as a simple rental fee, which has the advantage of predictability for the private investors, but also brings with it the complexity of establishing the market price of renting something that is unique. Where in God's name do you find the classic "comparable" against which to establish a fair rental price, when there are no comparable developments to what is a unique soccer franchise, a public park that needs to be decontaminated and a mixed-use commercial complex?

There are no comparables. Yet that did not stop the city fathers, and their special counsel, from trying to come up with a fair-rental rate. Knowing this, and sensing that the issue was paramount in terms of public policy – if not public politics – I had suggested to both Russell and Mayor Francis that another metric be added, based not on some elusive flat rental rate but on a simple percentage of gross revenues.

This was the formula that we had been using to set rental rates at the airport, which is a classic, government-controlled monopoly. It's quite simple. The flat rental is set based on whatever comparables or other analytical factors one can concoct. Then a percentage of all gross revenues produced by the tenant is imposed – typically in the 5% range. The higher of the two is the one that is then paid as rent.

The big advantage of using percentage of gross revenue as the rental rate is that there's very little chance of shenanigans in the calculations. By only using revenues, and not net income or profit, the government-as-landlord avoids worrying about the costs incurred by the tenant, which are often overloaded with cushy jobs for friends and family, including relatives of the governing officials.

Acting wisely on my advice, Russell and Francis added the provision for rental at 5% of gross revenues. Later, the metric was raised to 6% at the request of Alex Diaz de la Portilla. That may have been the single best public-policy move by Alex DLP in three decades of erratic, public misbehavior.

The final vote by the commission took place on a Thursday meeting that lasted some seven hours, interrupted by a recess which was invoked by Mayor Francis when the commissioners seemed to reach a stalemate in divvying up some $20 million of "community benefits" that the Beckham/Mas team had to pay in upfront incentives.

It is not my place to divulge details of the many negotiations that took place during those seven-hours, or to restate the nastiness of what in sports is called "trash-talking" and that in one instance led to a commissioner (who did not notice a live mike nearby) referring to a colleague as a "come-pinga."

All I can say is that, in the end, four votes were obtained for the 99-year lease. Mayor Francis X. Suarez had, once again, come out on top. His city would now have five major sports: football, baseball, basketball, Formula One and major-league soccer.

You want to know how many cities in the world, other than Miami, have those? Well, it's none other than Miami.

Who said that Miami is the classic sleepy tourist and flight capital mecca of the Americas? As per the *Financial Times,* Miami had become America's "most important city." Its mayor had become America's most important and accomplished mayor.

Only a few disgruntled bloggers and a couple of *Miami Herald* editors would dispute that. And that brings to mind one city hall vignette.

It happened that the president of *Time Magazine,* named Keith Grossman, was visiting Francis at city hall, when he saw the cover story of his magazine with the "next generation 100" most important world figures, featuring Francis. Next to it was an even more impressive ranking, by *Fortune Magazine,* rating Francis as the No. 20 most important world leader.

Francis couldn't help but gloat over the fact that *Fortune* had outperformed *Time* in the coverage of his notoriety. But Grossman had the last word: "Remember, Francis," he said, "that we were first."

68

Francis, the Fearless Leader

Many political biographers have underscored a trait that is considered absolutely essential for any leader. It is the simple quality of physical courage.

Francis exemplifies that. And a recent incident illustrates it rather vividly.

It happened in a little island in the Bahamas called Great Harbour Cay. It was a clear day in September, when the ocean in that part of the world cools down to about 78 degrees, which for us Miamians is not exactly copacetic to our body temperature, used as it is to surf temperatures in the high eighties and low nineties.

But my wife, my son and I were itching for a little bit of salt water magic, and the blue waters of the Berry Islands were as close to paradise as you can get in September. And so we waded in.

Leaving my wife and son to their conversation, I went off to do my schtick – a short, up-tempo attempt at setting my late summer record for swimming as many as 50 strokes without breathing. (On most years, by this time I am doing at least 50 strokes, though I have been known to do as many as 54…)

On this day, I could only manage 36, but the splashing effect must have resembled a wounded animal, struggling to reach some sort of safe harbor. For whatever reason, my wife alerted Francis to the danger of sharks. "Francis, please keep an eye out for sharks…"

She had just pronounced the words when Francis looked away from the shore and immediately yelled: "Dad, get out of the water; there's a shark!"

I did as he said, but before I headed towards the shore, I did sneak a peek towards the deep blue sea; sure enough there was the telltale fin, rising above the water and appearing to be heading in a very straight line towards me. Francis wasted no time in sprinting in a direction that would cut off the advancing predator.

Whether it was the shouting or the determined defense by Francis, the most feared of all water animals decided to change course and retreated back towards the deep.

Afterwards, I asked Francis what he would have done if the shark had not changed its course. "Dad, being inside the water, I would not have been able to do much with my feet; but I know how to pound the nose of that particular predator, and I would have hit it with my fists around its face and eyes."

It is entirely possible that he saved my life that day. Any shark bite in that isolated part of the island would have been enormously risky, given the fact that there is no hospital, no 911 one can call, no lifeguards or even a clinic nearby. We would have had to do with home remedies and hope for a medical-rescue helicopter to arrive from Nassau and then transport me back to a Nassau hospital for surgery.

It's not a pretty scenario, even assuming the shark did not drag me out and drown me as a preamble to a tasty Xavier meal.

Later on I had to admit that if the tables were turned, I might not have reacted so nobly. I don't mean if my son was attacked by a shark; I believe that the paternal instinct takes over and overcomes the survival instinct. What I mean is if I had been 44 years old and my 72-year-old father was the one in danger of a shark that could just as easily come after me, the instinctive part of me would insist that we should all get out of the water together.

I don't rightly know. All I know is that Francis is not physically afraid of too many things. In fact, this recent, close encounter with a shark was not the only one I witnessed. The other one was a couple of decades ago, and it was more poignant, because it was more real, although the shark was much smaller.

I had gone with Francis to the park close to our house, which borders the bay. We were chatting by the seawall when he told me he had spotted a small shark among the rocks below. He followed that by climbing down to the water's edge and crouching to be able to reach into the little pool of water that was surrounded by rocks. This is where he had seen the shark.

Next thing he does is swoop down into the little pool and try to grab whatever was there. He came up empty. But he didn't give up, despite my pleas that he should abandon what seemed an impossible feat, given how slippery a wet shark is and how sharp its teeth. Besides, I said, your arm is already scratched and the shark has already escaped.

But he assured me it had not and once again crouched down to try again. And, lo and behold, this time he actually grabbed the animal and sent it flying backwards towards where I stood next to the seawall. And the darn thing seemed to have my name in its forehead; when it landed on the ground next to me, it struggled to move forward on the grass as if trying to sink its teeth into my feet...

Neither of us had a camera or cellular phone with us that could record the event. And, of course, Francis sent the creature back into the water, where we could see it swimming away as if nothing had happened.

It was yet another reminder that we had someone special in our midst.

69

A Bid for Very High Office

The remarkable ascendency of Francis's political star was evident as he started his second term as mayor, which coincided with his first year as president of the United States Conference of Mayors.

He had been reelected by close to 80% of the vote. He totally overshadowed the other local politicians. His city was time and again proclaimed as the one with the lowest crime rate, the lowest tax rate, the highest rate of tech growth, the highest rate of capital formation, and the lowest rate of unemployment.

Other polls showed Miami as the happiest city and also the healthiest city. *The Financial Times* proclaimed it the "most important city in America." Atop it all, and leading the symphony that had become his city, sat Mayor Francis X. Suarez.

Francis was not just the conductor of the symphony. He was also the composer, the chief violinist, and the most powerful percussionist. His Instagram page carried a daily barrage of meetings, conferences, community outings, and "cafecito talks" with the best and the brightest in industry, the arts, sports and politics. One day he would interview Magic Johnson; the next day he hosted New York's Mayor Eric Adams; the day after it was the Mayor of Kiev, Vitali Klitschko, who was not only a world-famous politician but a world-champion boxer.

Everyone assumed that Francis would either challenge for the governorship in 2022 or wait until the incumbent (Ron DeSantis) was termed out in 2026. There would be no better launching pad for the presidency than being governor of the third largest state in the country – particularly given that Florida was prospering almost as much as Miami, with people flocking there at the rate of one thousand new residents per day.

That gradual ascent, from mayor to governor to president, was not my preferred course of action. Not by a long shot.

I saw the nation's two political parties stuck in a rut that would lead to a repetition of the debacle of 2020, when the two parties nominated candidates for president who were disliked by seventy percent of the voters.

It begged for a third alternative – preferably a next-generation, centrist leader who would unite the nation combining traditional values of faith and family with progressive reforms in areas like affordable housing, mass transportation and clean energy.

In politics generally, it is tough to stay at the top. In municipal politics, it is nearly impossible. Mayors don't get credit for much and get blamed for everything. You can be a great mayor, keep taxes and crime low and economic growth high, and still lose your popularity when a hurricane or snow storm hits your town while you are away on vacation with your family.

In Miami, if a tropical storm hits a neighborhood and the natural tendency to flood low-lying neighborhoods is compounded by drains that happen to be clogged with debris, the mayor is blamed for the flooding. If a condominium building crumbles due to bad maintenance, bad design or both, the mayor gets blamed. If a police officer uses excessive force on a suspect, resulting in the suspect's death, the mayor is at fault.

In an international city like Miami, the mayor is always under suspicion of caring too much for foreign policy issues. New York's mayor can refuse to let South African leader (and former President) Nelson Mandela use a city facility, but Miami's mayor cannot even criticize Mandela for saying that Fidel Castro and Muammar Ghaddafi are his "comrades at arms."

By any objective measure, Francis was a successful and popular mayor. By the middle of 2022, he had become an immensely popular figure at the national level. Yet his hometown newspaper (*The Miami Herald*) delighted in criticizing him with nitpicking editorials on things like the firing of a police chief (actually done by the manager) or the siting of a major league soccer stadium (approved overwhelmingly by the voters in a referendum).

When Francis somehow convinced a crypto currency company to pay the city substantial sums for the privilege of calling one of its products

"Miami Coin," his business acumen was questioned, as if he had involved the city in a bad investment. And even hinting at some sort of military support for the opposition in Cuba (not different from the help given to Ukraine in its resistance to Russian communism), brought Francis heaps of ridicule from *Herald* editors and columnists whose sole solution to the repression in Cuba was more dialogue and more diplomacy.

Nevertheless, the momentum continued to be in Francis's favor. The question was whether he could amass a substantial war chest. Would the tech and fintech moguls ante up with millions, as they kept promising?

That was the big question as we approached the halfway mark of 2022.

Epilogue

I n mid-2023, Francis did, indeed, file to run for President of the United States. A more complete story is told in a book that I have almost completed, to be titled Democracy in America 2024.

I don't want to spoil the fun for readers of that book, which will be the third in a series that dovetails with the classic one by Alexis de Tocqueville, which is aging so well, since its publication in 1835, that it has become the most quoted and most revered tome on American democracy.

In the end, the ultra-charismatic mayor of Miami was unable to meet the threshold requirements that were imposed by the Republican National Committee for those wishing to participate in the primary debates. There were a few miscues in the logistical aspects of the campaign, but the general view was that Francis performed well and pulled out of the race in a timely fashion.

Perhaps his most scintillating media appearance was in the Democrat-slanted ABC program called "The View," where he was well received by both the hosts and the audience.

Towards the end of his short-lived campaign, Francis made repeated appearances in Iowa, which is the state of the first primary. While the other Republican candidates huffed and puffed under the Iowa sun, Francis sported a blue polo shirt that made him look like a professional athlete, more than a politician.

A reporter for the Washington Post went so far as to contrast the travails of Nikki Haley, who didn't seem to be recognized by Iowa Fair goers, with the resplendent, youthful Francis, accompanied by photogenic wife and kids. She called him a "Republican John F. Kennedy."

THE END